EZRA POUND'S RADIO OPERAS

EZRA POUND'S RADIO OPERAS

The BBC Experiments, 1931–1933

Margaret Fisher

The MIT Press ~ Cambridge, Massachusetts ~ London, England

This book was set in Bembo by Graphic Composition, Inc., and was printed and bound in the United States of America.

Library of Congress Cataloging-in-Publication Data

Fisher, Margaret, 1948–
Ezra Pound's radio operas : the BBC experiments, 1931–1933 / Margaret Fisher.
p. cm.
Includes bibliographical references and index.
ISBN 0-262-06226-7 (hc. : alk. paper)
1. Pound, Ezra, 1885–1972. Testament of François Villon. 2. Pound, Ezra, 1885–1972. Cavalcanti. 3. Radio operas—History and criticism. I. Title.

ML410.P7875 F57 2002
782.1´092—dc21

2001044442

for Bob,
this side

Contents

Acknowledgments

THIS BOOK BEGAN as an incidental chapter for Robert Hughes's study of Ezra Pound's music from the perspective of the last complete large work, *Cavalcanti.* My job was to explain why that work was not produced in Pound's lifetime. Bob generously granted me access to all aspects of his research, and spent countless hours in discussion and review of the primary and secondary music materials, challenging my arguments, and helping me to formulate better ones. I met Bob in 1976, at a time when he thought his work with Pound's music was finished. When he acquired the *Cavalcanti,* a new phase of editing, conducting, recording, and writing began. His pioneering research has produced definitive performance editions of Pound's two operas and violin works, world premieres of the operas as originally composed, numerous recordings, and a recently completed analysis of the music and of Pound's composing process. Pound's music takes its place as one of the many fascinating and large-scale projects in Bob's multifaceted contribution to American music as composer, conductor, bassoonist, and champion of new music.

R. Murray Schafer's contributions to Pound's music and its study are bedrock to the field. Because he is one of Canada's foremost composers and was coproducer of the BBC's 1962 broadcast of *Le Testament,* friend to Pound and Agnes Bedford, and a producer for the Canadian Broadcasting Corporation, his perspective on the radio operas (intended as an accompanying volume to his edition of Pound's complete music criticism, *Ezra Pound and Music*) has an unparalleled basis in research, performance, radio, and personal acquaintance with some of the persons who first performed his music. I am grateful to Murray for reading and commenting on an early manuscript for this book, and for answering many questions.

The performance history of Pound's operas of course began with Pound and the professional musicians who befriended him—Agnes Bedford, Olga Rudge, Yves Tinayre, and Robert Maitland. In the years that followed, BBC producers A. E. F. Harding and D. G. Bridson and musicians Raymonde Collignon and Gustav Ferrari encouraged Pound's efforts in music. I wish to acknowledge the artistic contributions of these persons, apart from the factual information presented in my text. Bob Hughes introduced me to Olga Rudge, and I am grateful to have known her as a friend, in Venice and in California. Gavin Bridson generously provided me with information about the vast scope of his father's career, and provided leads to other radio producers. I wish to thank Charles Mundye, whose production of Pound's *Le Testament* at the University of York brought forward a fresh interpretation of the opera. I am grateful for his correspondence and interchange of ideas. I extend special thanks to Toyoji Tomita, an esteemed performer in his own right, who reviewed my approaches to some of the more arcane possibilities suggested by the *Cavalcanti*. I thank Charles Amirkhanian for permission to review materials in the George Antheil archives, and for his promotion of Pound's music over the years.

I thank Mary de Rachewiltz and Omar S. Pound for furnishing documents and many factual details, and for their generous permission to print previously unpublished materials.

Grateful acknowledgment is given to New Directions Publishing Corporation and Faber & Faber, Ltd., for permission to quote Ezra Pound materials. Peggy Fox at New Directions has been a mainstay to the field of Ezra Pound and music, and to this project. She read earlier manuscripts and guided me through the intricacies of copyright issues regarding the previously unpublished manuscripts included in this book. I also thank Declan Spring of New Directions for handling the myriad permissions issues that arose. I would like to express my appreciation to the British Broadcasting Corporation, and its agent, the BBC Written Archives Centre, Caversham, for permission to quote from material under their copyright. My work has been greatly facilitated by Jacqueline Kavanagh,

BBC Written Archivist, who read and commented on an early draft of my manuscript. She and her staff located many items for me, provided services whether I was on site or in California, and answered my questions in detail. It has been a privilege to work at the Beinecke Rare Book and Manuscript Library, Yale University, in New Haven, Connecticut. I am grateful to Patricia Willis, Curator of the Collection of American Literature, and the staff at the Beinecke for their assistance. The firsthand experience of seeing, and attempting to make sense of, the hundreds of pages of music among the Ezra Pound and Olga Rudge Papers was an important part of understanding Pound's process, second only to hearing the music. I thank the Lilly Library, Indiana University, in Bloomington, Indiana, for permission to quote from materials in the Ezra Pound Manuscript and the D. G. Bridson Manuscript Collections. I wish to thank Saundra Taylor, Curator of Manuscripts, Lilly Library, who arranged for me to work with the materials of the collections from a distance. I am especially grateful for her assistance with textual details, including reading the scant impressions of a typewriter that were not picked up by microfilm. I also thank the staffs of the Doe and Bancroft Libraries of the University of California, Berkeley, who provided invaluable assistance and procured many hard-to-find items during the course of my research.

I was assisted with archival research by the late Donald Gallup, who kindly permitted me access to his own collection of letters. He took the time to read this work in an earlier version and comment on the idea of the radio operas as a love trilogy. I thank Stephen J. Adams, who also read the earlier version and offered encouragement and comment, including insights from his research on Pound and music. I have profited from his many published articles on the subject. I am indebted to Madeline Sunley, who assisted me in the initial preparation of these materials. I am likewise indebted to Mark Griffith for reading and commenting on an early manuscript. He, with Janet Adelman, Mel Gordon, W. B. Worthen, and Margaret Wilkerson, arranged for invaluable institutional support for further study. Barry Ahearn and Leon Golden have each provided a forum for me to introduce ideas selected from this book, for which I am grateful. For their generous extension of time and counsel on my behalf, I thank professors Albert Ascoli, Michael André Bernstein, Steven Botterill, Bill Jones, Mary Ann Smart, Ruggero Stefanini, and Doug Tygar.

Dear friends and acquaintances-by-mail have similarly drawn from their fields of expertise and personal libraries to offer invaluable resources and perspectives: Amir Baghdadchi, Reid Davis, Martin Esslin, Abe Garfield, Lou Harrison, Lisa Kaborycha, Lem Kitaj, R. B. Kitaj, Marilyn McCully, Brian Mulliner, Penny Niland, Maggi Payne, and the editors at *Paideuma*.

I thank Frank Wing for permission to reproduce his photographs of the 1983 *Cavalcanti* world premiere. I also wish to thank Robert Paquette, Sr., for educating me about the microphones used in early radio, and for permission to reproduce photographs from his collection. I thank Bobbie Mitchell, BBC Picture Archivist; Lynda Barnett of the Canadian Broadcasting Corporation/Société Radio Canada; and Karen Lem Donahue of Color 2000, San Francisco, for the professional services they have extended to provide the photographs for this book.

I am indebted to my editor Roger Conover for steering this manuscript in new and unexpected directions. I thank Anne Marie Oliver, who edited the contents of this book and provided invaluable suggestions. I also wish to thank Matthew Abbate, Erin Hasley, and the production staff at the MIT Press, who guided the manuscript to print.

Specific acknowledgments of permissions to reproduce various materials can be found in the Credits that follow. I have made a good faith effort to locate the copyright holders for materials reproduced. In cases where my efforts have not succeeded, I have limited the number of words quoted to comply with standards of fair use. Should a copyright holder of words quoted in the text locate me where I have failed to locate them, please write to the author care of the publisher.

The BBC radio script for Ezra Pound's *The Testament of François Villon* appears here in print for the first time. This has been made possible by the kind permission of Mary de Rachewiltz and Omar S. Pound, as well as by the coordination of permissions and services among New Directions Publishers, the BBC, the Lilly Library, and the Beinecke Library.

Credits

Excerpts from the following works of Ezra Pound are reprinted by permission of New Directions Publishing Corporation and Faber & Faber Ltd., London, agents for the Trustees of the Ezra Pound Literary Property Trust.

ABC of Reading. All rights reserved.

The Cantos. Copyright 1934, 1937, 1940, 1948, 1956, 1959, 1962, 1963, 1966, and 1968 by Ezra Pound. Thirteenth printing, 1995, used herein.

The Classic Noh Theatre of Japan. Copyright 1959 by New Directions Publishing Corporation.

Ezra Pound and Music. Copyright 1977 by the Trustees of the Ezra Pound Literary Property Trust.

Ezra Pound and the Visual Arts. Copyright 1926, 1935, 1950, 1962, 1970, 1971, and 1980 by the Trustees of the Ezra Pound Literary Property Trust.

Ezra Pound's Poetry and Prose: Contributions to Periodicals. Copyright 1991 by the Trustees of the Ezra Pound Literary Property Trust.

Guide to Kulchur. Copyright 1970 by Ezra Pound.

Le Testament. Copyright 1972 by the Trustees of the Ezra Pound Literary Property Trust.

Literary Essays. Copyright 1918, 1920, 1935 by Ezra Pound.

The Rome Broadcasts: "Ezra Pound Speaking." Copyright 1978 by the Trustees of the Ezra Pound Literary Property Trust.

Selected Letters 1907–1941. Copyright 1950 by Ezra Pound.

Selected Prose 1909–1965. Copyright 1960, 1962 by Ezra Pound, Copyright 1973 by the Estate of Ezra Pound.

The Spirit of Romance. Copyright 1968 by Ezra Pound.

Pound/Joyce. Copyright 1967 by Ezra Pound.

Pound/Laughlin. Copyright 1994 by the Trustees of the Ezra Pound Literary Property Trust. Published by permission of New Directions, agents for the Trust.

Ezra Pound material quoted in David Anderson's *Pound's Cavalcanti,* Princeton University Press (Copyright 1983 by the Trustees of the Ezra Pound Literary Property Trust; published by permission of New Directions, agents for the Trust).

Ezra Pound material quoted in Mary Barnard's *Assault on Mount Helicon,* University of California Press (Copyright 1984 by the Trustees of the Ezra Pound Literary Property Trust; published by permission of New Directions, agents for the Trust).

Previously unpublished material by Ezra Pound including music and radio script of *Cavalcanti* (Copyright 2002 by Mary de Rachewiltz and Omar S. Pound; performance edition of the music and libretto, copyright 2001 by Robert G. Hughes; used by permission of New Directions Publishing Corporation, agents).

Excerpts from published and unpublished materials, artwork, and photographs of the British Broadcasting Corporation are reprinted or printed for the first time by permission of their agent, the BBC Written Archives Centre, Caversham.

Announcements and artwork from *Radio Times* copyright 1931 by the British Broadcasting Corporation.

BBC Engineering, 1922–1972 by Edward Pawley copyright 1972 by the BBC Publications.

Photograph of E. A. F. Harding copyright 1943 by the British Broadcasting Corporation.

Photograph of the dramatic control panel copyright 1930 by the British Broadcasting Corporation.

Previously unpublished letters and script notations of E. A. F. Harding copyright 2002 by the British Broadcasting Corporation.

~ ~ ~

The graphic waveforms that appear on the display pages in this book depict sound waves captured from recordings of Ezra Pound's music:

The word *amore* from Guido Cavalcanti's canzone "Donna mi prega," pages i, iii, viii, xii, 1, 2, 202, 204, and above plate 1.

From Sordello's "Tos temps serai," pages vi, vii, 8, 196.

The opening contrabass line of Cavalcanti's "Poi che di doglia," page 40.

From the anonymous thirteenth-century dawn song "Gaite de la tor," which Pound interpolated into his setting of François Villon's fifteenth-century ballade "Père Noé," page 84.

From the dance rhythms of Villon's "Père Noé," page 142.

The word *amare* from Cavalcanti's "Donna mi prega," pages 222, 296, 306.

EZRA POUND'S RADIO OPERAS

The BBC Experiments, 1931–1933

Introduction

OTHER THAN BRIEF REMARKS of an introductory nature regarding the BBC adaptation of Ezra Pound's opera *Le Testament* for broadcast in 1931, very little has been written about Pound's seminal radio activities, despite the severe consequences of his Rome radio speeches during World War II.[1] The tangible groundwork in radio technique undertaken by Pound for the opera broadcast overshadows the purely speculative but more commonly cited inducements for him to broadcast—an encouragement from Major C. H. Douglas in 1935, the English economist most lauded by Pound for his theory of "social credit," and his acquisition of a radio in 1940 from the American expatriate writer in Paris, Natalie Barney.[2]

Pound received an invitation to broadcast in 1931 from Edward Archibald Fraser Harding (1903–1953), BBC producer, pioneer of the "feature" program, and tireless advocate of microphone access to all classes of persons in Britain. Together, Harding and Pound broke technical and theoretical ground in the production of opera for radio. Harding produced Pound's opera-for-radio *The Testament of François Villon* on October 26 and 27, 1931. The transmission, a studio performance from the BBC's Savoy Hill headquarters on the Thames River, was one of the first electronically enhanced operas to be broadcast in Europe. It featured the use of artificial echo throughout the performance to distinguish scenic location, and the operation of an electronic audio mixing board to combine prerecorded passages with live performance. With access to the most up-to-date recording technology, Harding arranged for a steel tape recording to be made of the penultimate rehearsal to provide immediate playback for the performers' edification.

Agnes Bedford, Pound's collaborator and rehearsal coach for the broadcast, having worked side by side with Harding for days on end, enthused to Pound, "He is definitely your man."[3] When Harding proposed a new work composed specifically for radio, Pound wrote his wife Dorothy Shakespear Pound, "[Harding] also wants to have Possum read 'em part of How to Read = & to have me do 'another OPRY' ETC."[4]

While preparing the opera, Harding took it upon himself to tutor Pound in the theoretical and political potential of radio. Pound did not travel to London from his home in Rapallo, Italy, but met with Harding in Paris, on May 9 and 10, 1931. It was a crash course in radio technique, devices, and production principles by one of radio's most forward-thinking practitioners and theorists. Several of his "lessons" contained in letters to Pound are reproduced in this study.

Within a year of the opera broadcast Harding produced the world's first global radio linkup. He would also found and develop the BBC's first Staff Training Program. To appreciate the intellectual and creative relationship that characterized Pound's work with Harding, it is helpful to recall the general state of radio in the 1920s and early 1930s, radio's formative years. Program policy was often pieced together producer by producer, country by country, on a trial-and-error basis. British radio was a public communications utility under the auspices of the Post Office, which handled licensing arrangements for the radio industry. A conglomerate of industry representatives formed the British Broadcasting Corporation under royal charter (1927–1936), but, theoretically at least, the corporation operated independently of the government. Official policy opposed the politicization of broadcast material and prohibited personal, organizational, or governmental bias.[5] The experimentalist Harding challenged this policy from within the institution, leading British radio by the mid-1930s to play a greater role in social and domestic issues. He and his colleagues worked in a highly charged, production-intensive atmosphere where technological and artistic discoveries were daily events. They expressed a self-conscious awareness of the unique moment of their mission in history and engaged in passionate debate about the invisible, ephemeral medium of radio. For this book, I have provided examples from the debates, challenges, aspirations, achievements, and failures of early radio's first producers and artists to lend perspective to Pound's earliest radio projects.

His second radio opera *Cavalcanti* took for its subject the poetry of Guido Cavalcanti, Italian lyric poet of the thirteenth century. Pound composed the opera from 1931 to 1933, but it was never broadcast. It appears from the correspondence that Harding never explained the work's indefinite postponement. Because the materials for the opera became separated during Pound's incarceration, it was presumed unfinished. In 1982 the American conductor Robert Hughes pieced together the complete work from music deposited in the Ezra Pound Collection of the Beinecke Rare Book and Manuscript Library at Yale University, and the private collection of Olga Rudge, American violinist, at her home in Venice, Italy. Rudge had performed excerpts from *Testament* in several Paris concerts in the 1920s. She assisted Pound in the composition of a larger work, the *Ghuidonis Sonate,* from which the overture to *Cavalcanti* and many of its melodies were to be drawn, and helped to make clean copies of the opera's arias from Pound's manuscript.[6]

For the reader unacquainted with Pound, the background provided in this book may seem surprisingly broad in scope. To understand how the dramas are constructed, to whom they were addressed, why they end the way they do, and how they differ from radio experiments by other artists of the time, the information is essential. To accommodate the detail of the operas within the wider scope of Pound's experimentalism, I offer a very general and by no means comprehensive introduction to many of his literary theories and practices. The emphasis on drama is an artificial filter that I have applied to the vast panorama of Pound's interests toward understanding two specific works. I analyze the *Testament* radio script in terms of structure, language, time, and meaning in four distinct synopses. *Cavalcanti* is analyzed along similar lines; in the absence of any surviving broadcast script with producer's notes, my treatment of it depends on Pound's drafts, final manuscripts, and Robert Hughes's recently completed performance edition from those documents. I have set out to understand Pound's statement that the setting of words to music is a viable form of literary criticism. Is this a summary judgment drawn from the proof of his music works, and if so, what did he accomplish in this vein? If I have erred on the side of multitudinous detail, it is to represent the full spectrum of concerns in Pound's discontinued laboratory of music and radio art, and to point to relatively unexplored primary sources that would benefit from repeated performance and further consideration.

I have addressed these works foremost as a theater director in search of the inner life of the music and libretti. I have put aside assumptions of amateurism regarding Pound's abilities either as dramatist or composer on the premise that he brought his artistry and intelligence to bear upon a medium new to him, and that he intended to do something new within that medium. Some of the most compelling elements of these dramas were not the artistic high points, of which there are many, but the apparent nadirs of expression that were initially unfathomable but would nevertheless have to be resolved if a convincing performance, broadcast, or film were to be made of these works, the hypothetical goal presumably motivating Pound. In my view, Pound appeared to purposely insert the most blockheaded obstacles to a dynamic drama, pockets of forced humor and vapid symbolism. Without fail each of his underdeveloped characters, symbolic utterances, and gratuitous references to external people or events proved to be crucial to an understanding of the logic of the work once his formulation of a two-audience, multicentury script became apparent. It was maddening and impractical that Pound did not explain his work. Experimental performance productions never have the time or budget for the research he expected.

I have tried to provide enough background information to facilitate a recreation of the 1931 broadcast or a contemporary stage performance, film, or video production, by including discussion of theatrical models, sound design, interpretive comments, technical details, artistic trends in film and radio, differences in broadcasting organization and facilities, and professional differences in radio technique.

Pound's reasons for composing music differ from the usual reasons to compose. He sought to revive the troubadour art of "motz el son" through a recombination of words and music that would recover and transmit the voice, rhythm, and mind of the author over the voice of the composer or the performer. The persons most capable of determining whether Pound has succeeded in his literary goals for music have yet to come forward. Additionally, a performance work ultimately depends on the senses of hearing and seeing. Performance works are complete when performed, and each performance is an introduction to a future performance.

For his large poem *The Cantos,* Pound developed a new palette of literary styles and techniques to serve his perceptions about the world, the individual mind, and the organization of knowledge—a methodical upheaval that is traceable throughout his earlier body of work. My recovery of his "lost" radio dramas is only possible because the "thought" that generated the works has not been lost. I have directed my focus continually inward, into the crannies of a labyrinth that has had few visitors over the past sixty-eight years. I have selected examples from Pound's larger body of work to illustrate ideas carried over into his radio aesthetic and technique, and relevant examples from the work of other artists who, as contemporaries of Pound, also ventured into the field of radio before radio became implicated in the political affairs of Europe. I have attempted to be neither inclusive nor encyclopedic but have rather made selections to shape a handbook for the study of Pound and performance, and some uses of radio in the 1920s and 1930s.[7]

Given the climate of hostility at the conclusion of World War II against British and American citizens who broadcast from Axis countries, it is fortuitous that *Cavalcanti* was not produced on the schedule originally proposed by Harding. Had the radio opera been made public earlier, it might have impacted Pound's trial and incarceration in unpredictable ways. The opera's thirteenth-century narrative hinges on the transfer of a political cipher directly encoded in the music. Pound's story element was a clever and original turn on early radio plays, for which dramatists designed plots that exploited the absence of visual cues in radio.

Pound appears to have absorbed and utilized an endless number of subjects with fluid ease through his idiosyncratic organization of knowledge. His radio operas were well-designed first attempts to convey that knowledge to a large public. But the logic of his organization and presentation of ideas in the 1940s radio speeches seems, from our perspective, nonexistent. Only a residue remained of the carefully engineered contrast of elements within the operas—the alternation of speech (slang and dialect) with music, the imagined ignorance of the people surrounding great poets (friends, enemies, household personnel, passersby), and the use of radio as a personal bulletin board.

A detailed examination of Pound's unknown radio operas is doubly justified, for not only are they serious large projects that expanded Pound's artistic focus in the 1930s, but also, today, they provide new perspective to his war speeches. This study will demonstrate that Pound's interest in drama, music, film, and the broadcast media between 1931 and 1933 was linked to experiments in perception on the one hand and new forms of criticism and pedagogy on the other. When he broadcast from Rome in 1941, he had an insider's knowledge of radio technique and theory, practical experience, and a grasp of the political potential of the medium.

After the period of the broadcasts, Pound wrote the first Italian Canto LXXII, in which he engages in dialogue with the ghost of F. T. Marinetti, the artist who is more commonly associated with experimental radio of the 1930s. In his 1933 futurist radio manifesto *La Radia* Marinetti proposed the broadcasting of radio interference as a form of futurist art. Pound refers to the interference between radio stations and transforms it into poetry.

> *E come onde che vengon da più d'un trasmittente*
> *Sentii allora*
> *Le voci fuse, e con frasi rotte,*
> *E molti uccelli fecer' contrappunto*
> *Nel mattino estivo . . .*
>
> (LXXII/430)

> Confusion of voices as from several transmitters, broken phrases,
> And many birds singing in counterpoint/In the summer morning . . .
>
> (Pound's translation, LXXII/436)

A Dramatic Filter

1

EZRA POUND'S TWO BBC PROJECTS of the 1930s moved his ideas about history, religion, art, and prosody into the temporary domain of drama and all that entails—immediate and simultaneous reception, an audience, and the requisite entertainment that holds them—what Pound called the "tricks of the stage." The latter, he explained in his 1910 essay "The Quality of Lope de Vega," were its "rhymes and its syntax," independent of any appetite for subtlety, though inclusion of subtlety was not prohibited.[1] The essay, which drew upon his earlier graduate research for the University of Pennsylvania, was followed by a temporary wane in his interest in Western drama. He questioned the value of writing for the stage in a review of James Joyce's play *Exiles:* "Is drama worth while? Is the drama of today, or the stage of today, a form or medium by which the best contemporary authors can express themselves in any satisfactory manner?" And to Joyce he wrote, "My whole habit of thinking of the stage is: that it is a gross, coarse form of art . . . a play speaks to a thousand huddled together."[2]

Pound had tried his own hand at writing plays, aiming for an intimate and elite theater exempt from the populist orientation of a commercial stage obliged to recoup substantial outlays of capital risked for each production.[3] His theater experiment yielded four plays styled on the Japanese Noh theater, his understanding of this classical form drawn almost entirely from the research notebooks of the American Ernest Fenollosa (1853–1908). An art historian and former curator for the Museum of Fine Arts in Boston, Fenollosa specialized in Oriental art. His study of Noh in

Japan, taken up intermittently from 1883 on, and steadily from 1896 to 1901, led him to propose that the art of Noh was a literary art, "the living analogue of Greek drama in Japan."[4] When Fenollosa's widow asked Pound in 1913 to complete her husband's translations and notes for posthumous publication, he took the work with him to Stone Cottage in Sussex, where he would spend three winters as part-time secretary to William Butler Yeats, immersing himself, and Yeats, in Fenollosa's descriptions of the literature and art of China and Japan. During this time Yeats developed two dance dramas based on the Noh, with music by Pound's friends Walter Rummel and Edmund Dulac. Pound had hoped that one of his own plays would also be performed on the April 1916 private program of Yeats and Dulac's "At the Hawk's Well," but none of his four plays were ever performed.[5]

Although direct reference to the Noh in Pound's poetry, drama, and music must be determined on a case-by-case basis, Pound's notes and manuscripts testify to the fact that Noh remained a significant influence throughout his career. We will see that what Pound called a "complete service of life," the presentation of several Noh plays for one occasion, aptly describes the total output of his music dramas adapted or composed during the period of his work for the BBC, 1931–1933. As Pound understood Fenollosa's notes, the Noh service was comprised of five or six plays or play fragments: a piece connected with a rite to the gods, a battle scene, a play of women, a quiet play, a lively scene, and a play of praise.[6] The few short scenes of each Noh play are enacted by "personae . . . beyond life": gods, nature spirits, and the ghosts of warriors, murderers, and lovers who cannot free themselves from their past and who continue to live in the cultural memory.[7] Though he never stated that Noh was his model, Pound carefully guided the listener's hearing toward a culminating preternatural moment that required vision for fulfillment. His method expanded upon his observation that writing fell into two camps: "There are two kinds of written language, one based on sound and the other on sight."[8] It freed him from the demands of plot-driven work to concentrate his energy on the single image.

In the case of the radio dramas, Pound never employed explicit description in his dialogue. Though part of the art of radio plays is to evoke a visual image without reliance on description, certain final images in Pound's radio works depend on vision to understand the surprise ending.

Trying to explain the final image of his second opera *Cavalcanti,* he admitted that the pictorial effect would have to wait for film or television, and hoped that at least the important groundwork of listening attentively to the music would be accomplished.[9]

At Stone Cottage Pound tackled the logistics of writing a long poem, the work we know as *The Cantos.* It was conceived in the lineage of Western epic poetry, commencing with Homer, culminating in Dante, and resuscitated by Browning. With the stimulus of Fenollosa's research, Pound sought to reshape the epic form as a poem containing history and mythology from East and West. He would include translations of and direct quotations from both political and economic documents and literary sources. Pound conceived of the poem's mythological subjects as culturally interchangeable within a homeomorphic pantheon of gods and demigods.[10] All of these elements would be woven into a tapestry of voices, dialects, and languages. Having stated early in his career, "I am more interested in life than in any part of it," Pound would offer an image of the twentieth century by availing himself of all previous human endeavor he considered significant, condensed by the method of "Luminous Detail." His project required the creation of a new spectrum for poetry that could be compared to "the contemporary search for pure color in painting."[11] This search for a purity of language was conducted in relation to yet another—the search for a "permanent basis in humanity," or the hard palette on which the "colors" are arranged.[12]

Certain human traits underlie all human existence: the social impulse to form government, the religious impulse to consider the possibility of Mind or Other beyond the sentient world, and the psychological impulse toward greed or benevolence. These traits would be exampled throughout the poem, not to demonstrate progress from primitive to advanced society, but to mark a recurrence of the pinnacles and nadirs of human existence. As such, Pound's critical function for his poem escalated into an inquiry into psychology, perception, and physical science.

Pound's twentieth-century critic was drawn on the model of the medieval "natural philosopher," whose inquiry sought to articulate the inherent Form of things: how Form comes into being, its location, its nature, its effects. Pound brought this identification and definition of Form into the purview of criticism when he wrote, "It is the function of criticism to find out what a given work is, rather than what it is not."[13]

With the critical function of the philosopher-poet directed toward an awakening of perception, discursive language, with its inherent bias toward polarization of opinion and unnecessary cultivation of taste, became inadequate and restrictive. Music proved to be a more appropriate tool than discourse for the articulation of the Form within poetry. Pound presented five categories of criticism in a 1934 essay "Dateline," the final three of which could be directly related to his song settings. The essay confirms the fact that Pound's composing activities were a form of literary commentary. For his third category, "criticism by exercise in the style of a given period," Pound composed in a variety of rhythmic and modal styles to reproduce characteristics of music of the twelfth through the fifteenth centuries while, at the same time, availing himself of contemporary music techniques. Pound believed he could demonstrate differences in cadence and tonal nuance that otherwise could not be adequately perceived by means of written textual criticism of the strophic forms, the tropes, rhymes, and quantitative meters of poetry from these earlier periods. While his two completed operas are excellent examples of the third category, they were composed specifically to serve the fourth, "criticism via music, meaning definitely the setting of a poet's words." This was the "most intense" category save for the last, "criticism in new composition" (for which we have just one example from his musical oeuvre, that of *Guido's Frottola*).[14] Having devised a systematic approach to song-setting that would purportedly maintain the poet's voice in the music, Pound then used this voice as a persona or mask for himself. To explain the construction of this musical mask and the dramatic impulse behind it, I will turn back to Pound's earlier prose writing on psychology and to his three Ur Cantos.

As part of his informal study of the mind, Pound distinguished two types of persons exhibiting an awakened perception. The first type included those whose "minds are . . . circumvolved about them like soap-bubbles reflecting sundry patches of the macrocosmos." Pound called this mind the "phantastikon." The consciousness of the other type he termed "germinal": "Their thoughts are in them as the thought of the tree is in the seed, or in the grass, or the grain, or the blossom. And these minds are the more poetic, and they affect mind about them, and transmute it as the seed [of] the earth."[15] Those of the second type are the poetic minds that Pound chose to render through drama, music, and radio: François Villon (1431–?),

Guido Cavalcanti (c. 1250–1300), and Gaius Valerius Catullus (84–54 B.C.).[16] (Of these, none lived to old age, and only Catullus avoided exile.)

Pound's discovery of signs in Noh pointing to the "permanent basis in humanity" would greatly influence his portrayal of poets not commonly thought of in connection to gods and ghosts: Cavalcanti and Villon. As Pound understood it, the ghost psychology of Noh facilitated a momentary penetration or change of ordinary human experience that was the natural and edifying culmination of a spiritual or allegorical journey.[17] The traveler's sincere quest was often elaborated through a ritual of song, prayer, and meditation, permitting witness to psychic presence(s) within the voices and images that moved fluidly through the dramatic time and place of Noh. To perceive Japanese gods and ghosts was to enter that fluid state. In contrast, human perception of Greek and Roman gods often entailed falling victim to the gods' neuroses or being endowed with unsustainable powers, on the basis of a chance encounter or sentimental godly urge.

In the two completed radio operas, neither protagonist, Villon nor Cavalcanti, has invoked, wished, or prayed for the appearance of the ghosts or gods that Pound inserts into the works' concluding scenes. But each poet wrote at least one work invoking the gods or spirits, and Pound uses these poems, transfigured as music drama, to evince the dénouement of each opera. By using the words of the poets to resolve the operas, Pound was able to sustain the unique mystery or special quality of the poet's original voice addressed to the beyond, or other side, and impart this directly (enhanced, but not transformed, by his music) to those sincere seekers of new perception—the reward for attentive listening and questing. The voice of the poet-protagonist in each opera is double—Villon and Pound's Villon, Cavalcanti and Pound's Cavalcanti. A third voice, that of the poet's biographer and historian, may join in. A brief introduction to *The Cantos* will prepare us to examine the intermixture of gods and people represented by the voices in Pound's radio dramas.

Voices in *The Cantos*

Conceived as a "lengthy poem," *The Cantos* received its preliminary start with the publication of three cantos (1917), the result of the working winters at Stone Cottage.[18] All three were to undergo considerable revision before Pound felt he had effectively launched a poem that was to contain history. The first canto was peopled with the living and the dead, gods and goddesses, ghosts and "my own phantastikon."[19] Present as the narrator of the poem, Pound offers himself as the exemplar of a writer's true wisdom:

> avoid speech figurative
> And set out your matter
> As I do, in straight simple phrases:
> Gods float in the azure air, . . .

and

> . . . all the leaves are full of voices.[20]

When submitting the typescript of what are now called the "Ur Cantos" to his editor Harriet Monroe at *Poetry,* Pound canceled a comment on the manuscript originally intended to draw her attention to the similarity between the theme of his new long poem and the Noh play *Takasago* by Zeami (1363?–1444).[21] His explanation may not, in the end, have been satisfactory for the whole poem as he envisioned it, but it did, if only for an instant, select Noh theater as a parallel realm, one also inhabited by spirits and gods. The proportions of Noh, as he understood them from Fenollosa's notebooks, particularly held Pound's interest: "If one has the habit of reading plays and imagining their setting, it will not be difficult to imagine the Noh stage—different as it is from our own or even from Western mediaeval stages—and to feel how the incomplete speech is filled out by the music or movement."[22] Zeami incorporated quotations from two revered collections of Japanese poems to link the spirit of the Takasago Pine to the time of the most ancient anthology of the eighth century (the *Manyoshu* or Collection of Myriad Leaves) and the spirit of the Sumiyoshi Pine to the more recent imperial anthology of the tenth century (the *Kokinshu*). The spirits of the two pines appear together as man and wife within the dramatic present of the play, transcending the limitations of time and space. Reflecting its origins in the Shinto religion, *Takasago* presents nature and gods as one. The lines cited above from

Ur Canto I capture this sense of the gods within the given—within the air and the leaves. The theme of *Takasago,* spirit or "wireless" communication between two pines in different locations, leading to a vision of metamorphosis—revelation reserved for the most assiduous of audience members—identified the underlying technology, if not the explanation, of what was to come in the radio operas. That new technique would require a methodical division of hearing and seeing.

Pound's spirits and gods are spatially deployed, and therefore available to sight and physical sensation. They do not exist "back" in time, but "about" as in space, not only bearing time as decoration but forever restitched by time:

> . . . Ghosts move about me
> Patched with histories . . .
> (Ur Canto I)

And behind:

> . . . confuse the thing I see / With actual gods behind me?
> (Ur Canto I)

And within:

> He has a god in him,
> though I do not know which god. (II/9)

People (living and dead), events, ideas, places, and objects were also "patched with histories." Rarely were they pegged onto the historical time line we know as past, present, and future. They were characterized instead by a measure of transience or recurrence. Gods and their attendant spirits were deemed eternal, though it is difficult to pin down whether we are speaking here of a metaphysical state or a mental state that has endured and is always available to humankind through a form of shared consciousness. Pound's system has a certain fluidity and permeability that acknowledges the unstable nature of moral order and disorder.[23] By accounting for time beyond the human life span, Pound brings religion and history together under the gaze of Mind and subject to its pulse. *The*

Cantos provides the most extensive testing of that system, by insisting that one can only present a "subjective perspective of the facts."[24] Acoetes of Canto II states this clearly: "I have seen what I have seen" (II/9).

People described or given voice in *The Cantos* are either transitory figures who never recur in the poem, or figures that retain their currency and reappear elsewhere in the poem, according to Pound's subjective perspective rather than according to an "objective" time line. The words of the poet-heroes of Pound's radio operas, Villon and Cavalcanti, recur in the poem and are made current (i.e., relevant and contemporary). Outside the poem, they will be transformed from sound waves into electromagnetic current carried by the air. Art itself becomes molecular, economic, and historical, as well as dramatic, poetic and musical. Pound's goal is traduction—a transfer or "leading across," transmission by generation to posterity—through literature ("news that stays news"). Pound would often substitute the word *traduction* (from the Latin *traductio*) for *translation,* to point up the fact that he was employing an alternative process.[25]

Pound's resistance to chronological organization, "We do NOT know the past in chronological sequence" and "All ages are contemporaneous," calls into question our notion of a poet *looking back in time* to classical Greek, Roman, and Chinese civilizations, the Middle Ages (including Japan), the Renaissance, and so forth.[26] Inextricably bound to his revitalization of older forms of poetry is Pound's commitment to the actualization of the past in the present moment. These two themes run through all of his work, and are critical to the understanding of his poetry and music. We may enter the spirit of Pound's interactive potential of history, expressed in his axiom "Make it New," with the understanding that when he touched upon a subject he considered himself to be in some way not distant from that subject, but near at hand. He would later ask, "How is it far if you think on it?" (LXXIX/508).

This occult aspect of Pound's literary radicalism is at the crux of our interpretation of his dramatic figures whom we otherwise might presume to be "historical" and therefore fixed.[27] Because Pound wants us to know each poet intimately, he mitigates the distance of time, translation, and perception through a music that retains the sonic surface, texture, and movement of the original voice. The figures are borne through the operas by their own unmistakable sounds. Radio, with its intersection of voices in unbounded space and its quality of immediacy, provides an ideal mise-en-scène for Pound's dramatic figures, that is, for all but the final scenes of the operas, where revelation of some aspect of the "other side" might require vision as well as hearing.

Pound secured his poetic technique with Canto IV, begun in the first quarter of 1919 and published privately that October. The presence of the author as first-person narrator was abandoned, and the "phantastikon" of Ezra Pound as only one of many was substituted. The new method favored one thought cutting in on another "with clean edge," as happens randomly in life, among the inner voices of one's mind, and as would soon be possible on radio.[28]

What Pound referred to as the "plastic" quality of sound is everywhere apparent in the canto; it is the palpable surface left by the movement, the clear edges or outlines to the form of things or sounds and their transition to other things or sounds.[29] It is a surface demanding hyperacute senses and an active intellect to negotiate not an ordered time line of history, but a confluence of history. The presentation of images and events is as close to simultaneity as the poet can achieve with print on page. The canto introduces Pound's vision of poetry and civilization and is an important contextual source for the role of passion in the operas.

> Palace in smoky light,
> Troy but a heap of smouldering boundary stones,
> ANAXIFORMINGES! Aurunculeia!
> Hear me. Cadmus of Golden Prows!
> The silver mirrors catch the bright stones and flare,
> Dawn, to our waking, drifts in the green cool light;
> Dew-haze blurs, in the grass, pale ankles moving.
> Beat, beat, whirr, thud, in the soft turf
>   under the apple trees,
> Choros nympharum, goat-foot, with the pale foot alternate;
> Crescent of blue-shot waters, green-gold in the shallows,
> A black cock crows in the sea-foam;
> And by the curved, carved foot of the couch,
>   claw-foot and lion head, an old man seated
> Speaking in the low drone . . . :
>   Ityn!

Et ter flebiliter, Ityn, Ityn!
And she went toward the window and cast her down,
"All the while, the while, swallows crying:
Ityn! ["]
"It is Cabestan's heart in the dish."
"It is Cabestan's heart in the dish?"
"No other taste shall change this. . . ." (IV/13)

From an image of the destruction of Troy, Pound proceeds with a poetry lesson. He disliked the poetry of Pindar (518–c. 438 B.C.) but put it to good use in the canto's third line. Here, he places the first word of this Olympian ode in all caps to stand for Pindar's bellowing rhetoric, "Hymns that govern the lyre, what god, what hero, what man shall we sing of?" The six-syllable Greek address to the "hymn" contrasts the five-syllable Latin address to the bride by Catullus (84–54 B.C.) in his ceremonial wedding poem—"Do not weep. Aurunculeia, there is no danger any woman is fairer. . . ." (I suspect Pound was having some multilingual fun with gender as he highlighted the poets' sources of inspiration—the Greek hymn and the Latin her.) The epithalamium by Catullus was a poem that Pound admired and later set to music. The two words together form an eleven-syllable line, the preferred line length of the vernacular Italian lyric poets, Dante and Cavalcanti. The radio operas elaborate on exactly this kind of poetry lesson that makes its comparisons across centuries, but the lessons are set in music rather than in type.

The canto builds on the stories of Ovid (43 B.C.–18 A.D.)—Cadmus, Itys (Ityn), and Actaeon. Cadmus founded the city of Thebes, where the walls were built to music of the lyre. The "Golden Prows" recalls his legendary travels through Phoenicia, the *gold* standing for the artisan's craft as well as describing Cadmus's craft. On his return to Greece, Cadmus brought with him the Phoenician alphabet. Though Pindar was a citizen of Thebes, Pound seems to suggest that the music and words that were at the heart of the civilization built by Cadmus had, by the time of Pindar, become so much hot air. Cadmus wed Harmonia and received the blessing of the entire pantheon of Greek gods. Ovid recalls that such blessings were withheld from Procne and Tereus, the parents of Itys.

The "smouldering boundary stones" of Canto IV give way to Pound's own foundation stones for an earthly paradise, where the words and deeds of poets will construct a new civic order. Greece still catches in the mirror that Pound holds up, and blazes at "dawn, to *our* waking . . ." (italics added). The intimation is that Pound will craft from the post-World War I ruins of European civilization a new civilization, drawing heat out of the ancient stones of Greece. The onomatopoeic "Beat, beat, whirr, thud" keeps us in the present moment, as does "black cock crows," while the events of the poem recall the past in that present. "Goat-foot, with the pale foot alternate" reminds us that Greek verse stayed close to dance rhythms (and their ceremonial purpose). The old ruler on his throne considers the detrimental effects of passion on a civic order that, after Cadmus, depended on marriage to produce its protectors. When Pound later introduces Hymen (IV/15), the Greek god invoked by Catullus to bless the marriage bed ("Hymen, Io Hymenaee!"), he briefly directs the focus of the canto to the act of coition, celebrated by Greek religion in rituals separate from the marriage rite. Pound's paradise on earth will also celebrate and sanctify the act of coition.

The canto presents one revenge drama after another, laid "ply over ply," recurrence in different forms.[30] The revenge repast of a son served up hot, that is, as a meal—Itys, of Thrace—is remembered in the call of a bird that circles the air outside the scene of another murdered loved one, Cabestan, of France, also hot. Passion and civilization have always been linked. The distillation of a legend into two lines of dialogue is sufficient to understand that Ramon, lord of the castle of Rossillon, speaks first; his wife Lady Seremonda, Cabestan's lover, replies, "It is Cabestan's heart in the dish?"

From the line "Hither, hither, Actaeon," we deduce that it is Actaeon's companions calling him to the hunt, unaware that the stag they hunt *is* Actaeon, transformed by Diana. The full tragedy of the story can only emerge through this reading and not through a reading of the lines as Diana's. The pause required to locate the voice allows the trauma of the story to unfold and fully take hold in the reader. If the lines were delivered dramatically, the listener would have the advantage of vocal cues. But Pound chooses poetry, not drama. Accomplished with the utmost economy of words, the awful realization of the tragic turn of events relies on the rhythmic and emotional pull that reaches deeply within and moves the private mind of the reader toward an instant of understanding. The rhythmic play upon a theater auditorium scaled to the public mind would unfold over the course of an evening, the intensity aimed not toward a lasting perception but toward emotion, which lessens with distance from the stage and with time.

During the period in which he finished the first sixteen cantos and *Le Testament,* it appears that Pound also experimented with strategies to separate the senses of hearing and seeing. The sense of hearing becomes associated with the natural human world of the transient and recurrent. His attempts to reserve the visual and tactile senses for selected aspects of nature, gods, and things eternal are found in passages such as "And, out of nothing, a breathing, hot breath on my ankles" from Canto II, in which there is breath but no voice. (In the *Testament* opera, in contrast, the ghosts of Villon's "Frères humains" have voice but no breath.) No gods or spirits speak before Canto XVII. Thereafter, the systematization is not always upheld, but even within the deviations a special quality of difference suffuses the voice given goddesses, spirits, and ghosts.

Ezra Pound's Music: Revolution, Translation, Criticism

> It is an act of revolution when the educated musician wearies of Music's pampered doctrines and shoves them into the dogmahouse, even temporarily, but when the inquisitive man of literature ventures on the precincts of music he is obliged to cope with none of its encumbrances and therefore with none of the censure occasioned by "revolt." [31]

When he wrote these words in 1949, the American composer Harry Partch had in mind William Butler Yeats's theories about the setting of words to music (Yeats did not compose his own music). The thesis works when applied to Pound who, as literary man turned composer, fully intended "revolt," describing his music as "improving a system by refraining from obedience to all its present 'laws.'"[32] But Partch did not account for negligence, which could be worse than censure. Pound's musical oeuvre, being generally difficult, has yet to be performed in full; at this writing, only a few pages of it have been published. After hearing a concert performance of *Le Testament* in 1926, Virgil Thomson praised Pound's accomplishment: "The music was not quite a musician's music, though it may well be the finest poet's music since Thomas Campion. . . . Its sound has remained in my memory."[33] Pound's iconoclastic music can profitably be compared to that of his American contemporary Charles Ives. Both subjected melody to sophisticated techniques of juxtaposition and layering, Pound shaping melody with literary textures and Ives with harmonic and contrapuntal textures. Each experimented with a combination of different genres in a single complex work, Ives selecting from hymns, folk tunes, ballads, and minstrelsy, as well as instrumental pieces; Pound, from a vocal gamut of plain chant, homophony, troubadour melodies, bel canto and nineteenth-century opera clichés, as well as from twentieth-century polyrhythms.[34] The whore's aria of *Testament,* "Heaulmière," is composed in an eclectic medieval style. Pound suggested that it be delivered in a heavily inflected cabaret style.

Pound's reason for composing, to advance the arts of writing and poetry, is mirrored in his statement for the BBC, "As with *Villon* the poet here continues to follow his intention: that is, to take the world's greatest poetry out of books, to put it on the air, to bring it to the ear of the people, even when they cannot understand it or cannot understand it all at once. The meaning can be explained but the emotion and beauty cannot be explained. The poems are left in the original, the dialogue into English so that you can follow the story of the play."[35] A poem's movement was of greater importance than its message, Pound believed, and could not be obfuscated by the foreignness of its language. The study of Provençal verse was essential for writers of English verse: "To know the dimensions of English verse melody a few centuries later," wrote Pound, "you must find your measures or standards in Provence. . . . Without knowing Dante, Guido Cavalcanti and Villon, no one can judge the attained maxima of certain kinds of writing. Without the foregoing MINIMUM of poetry in other languages you simply will not know 'where English poetry comes.'"[36]

The Middle Ages provide the underpinnings of Pound's song settings. Dante's definition of the poetic author in *Convivio* (IV.6) tells us that a poet binds words with the art of music. Pound restates this as "Poetry is a composition of words set to music."[37] His statement that "Rhythm is a FORM cut into TIME" distinguishes his twentieth-century medievalism from contemporaneous SPACE/TIME theories of modern music, which sought pure abstraction.[38] Pound's theory requires that the listener discern FORM, which intercedes between the pure sound and the physiological reception.

Pound's insistence on the inseparability of words and music refers us to the beginnings of humanism—a time in which, Pound explains in his essay "Cavalcanti," the arts of Provence and Italy underwent a transformation. A new tensile strength entered the aesthetic, a result of the engagement of the individual artist with the thirteenth-century scholastics and their new methods of inquiry into natural philosophy and theology. The emergence of an exegetical strain in literature entered the tradition of *motz el son*. Words and music for Pound had not yet come undone at the end of the thirteenth century: "Guido's poetry in general, and the poems of medieval Provence and Tuscany . . . , were all made to be sung. Relative estimates of value inside these periods must take count of the cantabile values."[39] A medievalist may dispute the claim that these poems were "made to be sung," but it is this premise that motivates Pound to compose. The theater or opera director must investigate and promote this premise. Most importantly, she or he must determine what the cantabile values in twelfth- and thirteenth-century Provençal and Tuscan lyric poetry could mean to the twentieth century in terms of values that otherwise could not be communicated by written words alone.

R. Murray Schafer's study of Pound's translation notebooks confirms that the poet habitually fit "the rhythms of poetry to the curves of a musical line."[40] Pound was devoted to translation as a means of teaching the ear new rhythms. Having translated texts into English from Old English, French, Italian, Provençal, Spanish, Latin, Greek, Egyptian, Chinese, and Japanese, he included the practice as the second type of criticism catalogued in "Dateline." To encourage young poets to find their own voice, Pound challenged them to train their ear with translation work: "Rhythm is the hardest quality of a man's style to counterfeit."[41] But translation was not always possible: "The grand bogies for young men who want really to learn strophe writing are Catullus and Villon. I personally have been reduced to setting them to music as I cannot translate them."[42] In this case, the setting of words to music replaced translation as a means of elucidating the verse. Music could also keep a perfectly good poem alive when the sense of the words was irretrievable or no longer meaningful. In the poetry of Sordello of Mantova, Pound wrote, "there is nothing but the perfection of the movement, nothing salient in the thought or the rhyme scheme."[43]

Pound made transcriptions of music by the Renaissance composers Le Duc de Bourgogne, Pétrus Convitortio, and the troubadour poets Gaucelm Faidit and Arnaut Daniel.[44] He taught himself to read several forms of early music notation, working directly from parchment manuscripts in the archives of the private and state libraries in Europe. From 1917 to 1920 he wrote music criticism for *The New Age,* a London weekly.[45] With few lessons in music composition, he produced a small body of work, including a setting of Dante's sestina "Al poco giorno," among his original works for violin. His most important output is the pair of operas intended for dramatic production for stage, radio, film, and possibly television (1919–1933).

Pound's technique for setting words to music adhered to the principle that the melody of a song arises from the "tonal leadings" of the words themselves; the rhythm emerges from the spoken proportions of vowels to consonants, and is also established by the words. For the cadences to properly reflect the emotion of the poem, the governing tempo of the poem (or its sections if there are several tempi) and the durations of the notes have to be precise in their relation to the poet's words. "The difficulty in WRITING music is in the RHYTHM NOT in pitch . . . anybody can tap a pyanny till they find the pitch they want. The question of the DURATION of the note, is another job altogether. . . . Get a metronome and learn HOW long the different syllables, and groups of them take."[46] Rhythm will be Pound's equivalent to "pure color" in painting. Particularly irksome to Pound was a performer's liberty with tempi as a means of coloring the words with emotion, for example, the common tendency of singers to add a ritard to the ending cadences of phrases. The "absolute rhythm" already inscribed in the words requires a steady tempo to bring across the poet's emotion:

> As for the verse itself: I believe in an ultimate and absolute rhythm as I believe in an absolute symbol or metaphor. The perception of the intellect is given in the word, that of the emotions in the cadence. . . .

> . . . Music is . . . pure rhythm; rhythm and nothing else, for the variation of pitch is the variation in rhythms of the individual notes [i.e., the frequency of vibrations], and harmony the blending of these varied rhythms.[47]

According to Pound's system, it is the poet, not the performer, who is responsible for emotion in the music. The performer's craft is to mechanically incise the sonic contours with breath and voice within a given tempo. The distinction is important in the production of the operas because, theoretically, addition of emotive interpretation would obfuscate the poet's uncounterfeitable rhythm, the single most important element.

In 1923, Pound engaged the precocious American composer and concert pianist George Antheil to collaborate with him in what became the first of several Paris experiments undertaken by Antheil—the precise representation of the speech patterns of *Le Testament*'s Old French in microrhythmic notation.[48] Antheil worked from the original score prepared by Pound in 1920 with the help of Agnes Bedford. The new Antheil edition used irregular meters that were considerably more elaborate than Stravinsky's benchmarks of the period—*Le sacre du printemps* (1913) and *L'histoire du soldat* (1918).[49] In particular, there was little musical precedent for many of the shifts from one meter to the next. The challenge for the conductor was to be able to hear the beat of the upcoming problematic measure internally while conducting a preceding measure in a different time signature.[50] When the music was prepared for broadcast by the BBC in 1931, conductors were still learning to prepare themselves and the musicians for difficult mixed meter.

The difficulty of the music was contested by Olga Rudge, who had played violin in the Paris 1924 and 1926 excerpt performances of *Le Testament*. Because of the complexity of the microrhythms, Pound was obligated to compose simpler arrangements of the music for violin and voice to substitute for various numbers of the Pound/Antheil score, which Rudge and Bedford both considered impractical. Nevertheless, Pound wrote a publicity piece for the BBC describing the music as obvious: "The technique is so bare and simple as hardly to need explanation. The interest held by the single melody then by that melody sustained or 'forced onto' a ground tone then successively against another melody, against another scale system; one rhythm forced against another."[51]

The articulation of the poem's movement by music upheld one of the basic laws of modernist poetry: "The music of poetry is not something which exists apart from the meaning."[52] Working idiosyncratically but very much within the current of ideas regarding music as criticism and experimentation with meter and counterrhythms, Pound's specific intent for the opera was to demonstrate the influence of Villon's poetic movement, or vigor, upon English poetry. Modernism's debt to Villon is found in its second law: poetry should not stray far from the language of everyday speech.[53]

Melodrama

On October 23, 1931, the BBC's in-house publication *Radio Times* announced the newly adapted, newly titled Villon opera "The Testament of François Villon, a Melodrama by Ezra Pound."[54] The word *melodrama* is formed from the Greek roots *melos* (song) and *drama* (actions, events). Considered in a musical context, it refers to the dramatization of spoken words against a musical accompaniment. Within the theatrical tradition, the primacy of this relationship between words and music diminished as the genre, responding to commercial pressure, developed a sentimental and sensational style that took precedence over form. The drama of choice in England since 1800, melodramas produced on the English stage a century later represented a rich store of vernacular speech and dynamic rhythms that were taken up by the cinema. The simple stories of heroes, heroines, and their villains were stretched into three- to five-act extravaganzas. Violence, farce, and pathos were played in rapid succession, accompanied by music that either created or underscored the emotion. The dramas climaxed in an impossible rescue and happy ending that reversed a series of episodic defeats and delivered a moral tonic by the final curtain. The French romantic drama, though it used elevated speech and concluded on a dark note, thrived commercially by resembling melodrama, and came to be recognized as a variant of the genre. The action and intrigues of the early Gothic melodramas took place within medieval castles and monasteries. Some of the characters and themes of these plays—outcasts, ghosts, long-lost relatives, and long-concealed crimes—are resuscitated in Pound's melodramas, even if the formulaic plots are not.

Despite the flights of imagination, all of these trends in melodrama gave way to realism. The portrayal of ordinary people in realistic clothing was already considered a form of realism, as was the on-stage assemblage of soldiers, jugglers, and horses, for example, in scenic spectacles that included battles, waterfalls, fires, and snowstorms. By the 1830s the template for melodrama had changed, and theatrical realism would increasingly be associated with scientifically exact behavioral studies within the theater environment, usually domestic interiors. In England, the public interest in a more introspective realism led to further hybridization of melodrama by the London stages constrained by law to produce a lighter fare of drama. These "minor" theaters were, until 1843, subject to governmental restrictions that prohibited them from offering "legitimate" or spoken-word dramas—religious plays or Shakespearean and Restoration dramas. Interested in expanding their repertory to appeal to the tastes and social aspirations of a burgeoning middle-class audience, these theaters adapted the "royal theater" repertory to the "official" requirements of melodrama—three acts and a musical accompaniment.[55]

The publicizing of the Villon one-act radio opera in 1931 as a "melodrama" conformed to this liberal tradition of exploitation that had become endemic to the genre. For the design of a graphic announcement in *Radio Times,* the BBC drew forward melodrama's faded history of gothic thrillers and adaptations of verse plays (see plate 5). Though the designation of melodrama undoubtedly met with his approval (or was suggested by him), Pound, in his writing, consistently referred to the Villon as an opera. It was originally conceived as an intimate chamber piece during the period of Europe's "little theater" rebellion against grandiosity. The transformation into a melodrama for a mass audience had its basis in Pound's dual career as a music and drama reviewer. At least one year prior to the first sketches for *Le Testament,* Pound was evaluating the suitability of a number of dramatic forms that could accommodate music, the vernacular tongue, and the Poundian aesthetic. He had already published a number of independent articles on the subject of drama when he took on temporary employment as the drama critic for two London weeklies—*The Outlook* (October 1919) and *The Athenaeum* (March, April 1920).

Reviewing a melodrama at the Haymarket Theatre, Pound placed "sentimentality, exalted platitudes, [and] rant" within the scope of "sentimental realism," or bad melodrama, but insisted on looking past current practice to melodrama's potential:

> The language of this or of any other melodrama is capable of exposing the course of events, and of giving "character" in comic relief. It is, however, utterly incapable of expressing emotion. This or any melodrama is likely to contain several roles which only a Duse or Bernhardt could make plausible, roles which only French Alexandrines or the Best Aesculean or Shakespearean stylisation could make speakable. . . . Melodrama is the only mechanism of the contemporary stage, or almost the only working mechanism, by which an author can recall the "larger issues."[56]

The reviewer denies the potential for plausible human emotion within the language of melodrama, and locates such emotion only within the purview of the best interpreters of theatrical language and gesture. Though we do not think of Pound as a dramatic theorist, we here find him attempting to replicate one of the main tenets of his literary theory for a nascent drama theory—the effective use of separate sources for meaning and emotion. In this article, he considers the advantages of melodrama, once it is divorced from emotion and sentimentality, for a treatment of the "larger issues," which are linked to an exposition of "the course of events." One presumes that the "larger issues" Pound refers to are the intellectual, moral, and spiritual questions that repeat in history—part of the "permanent basis in humanity." He goes against the grain of English drama since the 1600s, when legal penalties insured that serious issues were equated with the elevated speech of tragedies, or religious and historical plays, and not with plays of everyday speech, such as political satire and comedy. The language of melodrama, directed to an unsophisticated audience, could expose "character," but only in "comic relief," and, presumably, related to the larger issues. In Pound's view, emotion was manufactured and circulated at will by the actors. It was external and distinct from the written contours of comic relief that were integral to the play text.

Comic relief, a technique or device, must be further distinguished from the modern genre of comedy. Pound wrote of them interchangeably, positioning contemporary comedy under the author's aegis. If we follow his trend, we will find him attempting to redirect comedy for his larger purpose. The emotion facilitated by our notion of modern comedy, however, is a pastiche drawn from three sources—the play text, the play's characters, and the audience. It is at the service of humor and subject to a system of checks and balances. If one source fails at humor, the others will also fail. The emotion that Pound identified in melodrama does not conform to such a contract with either author or audience. In the hands of the performer, the dramatic situation presents the same problems he identified with the vocal and instrumental interpretation of music, cited above. He sought to recover artistic control over emotion through a strategic use of comedy as criticism. The comedic writing he settled on for his radio laboratory is no more than a scattering of punch lines throughout the script, placed for comic relief. There is little interchange that builds directly to, or feeds on, these lines. He reveals a distrust of performer and audience, and exploits this skepticism to comment humorously and critically on the operas' more trustworthy sources—the music and poetry.

For his 1930s radio scripts, he augmented the number and type of character roles in order to more brazenly stand comic relief against the classical literature that constitutes each opera's primary libretto. His characters' speech is not particularly funny; rather, it is dry, terse, and aphoristic. Its merit is that it stays in the ear after the details of the scene have dropped away. The moods expressed (awe, cordiality, annoyance, arrogance, despair, confusion, impatience) are *symbols* of psychic states rather than grist for narrative development. These psychic states are responsible for the inertia and momentum (the rhythms of his dramas) that, with fate, determine the "course of events."

We can better anticipate the neoclassical trend of Pound's intentions for a new drama theory by reordering his statement "Melodrama is the only mechanism of the contemporary stage . . ." to read "Melodrama is only the mechanism of the contemporary stage . . .". Pound endeavors to bring forward a technique with a rich history, without trying to recreate the emotion with which it is associated. This, at first glance, is the early twentieth-century neoclassicism of Stravinksy, though Pound's inclination toward it slightly predates his involvement with the music of Stravinsky. The music reviews for *The New Age* demonstrate his intellectual engagement with the neoclassicism of early seventeenth-century music theater (for example, Caccini, 1551–1618, and Monteverdi, 1567–1643), spanning well into the eighteenth century (as represented by Mozart, 1756–1791).

The neoclassicist doctrine in theater demanded attention to a philosophic truth that could be drawn from encapsulated dramatized events, and moral lessons that reinforced this perspective. Today, we recall this movement as part of the baroque period, remembered not for its intellectual lessons but for its emotion, expressed as an excessive yet essential embellishment, characterized in music by mathematical precision. In the most general terms, a neoclassical technique developed by which the artist identified a temporal emotion and, through craft, diverted it to serve a structural purpose. Pound's statement of a process concerning the creation of an absolute symbol in poetry, quoted earlier, resonates with, but does not duplicate, neoclassical technique. Pound relocates the source of emotion in art in the structure of art: the intellectual perception—given in the meaning of words—is separated from the emotional perception—heard in the sonic contours of words. The vernacular genre of melodrama, an art of music and words, offset by Pound's newfound structural purpose for comedy, offered the author a palette on which to experiment with the combination of emotion and ideas. Humor was to be the built-in safeguard to inhibit the interpreter's emotion.

Aldous Huxley's *Athenaeum* drama review the following spring characterized melodrama as a genre of intense but false emotions, which the audience encounters only in the theater. For Huxley, melodrama was wholly divorced from life, incapable of exposing even hackneyed truths. Only tragedy could handle the "larger issues":

> Melodrama deals with harrowing emotions *in vacuo,* with hypothetical agonies that have no real connection with life as we know it. However painful these emotions may be, they affect us only temporarily and superficially; we recognize them as something

apart, inapplicable to our own lives or to life in general. Tragedy is distinguished from melodrama by possessing this universal applicability; it affects us intimately, for we recognize in tragedy a truthfulness which is absent, whatever its realistic plausibility, from the melodrama.[57]

Tragedy had long been out of favor on the English stage, having yielded to melodrama, comic opera, grand spectacle, and illusion—in other words, to a thriving theatrical commercialism. Pound, like Huxley, condemned the grand crowd-pleasers. He viewed the scenic innovations brought about by the installation of stage elevators, hydraulic lifts, and treadmills as "Semitic luxuries" intruding upon the literary worth of the theater. Less ambitious vaudeville theater provoked Pound's epithet "Malebolgic."[58] The promise of melodrama to unite music with the vernacular language, however, sustained an allure for Pound.

When he considered the potential of melodrama in association with comedy, he offered the patronizing view that the two genres succeeded precisely because they lacked artistic vision and direction: "[Melodrama is] a play neither written nor acted; it is a convention, as much as the Italian commedia del arte or Punch and Judy is a convention. . . . It deals in, or rather, is based on a set of moral clichés and platitudes, but these, like the propositions of La Sainte Foi Catholique [that is, the propositions of the Catholic faith], hang together in a perfectly harmonious fashion."[59] Six months later he examined musical comedy under the same light: "Musical Comedy is a convention, and therefore permissable; it is a convention which has never quite decided on itself, and is therefore without standards."[60]

The title of his first review for *The Athenaeum* had settled the matter by declaring melodrama a kind of in-between state of "dramedy."[61] Pound perceived that the genre could handle more play and substance. Certain conventions of melodrama he dismissed as de rigueur jokes—the balcony scene, a corps de ballet that cannot dance. Within ten years we find him scripting for his own dramedy *Cavalcanti* a balcony scene and a flowerpot joke that is pure slapstick.

It is in the area of musical convention that Pound questioned if it were not possible to render something more dramatic, better constructed, and of higher musical standards than the outdated tunes and rhythms heard on the stage. He advocated better musicians and an occasional "serious" song.[62] As for finding the appropriate English verse to set to music, he complained, "it just wasn't THERE to be musick'd. . . . The technique of British verse-writing is so woolly, so lacking in variety and strophic construction when it is even singably efficient, that a good musician like [Henry] Lawes, interested in the relations and counter-tensions of words and melody went on to a field of greater interest [i.e., setting Greek and Latin verse]."[63] Pound refused to set to music English verse or verse in translation. His task, as he saw it, was to carry across through music the untranslatable strophes of important poets (the protagonists) such as Villon and Cavalcanti, to preserve the freshness of their sound, the larger issue being the advancement of poetry—the specific bequest in the case of Villon, and the general theme of a poet's legacy in the case of Cavalcanti.

Pound's interest lay in restoring a primacy to melodious inflection and rhythmic qualities of the words, as had been the case in the Greek classical drama, and in the troubadour tradition of *motz el son* (words and music). Melodrama, as it was practiced in the English and northern European traditions, consisted of a musical accompaniment to a spoken text, where the languages, often monotonic in their acoustic properties, contrasted rather than united with the music. Pound's eventual adoption of the genre for his radio operas sought the best of both practices. His song settings would unite French, Provençal, and Italian verse with music; the English dialogue, characterized by strongly inflected vernacular speech with a stylistic unity of expression, would contrast the music with comic relief.

A production of the comedy "Society" at London's Scala Theatre contained a brief and memorable allusion to the war, which Pound judged more effective than the elaborate treatment of similar topics in current "serious" plays. "Society" prompted Pound to consider musical comedy in relation to the classical Japanese drama: "The remaining convention [following the dramatic and musical conventions] of musical comedy is the journey; this, I believe, exists as a convention in the classic plays of Japan, whence it can hardly be derivative, but it has no regular prototype in European drama."[64]

When he scripted his operas for radio, he loosely adapted the notion of the journey to depict the transportation of dramatic characters. This was achieved obliquely in the Villon (a biographical journey through the life by means of a legal document, the will) and directly in *Cavalcanti* (a biographical journey through the adult life). The concept of journey is particularly apropos to the intricate design of the works. Each opera "tracks" its poet-protagonist on three simultaneous trajectories: one path moves through the poet's language; another through Pound's selection of the poems, their ordering and assignment to different characters; and the third through Pound's music, made from the poet's words. These "journeys" transpire in acoustic space rather than in geographic or emotional space.

The remainder of the review of "Society" offers a further glimpse into Pound's procedure. Observing that the transportation of the characters "*en masse*" broke with the classical rules of unity for Western theatrical time and space, Pound found the appeal of the play "neither to ear nor to dramatic sense" but rather to the uncritical eye hungry for decoration and "a profusion of variety."[65] Pound constructed for his reader a blueprint for the effective interrelation of dramatic elements of the stage:

> The value of multiplicity on the stage is the same for these group scenes as for ballet; it follows the simple aesthetic principle that when the single object is not interesting enough to retain the eye, the entertainer must provide so many objects that no eye in the audience can quite exhaust its analytical process, the search for perfection must not receive a convincing negation. This profusion of variety should alternate with exactness of pattern.[66]

Pound aimed his dissection of the principal parts of drama toward understanding the basis and potential for those elements apart from their tradition of execution and any rules to which they were compelled to conform. We find in these comments a source for the eclecticism of his music and radio operas, especially in their attempts to separate the source of meaning from that of emotion, and to discretely appeal to the senses of eye and ear. Pound's approach to repetition and pattern through the kind of excess called for above would be reserved for his operas' central arias, Heaulmière's "La vieille en regrettant le temps de sa jeunesse" and Cavalcanti's "Donna mi prega," respectively. Heaulmière and Cavalcanti would each be interrupted by comic figures (Gallant and the Bianchi, respectively) who contradict the sentiments of the main characters. By their pointed comments, these figures provide a context for each song's envoy (the final verse that dispatches the poem) that immediately follows their words. These poetic sentiments, having been scrutinized by fools, may go out into the world with renewed authority and audacity. Fortified by excess and humor, the arias demonstrate that Pound was prepared to entertain his audience.

The Villon Opera

Villon's life is known through his semiautobiographical poems and the police records of the City of Paris. His large poem *Le testament* plays freely upon conventions of the Church (liturgy, psalms, prayers) and State (legal documents). It conforms to prescribed legal format and follows the forked example of the legitimate and parodic legal testaments of the day. The latter were a literary prototype of great mockery, including obscenity and satire directed against the Church.[67] At the close of the poem ("De tout ce testament . . . A tout cecy je m'y consens"), Villon grants authority to the notary Jean de Calais to gloss, define, build up, abridge, add to, cross out, interpret, or annul his will. Pound rearranges its order. By doing so he arrives at an original and overarching dramatic design that draws from among Villon's verse and biographical comments a small selection—one could call it an amulet for a French epoch. The selection stands in contrast to the great subjects of Canto IV—passionate love and the building of cities—with its squalid square, brothel and tavern, and a desolate hill of fifteenth-century Paris.

Le Testament (1920–1923)

The opera *Le Testament* began to take shape the same year as Canto IV, with Pound's observation that the music for two of Villon's poems already existed in the words themselves.[68] By 1921 the approximately fifty-minute, one-act opera contained eleven poems from Villon's fifteenth-century *Le testament,* and the miscellaneous ballad "L'épitaph Villon," added for the separate final scene. The poems are strung together as a series of entertaining vignettes performed by Villon and characters from his world. The staged version of the opera should be dramatized as a series of discrete songs, each portrayed by its appropriate musical idiom—troubadour song, women's song, jongleur's song, drinking song and group dance, and prayer—in a riotous processional that converges in one lowlife corner of Paris.

Villon's *fals'amors,* or "love by the hour," had no place in Canto IV, and little place throughout *The Cantos* as a whole.[69] The canto's concluding references to remnants of pagan goddess worship and to Cavalcanti's *fin'amors* help to explain why Pound devoted himself to a large Villon project outside the long poem. Pound valued Villon's language, its vigor and accuracy, more than almost any other French poet, but whores for hire did not fit with Pound's vision for his epic—the building of an earthly paradise, in which coition would once again be sacred, its potential for mysticism and revelation reestablished according to the ancient mysteries.[70]

Villon's position in relation to the Church in the opera *Le Testament* is portrayed by Pound as a state of symbiosis rather than antithesis, despite the crimes and heretical taunts of the foul-mouthed bard. To Pound, Villon and the Church were partners in the abnegation of the sacred mysteries. Stage instructions for live performance of the opera call for a church wall as backdrop to the action outside the tavern and whorehouse.[71] The point was emphasized in the 1931 radio portrayal of the character of the priest. Given just a few jaunty bars to sing, his passage from church to whorehouse was marked by an increase in echo effect once he arrived at the brothel door. He transported the stony sound of the church with him. His role was not to engage in the sacraments of the Church, but to engage in a spoiling of the sacrament of coition.[72]

The distance between Pound's earthly paradise and the Paris square can be heard in Pound and Antheil's microrhythms, which are calculated according to supposed speech patterns of Old French. These add up to a rhythm of unending difficulty. Listening to the music, we discover no predictability or real polish of manner, no comfort zone for singer or listener, no rests or breath marks, not even in the mother's prayer. These are not the rhythms of people secure in their own beds each night. The music admits the corporeal rhythms (human bones are called for in the percussion part)—scratches and hiccoughs, physical obsessions and physical limits—nothing that would be admissible to courtly etiquette. Even the repetitive syncopated dance patterns of "Père Noé" are made to lurch in counterrhythm one against another. It is a rhythm of poverty and industry combined. Not everyday workaholism but craftsmanship. With melody against ground tone and forced against another melody, with a polyphony that spurned traditional laws of harmony and spurned counterpoint, the Pound/Antheil score managed to graph not only the voice but the reciprocity between life and voice that contributed to the potency and originality of Villon's verse. It was a test of Pound's idealized abstraction of "absolute rhythm" against a practical, if extreme, system—a test conducted in the laboratory of someone obsessed with the relationship between words and music.

Synopsis of Action

The action of Pound's opera does not quite add up to a plot or dramatic story: the outlawed Villon moves back into Paris despite an outstanding warrant for his arrest in that city. His closest friends gradually assemble around him—Ythier, a former girlfriend nicknamed Rose, the old prostitute Heaulmière, her protégés Gantiere, Blanche, and Guillemette. Joined by Villon's mother, the group urges Villon to flee for his life, but to no avail. Villon pens his last will and testament. By evening the gathering crowd has grown quite large and quite drunk. Their singing and dancing attract the attention of the police. Villon is arrested. A final tableau depicts six lads hung by the neck. Each director mounting the production must decide if Villon is among the six, as history has left no trace.

Selection of Music

The opera's first number, "Et mourut Paris ou Helaine," is about Troy, and, following its destruction, the beginnings of Western civilization—the theme developed in Canto IV. The second song, "Dictes moy ou . . . est Flora la belle rommaine," recalls virgins, courtesans, and women who took the veil from Roman time to the Middle Ages. Ythier's "Mort, j'appelle de ta rigueur," the only gesture to twelfth- and thirteenth-century

Table 1 **Pound's selections from Villon's *Le testament* (1461) in their original order**

Line	
169	Je plains le temps
313	Et mourut Paris
329	Dictes moy (Ballade)
453	Advis/Ha, vieillesse felonne et fiere
533	Or y penser belle Gantiere (Ballade)
625	Pour ce amez tant que vouldrez (Suivez beauté) (Double Ballade)
713	Je regnie amours
873	Dame du ciel (Ballade)
910	Item, m'amour, ma chiere Rose
942	False beauté (Ballade)
978	Mort, j'appelle de ta rigueur (Lay)
1238	Père Noé (Ballade)
1591	Se j'ayme et sers la belle (Ballade)
1996	Icy se clost le testament
Frères humains (from Villon's miscellaneous poems)	

fin'amors in *Le testament* (explained perhaps by the fact that it was commissioned of Villon by another), introduces the chivalrous tradition of devotion to one woman. Penniless and old, Villon responds that his only regret, "Je plains," shall be for his own youth. The old whore Heaulmière turns the focus onto her ravaged body, "La vieille en regrettant le temps de sa jeunesse." Characters continue to come forward in a procession of fabulously entertaining and silly rationales for what has already been perfectly well settled through time and commerce: love should be sold, by the hour. It is sheer folly to think that love endures or that man has *virtù,* but this thought has driven history and literature for millennia. Villon, testator-scribe of the opera, reads from his will,

> *Item, m'amour, ma chiere Rose, Ne luy laisse ne cuer ne foye,*
> *Elle ameroit mieulx autre chose.*
> [Item: to my well-loved Rose, I leave neither heart nor liver;
> her taste falls well below those things.][73]

Table 2 **Pound's ordering of selections for his opera *Le Testament* (1923)**

Et mourut Paris
Dictes moy
Mort j'appelle de ta rigueur
Je plains le temps
Advis/Ha, vieillesse felonne et fiere
False beauté
Item, m'amour, ma chiere Rose
Or y penser belle Gantiere
Dame du ciel
Mère au Saveur (by Willaume li Viniers, 13th century)
Suivez beauté (Pour ce amez tant que vouldrez)
Se j'ayme et sers la belle
Je regnie amours
Père Noé
On ne les ayme que pour l'eure (spoken, 1931 radio opera only)
Frères humains
Icy se clost le testament

The opera's "great aesthetic arc," upheld above all in the music, keeps the work within the borders of the kind of teleological doctrine that informs ritual, and prevents it from emerging solely as personality and psychodrama.[74]

A Model for the Opera

One can only guess what Pound meant when, writing to Yeats to inquire about the possibility of a production at the Abbey Theatre, he described his work as modeled on the Greek theater rather than Noh drama: a "single act and final tableau."[75] Pound could have meant no more than to give a practical idea of requirements for program time and scene change.[76] The frenzy of the crowd that bursts into dance while singing "Père Noé" (Chorus of the Drinkers) suggests the Greek model, where the chorus danced in honor of the god (in the case of *Testament,* they honor the Biblical figure Noah).[77] Pound's specification of a gibbet rather than a gallows carries an echo of Greek drama: the *ekkuklema* or "rolling cart" bears the bodies of the victims onto the stage for the final scene.[78]

But, in fact, the elements of the opera appear to equivocate between the Greek and Noh models. Pound's staging instructions call for masks, wigs, and stylized gestures; they demand stillness when the characters are not singing, and articulated bodily isolations when they are.[79] The restraint seems well suited to the classical Japanese drama, but this can be said only because the living tradition of Noh survives whereas Greek drama does not. Pound's dramatic structure also straddles the Greek (scene change, ritual and dance, songs) and Noh (journey, ritual and dance, songs) models. Further complicating the issue are Fenollosa's many comparisons to Greek theater within his notes.

Le Testament's source of emotional power lies within the poetry and music, inclining it toward the Noh drama. The vague story carries emotional resonance as well. For example, the verse "Frères humains," popularly called "Villon's Epitaph" and catalogued among Villon's miscellaneous poems, is a plea for mercy for five or six young men who have been condemned to death by the royal court. Their criminal lives are made noble by their prayers (even beyond the grave, the urge to be noble will dog us all). The expression of humility elevates the common person's plight, fulfills their need to be recognized, and solicits prayer. It is an emotion closer to Noh than to Greek drama.

Several explanations could account for the ensuing confusion regarding models. The first is that Pound again withheld naming Noh as a source for his organization of elements, as he had done with *The Cantos,* for unknown reasons. Second, he undoubtedly drew inspiration from the *Commedia* by Dante and may have also drawn on other models, such as twelfth- and thirteenth-century passion plays or works by individual playwrights.[80] Third, he thought of his models as interpenetrable, bridged by a spiritism that he had already adapted to his poetry in what Hugh Kenner has referred to as a "homeomorphism of spirits."[81]

When Pound rescripted *Le Testament* for a large radio audience, he made additions to the music score, expanded the dialogic "joins" into a dramatic plot that moved through fictional time by means of flash-forward, and flashback, worked within conventions established by opera and by film montage, and called the new work a "melodrama."

For Pound the modern dramatic play text was stillborn. It was neither the impetus that brought an audience to the theater nor the provocative aspect of theater that stayed with them when they left. The "rhymes and syntax" had been taken up by cinema. Radio could do nothing to fulfill the promise of gesture or visual design. Why should Pound turn to drama then, in 1931, with a work adapted for British radio? What could radio provide? *Voice.* Voice was the smallest unit to which the practice of words and music could be reduced, the lowest common denominator to which the production of *melos* and *drama* could refer. Radio plays were about voices.[82] Theoretically, radio voices would be free of the usual visual distractions of bodies, gestures, props, and environment. Voices on radio offered the promise of pure sonic contour in a time-based medium, the opportunity "to cut a shape in time."[83]

2

The Cantos and the Parallel of Radio

POUND WAS THINKING ABOUT RADIO in relationship to *The Cantos* at least as early as 1924, the year he moved to Rapallo, a small town on the Ligurian coast with an established residential foreign population. The first radio transmissions received there in 1925 emanated not from within Italy but from the new BBC thirty-kilowatt transmitter at Daventry, England, which employed a long wavelength of 1,500 meters, powerful enough to be heard throughout most of Britain as well as on the continent under good atmospheric conditions. Italian broadcasting soon followed suit, and was licensed by the Mussolini government as the Unione Radiofonica Italiana (URI), with its first and main station in Rome, and, later, regional stations in Naples, Palermo, and Milan.[1]

In correspondence with his father concerning *The Cantos,* Pound wrote, "Simplest parallel I can give is radio where you tell who is talking by the noise they make."[2] The letter describes two cantos from the "Hell" section of his poem in terms of a different radio poetic:

> You hear various people letting cats out of bags at maximum speed. Armaments, finance, etc. A "great editor" or at least edt. of the woilds best known news sheet, a president of a new nation, or one then in the making, a salesman of battleships, etc. with bits of biography of a distinguished financier, etc.
>
> Mostly things you "oughtn't to know," not if you are to be a good quiet citizen. That's all.

> Who made the bhloody war? The cantos belong rather to the hell section of the poem; though I am not sorting it out in the Dantescan manner . . .
>
> Am leaving the reader, in most cases to infer what he is getting.[3]

Radio offered a great variety of aural events. The juxtaposition of voices required listeners to identify who was talking and what was being said, without visual aids or program notes. It was the first time in history that random snippets of conversation and music could be heard as foreground material. "Skip anything you don't understand and go on till you pick it up again," Pound advised Sarah Perkins Cope regarding *The Cantos.*[4] He could have been talking about the radio dial. Figures from the past are brought together in the present, the foreground, which is the poem. Pound later claimed to have anticipated radio in the early cantos' presentation of personae and their intersection in radio time and space.[5] "All the first fifty Cantos are simultaneous," Pound told a visitor to St. Elizabeths.[6]

Pound's anticipation of broadcast radio, and his eventual use of it in the 1930s as a medium that could cut between and juxtapose the transient, recurrent, and eternal voices of his poetry and music, was shaped by radio's earliest voice experiments in the opening decade of the century. The first documented American radio broadcast was an experiment conducted by R. A. Fessenden from Brant Rock, Massachusetts, to ships at sea on December 24, 1906. Fessenden's program included a short talk, the singing of carols, a work by Handel, and the recitation of a poem.[7]

The first land-to-land vocal transmission was surrounded by an atmosphere of fantasy. It concerned the reception of a voice from an unidentified source over a wireless set at the Brooklyn Naval Yard in 1907. The story illustrates the shift not only from military to civilian use, but from military to civilian concepts about content. Dr. Lee De Forest maintained a radio laboratory at 19th Street and Park Avenue in Manhattan. A journalist who was accompanied by a singer visited him one evening for a tour of the laboratory. To demonstrate the apparatus, Dr. De Forest asked his guest to sing into the experimental transmitter. The radio operator at the Naval Yard, expecting to hear only the short and long pulses of

Morse code, heard instead the sound of a woman singing the popular tune "I Love You Truly" through his earphones. He couldn't believe it and is reported to have shouted, "Angels singing in the air!"[8]

For a very brief period of time just after the introduction of wireless voice communications technology, a gap existed between people's understanding and experience of the physical world; they had no conceptual preparation to accommodate the new phenomenon of radio that had been brought into their world. Though the time period required to adjust to the new concept of radio space would prove to be nominal, the very first experience of living in a world that seemed to defy human reason was momentarily profound. Radio listeners had to learn to make sense out of dislocated sounds and disembodied voices. The first step was to accept the simultaneity of the radio speakers' real presence in the radio station and their spirit presence in the home (their virtual presence). A columnist for the October 29, 1923, *Manchester Guardian* described his experience of radio: "Like the traditional ghosts that wander in space, seeking to find a way within human cognisance, the ether was chock-full of voices striving to gain one's ear. If it goes on, some angel will have to read the Riot Act. Normally, of course, you pick up what you want and hear it through; but we were just experimenting, and the man at the levers switched us all over the kingdom."

Pound would later judge the spirit presence made possible by radio a blight, "the personae now poked into every bleedin' 'ome and smearing the mind of the peapull."[9] But between the first experiments and the early years of institutional broadcasting, the collective imagination was exposed to a surrealist world of noise fragments, a chansonnier of angels singing and reading on the air. Pound's radio dramas would resuscitate some of the flavor of the thirteenth- and fourteenth-century chansonnier, a compilation of poems, with biographies and anecdotes related to the poets.[10]

Futurism, Dada, Surrealism

In this section we will consider Pound's development of a radio aesthetic in the context of futurism, dadaism, and surrealism with the aim of delimiting Pound's specific objectives for performance and radio broadcast. The diverse goals of these radical art movements at times overlapped and coexisted so that their revolution in language and literature from the 1910s through the early 1940s was fueled by reactive and reciprocating stimuli.[11] Except for certain aspects of surrealism, the individual and collective interests (as opposed to styles) of these movements diverged in a pronounced way from those of Pound. This review briefly considers their major differences, with more extensive passages devoted to the futurist artist F. T. Marinetti, whose work, produced before and after Pound's radio operas, provides a variety of perspectives, political and artistic.

The artists of these radical movements, in their fractious, cubist, simulacral, amplificatory, and recombinatory manipulations of words and sounds in performance, could be said, like Pound, to have anticipated radio's potential to achieve a plasticity of voices, words, and sounds. Broadcast producers, literary and drama directors, and their fiscal controllers generally, however, did not reciprocate the vision by drawing from among these particular artists to shape radio's future. They asked some of the same questions, pondered similar theoretical issues, and were impacted at least indirectly by these revolutionizing trends in cinema, performance, and language arts. Radio learned to design, manipulate, and disseminate its own radicalized bits and blocks of sound. But radio could do quite a bit more; it could appear to collapse or expand distance as well as time; it could manipulate the illusion of time and space together or alternately, achieving its effects by means of cinema-derived techniques of montage and specially engineered-for-radio electronic devices that controlled timbral differences. Radio sound would achieve effortlessly and silently that which futurism attempted through machine-induced cacophony—erasure of its own history—and that which dada attempted through human pandemonium—erasure of the singular persona or artist. Of course, radio could invent history and glorify the persona as well. When it did so, these new constructions were divorced from a tradition of text and gained a tensile strength, like music, from their imposition upon a primary base of silence (or atmospheric noise). Because the radio wave left behind no physical trace of its source, it inherently held within its physical transmission the unrealized promise of an ideological platform for the antihistory agenda of futurism, and the anti-art, anti-artist declarations of dada.

Admittedly, there would have been difficulties had the dadaists gained access to broadcast. They were first and foremost artists who espoused an anti-artist program that succeeded by confrontational tactics. They were not prepared to infiltrate radio and launch their attacks from a vantage point in which they would lose their visible identity as artists. Further, anti-art, to succeed, had to come from and attack from within its own circle of persons who cared deeply about art.[12] Dada proclaimed war against the subjective states of mind that conjured, nurtured, and believed in art. Unlike the futurists, dadaists held machines to be a pox on the human spirit and not a substitute for art. Dada's staged events, like those of early futurist theater, were often a loose assemblage of variety acts with a gamut of textual styles that ranged from pure nonsense to the surreal, from the expressive to the emotional, but were rarely narrative or sentimental. The rearrangement of sounds as purely formal elements took inspiration from cubism as well as from photographic and cinematic montage. Those formal elements included rhythm, pitch (or sonic contours), repetition, and extremes of duration and dynamic for purely plastic effect. Reading aloud the first two lines of Hugo Ball's *Gadji Beri Bimba,* one can hear beyond the nonsense the play of these elements, "gadji beri bimba glandridi laula lonni cadori/gadjama gramma berida bimbala glandri galassassa laulitalomini . . .".[13]

For all intents and purposes, dada and Pound were opposites.[14] Bypassing for a moment the issue of Pound's embrace of the potential of technology, the prime objective of this book, it will suffice here to point out that Pound infused his writing with persona and meaning: The individual was important and the important individual became the durable persona; that is, he or she would bear up through history in many incarnations—myth, fact, fiction, document, and art. The meaning of Pound's words was critically incised, contrasted, repeated, framed, traduced, disguised, and layered, but never abandoned, even when he injected his poetry with isolated strings of words intended to impart a dadaist effect.

The dada movement, born in neutral Zurich in the middle of the First World War and then transplanted to France, Germany, and Holland, was already dying out when these nations institutionalized their first broadcast facilities. Even if dada's artists were not living on the fringes of society, avoiding the draft, using forged passports, and frequently moving across borders, the question of foreign accents would have hindered their access to broadcasting facilities.[15] Neither state nor commercial radio would have an open microphone policy until after the Second World War. Controlled access to radio equipment and facilities undoubtedly also prevented the futurists from participating in early radio experimentation. Unlike cinema, the new radio art was evanescent, practiced behind the walls of commercial or state officialdom, largely by producers and technicians who did not operate like an avant-garde and, according to film and art historians, achieved little of artistic significance.

F. T. Marinetti and Radio

The figure one generally associates with radio from this period of revolutionary art and anti-art is the Italian Filippo Tommaso Marinetti (1876–1944), dynamic founder and tireless leader of futurism. A painter, poet, novelist, dramatist, soldier, and visionary, he had a particular knack for publicity and propaganda, and kept a plethora of pamphlets and books on futurism in continual circulation. His "Manifesto of Futurism," published in the February 20, 1909, Paris newspaper *Le Figaro,* reached South America that same year, provoking ongoing debate among Brazil's modernists.[16] The debate came to a boiling point when, in the late spring of 1926, he arrived in Rio de Janeiro to promote futurism as the germinating force behind the Fascist cause, and to rally Italian nationals in Brazil to organize for Fascism.

On May 21 and 22, 1926, Marinetti delivered a talk on futurism and declaimed some of his futurist poetry on Brazilian radio for the Italian- and French-speaking sectors of the population. The following day he addressed a conference of Italians on the interventionist and futurist origins of Fascism, "Origini interventiste e futuriste del fascismo," and dispensed advice on how to appeal to the anti-Fascist forces in the country.[17] He received a warm reception from the governmental dignitaries who had been in the audience at the broadcast studios, and especially from President Arturo Bernardes, waning leader of a federalist party struggling to cope with the country's dire economic and political crises. The political alliances presented special challenges for the remainder of his tour.

Inaugurated in 1922 on the occasion of the centennial of the country's independence, Brazilian radio was launched as an integral force for continued independence. South America's largest country vacillated between the need for individual states' rights to govern an extremely heterogeneous population spread across a large geographical area, and the need for a national identity. Radio was just beginning to offer a veneer of homogeneity to the country's diverse classes, races, and regions through the national language of Portuguese.[18] Though Marinetti's radio discourse was largely on art and poetics, several factors were at odds with a population seeking to unite itself through radio: his delivery in foreign languages, his self-described bombastic and rhetorical style "con voce stentorea" (in a stentorian voice), the militaristic preoccupation and confrontational posturing of futurism (as well as the possible mention or promotion of Mussolini or Fascism).[19] Sounding like a foreign provocateur whose job was to promote futurism as the diplomatic face of Fascism, Marinetti quickly discovered, halfway across the globe, that radio deprived him of the physical charisma on which he depended to deliver a message that was meant to entice and provoke. Without the carefully groomed persona and the ubiquitous visual announcements (posters and advertisements) that accompanied his public presentations, the focus of attention shifted from the content of his talk to the foreignness of his delivery. The political fallout from his radio talk was an organized protest against futurism by anti-Fascist organizations.

He would eventually make his appeal to the anti-Fascists, but not before an encounter with a well-prepared political offensive in the south of the country. After the Fascists welcomed him on his arrival at the São Paulo train station on May 24, a group of anti-Fascists—artists and students—disrupted his planned appearance at the Teatro "Casino" Antartico with an anti-futurist demonstration. Marinetti's description of the scene in the theater—"explosions" on the stage floor caused by a rain of vegetable "bombs" hurled at the rising curtain—lent the protest a decidedly futurist disposition despite the anti-futurist sentiment. Forced to shout over the commotion to make himself heard, he abandoned the crowd after only a few words and retreated to the nearby Grill Room, accompanied by his wife and friends.[20]

Better prepared for the crowd at a second Antartico appearance on May 27, Marinetti managed to sustain his voice against the uproar provoked by the Italian anti-Fascists in São Paulo long enough to win the "attentive, admiring and thoughtful" interest of the others present. As recorded in his notebook, the newly enraptured audience was eager to hear about the futurist platform: velocity, simultaneity, a "hot" and virile dynamic, a fusion of metal with flesh, flora and fauna, a call for differentiation between the sexes, and a stand against fashion and luxury. The notebook claims a personal victory rewarded by endless waves of ovations. This time Marinetti made his exit with the crowd, while adversaries pressed his hand to confess their admiration for his prowess despite their differences.[21]

For the rest of his visit to Brazil, he relied on personal appearances and not on radio to interact with the public. The incidents offer perspective on the innate nationalistic bent of radio and the problems presented by the broadcast of foreign views, particularly by foreigners, on radio. Marinetti would draw upon his political experience of radio for his first Italian broadcast of national significance in August 1933, and for the manifesto *Il teatro radiofonico,* published in October 1933.[22]

Marinetti's delay in accessing radio in his own country was partly the result of the preceding decade of tension between his own politically charged artistic activities and Mussolini's government. From its beginning, Italian radio censored all material that violated Fascist policy. In 1927 the government established a new bureaucratic monopoly, Ente Italiano per le Audizioni Radiofoniche (EIAR), which placed all programs under even tighter control by a Supervisory Commission comprised of officially chosen leaders in Italian art, literature, politics, and science. A brief digression to consider Marinetti's political situation in Italy at this time will show that his particular use of radio, like Pound's, was not a flash in the pan, but had roots in the theater as well as in a comprehensive philosophy of art and politics developed over the course of a brilliant career.

That career suffered a major political setback when Marinetti's alliance with Mussolini, formed to combine the resources of futurism and Fascism, was soundly defeated in the November general election of 1919.[23] When Mussolini reacted by rejecting a revolutionary platform, Marinetti aligned the futurists with the socialists and anarchists. Fearing that futurism would be left behind in the growing Fascist regulation of art in Italy, Marinetti used the decade of the 1920s to position himself and the futurists to eventually return to Mussolini, not repentant but triumphant, at the vanguard of a vibrant national and international movement that Italy could not afford to ignore.

Marinetti's relationship to official government had been blatantly oppositional at worst, and marginalized at best. If futurists lacked access to the microphone, this was the main reason. In 1925 a special Rome tribute to Marinetti, *Onoranze a Marinetti,* brought him honorary status as a Blackshirt and personally telegrammed assurances from Mussolini that any differences between Fascism and futurism, being largely a matter of appearance, were surmountable. When in 1929 Mussolini inaugurated the Accademia Reale d'Italia (Royal Italian Academy) he personally selected Marinetti for the first honored group of "immortals" (Mussolini's term). The inductees would receive a handsome yearly stipend with no strings attached except that they pledge loyalty to the Fascist party and salute Mussolini at the opening of their meetings. Marinetti's personal circumstances did not extend to the other artists of the futurist movement, who were still held in suspicion by the strong conservative faction of antifuturists within the Fascist party, and kept marginalized until the 1930 Venice Biennale exhibition.[24]

Futurist Drama

Seeking a futurist wedge into mass culture, Marinetti had marshaled his poets, painters, and musicians since the movement's earliest years to challenge the mediocre and commercial Italian realist theater.[25] Their innovations were originally limited to a new kind of dramatic literature, the futurist *sintesi,* or short scenes of modern life. Slowly turning to technical concerns of the theater itself, futurist drama offered variety programs of body madness (*fisicofollia*), primitivism, eroticism, film, audience singalong, and so forth under the name Theater of Amazement. The futurist Synthetic Theater promoted improvisation and intuition, sensory experience, abstract cerebral energy, and the play of theatrical color, light, and shapes until theater seemed inseparable from the life force itself. Fortunato Depero's Plastic Theater introduced a pure language of form and color, using cubo-futurist constructions, shadow play, puppets, and grotesque animation. Experiments continued in a cascade of new forms: Theater of Light, Theater of Surprise, Theater of Touch, Theater of Visions, futurist cabarets, artists' festivals, and artists' banquets. Until 1924 many of these events were personally subsidized by Marinetti.[26]

Surprisingly, Italian futurist theater made no special contributions regarding the cult of the machine, particularly when compared with futurist theater in Germany and the Soviet Union.[27] This was to change with the participation of Fedele Azari, decorated pilot of World War I. Azari's 1919 manifesto for an Aerial Theater proclaimed the airplane a major protagonist in the new futurist drama.[28] After Azari's death, Marinetti expanded the manifesto and published it under the title *Il teatro aeroradiotelevisivo.*[29] Recognizing the potential of Aerial Theater to increase the influence of futurism in the public sector, Marinetti omitted the word "futurist" from this manifesto to garner political support that would not enrage the antifuturists within the Fascist party.[30]

Following Azari, a number of futurists wrote theatrical treatments of outdoor aerial dramas, with airplanes as the main protagonists, engine noise for music, and the vast panorama of the sky as backdrop. Marinetti's leadership and influence were required to move the scripts into production, and, even then, the productions appear to have gotten no further than one ambitious demonstration on January 28, 1932. Mino Somenzi was credited with the foresight to combine Azari's vision with a dramatic use of radio. Somenzi and Marinetti arranged for a fleet of airplanes to perform a generic episode culled from the growing pile of proposed spectacles. One airplane sent music and speeches to the ground from an extremely powerful loudspeaker. Lower-flying airplanes suspended primitive cathode ray monitors over the heads of the spectators.[31] "Radio" did not refer to public broadcast over a state transmitter but to the concept of dramatic action unfolding in all directions, "sopra sotto, sotto sopra e in tutte le direzioni,"[32] and to wireless communications between airplanes and the ground, radio transmission of television signals to a closed circuit of monitors, and amplification through loudspeakers.

Futurist Radio: *Violetta e gli aeroplani*

Another year passed before Marinetti would broadcast on Italian state radio. *Violetta e gli aeroplani,* a radiophonic drama in three parts, was broadcast January 19, 1933.[33] Geared to a broad public, it offered stereotypical characters, a fairy tale plot, and a chorus of loyalists. The play communicated the first "intention" of the 1909 futurist manifesto, "We intend to sing the love of danger, the habit of energy and fearlessness."[34]

Futurist ideals of leadership and energy were invested in the play's young children, who cavort by the sea in southern Italy. To distinguish between sexes, Marinetti gave the children names that personify certain traits as feminine or masculine. The young girl Violetta personifies the field flower—one like the other, delicate and lovely. Her roots are in the earth. In an act of poetic fancy, the flower dreams of airplanes. Her dream will be realized by her fourteen-year-old cousin, Giunco, personification of the bare-stemmed rush of the wetlands. Nicknamed "motorino," or "little motor," Giunco is the undisputed favorite among the boys at the beach, the singular, creative, energetic leader and aspiring futurist hero whose task is to overcome evil forces lurking in the high cliffs near the sea.[35] Violetta proves herself a loyal friend and resourceful companion to Giunco, but at play's end he disengages himself from her and his nonfuturist world in an act of metallic transcendence.

The script, not totally devoid of the kind of useless dialogue and inessential characters strongly condemned in Marinetti's 1915 theater manifesto, calls for choruses of children's voices and birds, sound effects, and silence—elements forecasting the manifesto on radio yet to be written. Indebted to Luigi Russolo's 1913 manifesto "The Art of Noise," and futurist experiments of the *intonarumori,* or noise machines, Marinetti writes into his script the sounds of different engines—an outboard motorboat had to be distinguishable from the roar of airplane propellers.[36]

Marinetti's method was to create a catalogue of sonic qualities assigned point for point to the diverse elements of the story. These included voices spanning and traversing distances, echoing across rock face, muffled by the sound of surf, emerging from above and below. Marinetti's scripting of voices from above and below, a reminder of the January 1932 aerial demonstration, would not, in fact, be perceived as such on radio. The only hard-and-fast law of aural perception harvested from early radio experiments was "Only distances are heard, not directions." Aural perspective was the artist's new tool: "The perspective element is one of the most effective means of representation in broadcasting . . . the radio artist is bound to call in the spatial properties of sound for representational purposes."[37] Marinetti's futurist script exploited artistic trends in radio, making its mark with a reflexive and conceptual sound design. It proposed to utilize modern radio electronics to convey the more primitive concept of radio as omnidirectional sound as had been done in the previous year's aerial demonstration: Giunco, Violetta, and the wanna-be tagalong Plomplom are always moving up, down, and in all directions; they dive, climb, clamber across trees, fall, and run. They transmit their voices through field radios. In the play's final scene, Giunco, victorious over the evil bird-catcher Gozzonero, hitches a ride on the mail plane to "paradise." The children's shifting locations take place within a shifting environment represented by sounds that, by their nature, move through space—thunder, waves, birds, hurricanes, landslides, wind, and rain. The one sound that does not travel is that of Gozzonero's snoring, the sound of the futurists' enemy. The moving beam of light from the lighthouse in the final scene would have to be imagined visually, as would Giunco's voyage to paradise.[38]

The characteristic infusion of a triple dynamic of speed, simultaneity, and surprise into futurist art creates an expectation that the elements of this play should be in continuous flux, but Marinetti scripted so much dialogue between the characters that a producer would be challenged to keep the voices and sonic elements in constant movement. Rather, the play is built on a rhythmic alternation between moments of perceived corporeal movement through space and moments of perceived stasis (in which exact denotation of conversational words matter). In an attempt to sustain aural tension between movement and dialogue, a drama of space was bravely pitted against the drama of time (as measured by words). The script might have entertained a live audience but over radio the persuasive charisma of Marinetti and the futurist visual presence fell silent. Marinetti would never write for radio in this vein again.

Master of Ceremonies

The significance of radio for Marinetti's career took another interesting turn on August 12, 1933, when he broadcast a poetic welcome and on-the-scene coverage of the arrival near Rome of the celebrated pilot and former commander of the fascist militia Italo Balbo. The expedition, *crociera del Decennale,* ended with a dramatic touchdown of twenty-three aircraft at the mouth of Rome's Tiber River, concluding Balbo's second round trip over the Atlantic, a demonstration for the Chicago world's fair. The Italian royal family joined with government dignitaries for a two-day homecoming of speeches, gun salutes, and a large parade through Rome. It was a triumph for Balbo, given his history of oppositional challenges to the Fascist party over the decade, but an even bigger triumph for Mussolini, who was on hand to aggrandize, kiss, and parade his national hero, the hero's airplanes, and the *atlantici* (as Balbo's flight crew were called), in a gesture to the world of a united Fascist party.[39]

The radio broadcast brought Marinetti onto the world stage with Mussolini, and there the laws of aural perspective proved their political worth. The aural imagination of the Italian radio audience interpreted their presence as a show of unity. A speech by Mussolini suggested a picture of the two men side by side in space. The simple fact of Marinetti at the microphone led the audience to imagine Mussolini in the background, lending Marinetti enormous official presence and authority. Marinetti took the role of master of ceremonies into his own hands, poetically declaiming the event for radio in terms recalling *teatro aeroradiotelevisivo.* To conclude, he mixed the crowd's wild cries with his own: "Eccolo, eccolo, eccolo! [Here he is!] Duce! Duce! Duce! Italia! Italia! Italia!"[40] It was through radio's aural conveyance of these two individuals that the reconciliation of futurism and Fascism was publicly enacted.

Radio as Pure Sensation: *La Radia*

In the October following Balbo's homecoming, Marinetti published, with Pino Masnata, a surgeon and playwright loyal to the futurist movement, the oft-cited manifesto *La Radia.*[41] It is this document that links futurism and Marinetti to the young art of radio, or the possibilities of a radio art. But radio, though young, was not neutral; its use as an arm of politics in the years preceding the Second World War and its nationalistic bias led to diminished prospects for artistic experimentation. *La Radia* did not so much launch futurist influence into the airwaves as it did gesture to a rapidly disappearing freedom to experiment.

The manifesto was published even as the Fascist government was in the process of responding to Goebbels's May 1933 Italian visit regarding reorganization of cultural policy along the lines of the Nazi model.[42] With this in mind, *La Radia* comes into focus as an attempt to secure futurism's place in official history while acknowledging an allegiance to Fascism. The opening statements include a celebratory summation of futurism's accomplishments, the current goals of futurism's second National

Congress, including a new "authentic religion of Fatherland" coupled with anti-Semitism, a new focus on radio ("We futurists are perfecting radio broadcasting which is destined to . . ."), and an offensive attack against radio art of the past ten years.[43] Radio was a new weapon with its own sensations and sounds, like those of the machine gun in World War I; it could be brought into pragmatic use (communication, music), or aesthetic focus (interference, silence, sensations), or could serve futurist ideology (simultaneity). Set against this background, *La Radia* offers a picture of futurism undergoing significant political changes.[44]

The document's attack on the field of radio as timid, staged, and tied to its audience, and on specific instances of French, Belgian and German radio drama as too realistic, differed from the futurist tone of the early scathing attacks on commercial Italian theater begun in 1911. These early declarations had imagined futurism as an entirely new venture seeking to replace what existed, though futurism had not yet had any experience in theater. *La Radia* proclaimed that contemporary radio drama, striving to achieve a futurist synthetic theater, had fallen short of its true goals. *La Radia* would abolish even the futurist Synthetic Theater. By posturing as an authority quasi-institutionalized not only in Italy but in Europe as a whole, and in terms of drama rather than radio, futurism tempered its criticism of a medium that was controlled by the government. By this time the future of radio as propaganda was obvious. Provocation of the radio audience at large was too dangerous, and therefore off limits, while provocation of the theater audience, even if accomplished through radio, could still be tested without dire consequences. A certain recklessness characteristic of earlier futurist challenges was absent.

A stronger challenge to radio to reinvent itself had been launched the previous year from Germany. Bertolt Brecht had complained that radio naively constructed itself into a substitute for the experience of theater, opera, and concerts. In "Der Rundfunk als Kommunikationsapparat" (The Radio as an Apparatus of Communication), he demanded an end to radio as a cheap attempt to wholesale human experience, and called instead for an interactive radio communication dependent upon listeners' input.[45] Marinetti and Masnata in turn called for the elimination of the concept of an audience altogether. It is arguable whether their position advances Brecht's advocacy of two-way communication or falls short of it.

La Radia's insistence on the simultaneity of the two-part process inherent to radio (broadcast and reception) can be seen as an attempt to retain a function for radio that closely resembled the actual experience or sensation of radio. In contrast, the ideas of theorists like Rudolf Arnheim and Brecht depended upon the articulation of a sequential two-way process in order to promote and politicize radio as a form of social communication. The futurist manifesto emphasizes the objectness of radio, "La Radia shall be . . . Essential art" (no. 14). Its platform advocates elements common to both futurism and dada (simultaneity, pure sensation, and break with tradition; nos. 1, 6, 8) and characteristic of surrealism (a new spiritism; no. 9), but overall retains the tenor of futurist demands for a new artistic syntax (*parole in libertà;* no. 12), the celebration of life (gastronomy, love, music, and exercise; no. 15), and the boundless human spirit (art free of time and space; no. 7). Sensation rather than communication is the operating principle of futurist radio.

Marinetti and Masnata's utterly original radio theory—it would do away with communication when activated—is written in language that endows the manifesto with an aura of speculation, abstraction, and unreality, but, above all, optimism. Certainly, the value of the document exceeds its own immersion in futurist concerns by its potential to fascinate later generations of artists. *La Radia* is accorded a certain status as the emblematic, if not historical, beginning of a new audio art and the precursor to post–World War II developments in audio art.

Though the document comments on concurrent radio practice, offering both a cure and vision, its application as a tool for historicizing developments up to and current with its own time has, to my knowledge, remained unexplored. Jeanpaul Goergen suggested this line of inquiry when he posed the question, Why was Walter Ruttmann excluded from *La Radia*'s criticism of French, Belgian, and German radio experimentalists?[46] *La Radia*'s original project, transformation of radio practice, limits its criticism of early radio to radio drama. If we understand the manifesto as a palinode, the reason for rejecting well-respected radio avant-gardists will become clear: futurist art must erase its own history. By claiming that particular avant-gardists aspired to a futurist Synthetic Theater, the futurists were free to erase their own work as well.[47] The attack on experimental narratives for radio that employed actors and divided into scenes was a rejection of Marinetti's own *Violetta e gli aeroplani*. Five conceptual radio scripts written by Marinetti in 1933 rejected dialogue, actor, and story; vocal presentation was limited to fragments of song and soundscape ("Dramma di distanze"), and was stripped of its traditional hegemony in a world of noise.[48]

Radio as Communication

Arnheim's *Radio,* the first publication of a comprehensive radio theory and microphone technique (1936), analyzed the ear's capacity to perceive sound without visual stimulus to arrive at an interpretation of the imagination's processing of the aural perception. It would be misleading to call this a study of passive reception, but in relation to *La Radia,* it can be said to represent the processing of signals by a minimum of intelligence and a maximum of instinct according to unstated assumptions about normal cognitive processes of the new mass audience.

Arnheim wanted a new intimacy in radio, soft voices rather than declamatory ones, a radio addressed to the individual rather than the masses.[49] Private reception of the radio voice was theorized to be quite different than reception by a crowd of people. Though the following conclusions were drawn about American radio, they were meant to apply to the medium in general:

> The microphone is the deadly enemy of the demagogue—a ruthless revealer of "hokum." Two thirds of the appeal of the old-fashioned political oratory and the mob-stirring of the rabble-rouser lay in the hundred-and-one tricks of posture and voice that catch on when the crowd is massed and the speaker looks it in the eye. But what was rousing in the old mass meetings may become ridiculous when it comes through the radio to the single listener. The radio will increasingly tend to put the rhetorician to rout and exalt the realist. Even the most average of average Americans is a more critical listener when he is not part of a mass meeting. The slightest trickery of phrase or voice shows up on the radio.[50]

Arnheim's persuasive communication, with its promise of entrée into subliminal states of mind, proposed to replace the ubiquitous microphone technique—stentorophonic broadcast to the imagined crowd of millions. (Note the reliance upon imagination on both sides of the microphone!) Arnheim wanted the more subtle art for communication's sake.

As Arnheim's ideas were being formulated, the Hitler regime was resuscitating the power of the political rally over radio. By including in its broadcasts the sounds of a euphoric crowd, German radio found it could cancel the listener's critical response as an individual and restore his or her sense of belonging to the group. Arnheim misjudged the power of radio and predicted it would have a receding influence in the wake of television (envisioned as the technological marriage between radio and film). He turned his efforts toward providing tools to prepare for the unknown future impact of television.[51]

The True and False Radio

With opposing methodologies, radio imagination and perceptual studies yielded one overriding conclusion that had very different implications for different individuals, professions, and governments: to discriminate between radio truth and fiction, one must have some experience of the subtle truths and fictions possible on radio. What distinguishes *La Radia* from perceptual theories as a tool for historicizing radio art, and also recommends it, is its emphasis on expanding rather than explaining individual experience and perception.[52] Though *La Radia* transmits its message through the poetic language of sensory promise, for example, the wish to record, amplify, and transmit the vibrations of a diamond ("La Radia sarà" [La Radia Shall Be], no. 5), the underpinnings of a technical document run through it. This particular entry exhibits an awareness of amplification and conversion technology such as Walter Ruttmann employed in the making of his acoustic film *Weekend* (examined below). *La Radia* aspires toward an art-science that refuses to set boundaries to knowledge at a critical moment in history when science, especially radio, was constrained by politics and economics to do so.

Marinetti and Masnata's desire to explore the essential sound of objects, their silence and their vibrations, can be understood as a search for incontrovertible truth. This was one of many fronts on which they fought, alongside the promotion of the principle of war, public relations, and the popularization and commodification of art. The futurist strategy of simultaneity charged with a maximum of dynamic tension precluded contradiction or cancellation. Within futurism, subtlety could be fought for.

Before returning to Pound's relationship to futurism, and then to surrealism, I offer a cursory application of *La Radia*'s proposals to a few of the key artistic radio events of its time. My goal is to introduce by way of this futurist snapshot certain acoustic experiments in radio and film that contributed to the development of a radio technique. This is followed by a closer look at the work of several audio avant-gardists whose work is directly or indirectly related to Pound's radio work for the BBC.[53] When we return to Pound, the nature of his endeavor can be more accurately registered on the overlapping maps of criticism, theory, and voice used to chart his radio career.

La Radia Sarà . . . (twenty proposals)

After stating what La Radia must not be (theater, cinema, or books) and what La Radia will abolish (theatrical space and stage [including the futurist Synthetic Theater], time, unity of action, theatrical personages, audience as self-elected mass critic), the manifesto lists twenty proposals for what La Radia should be.[54] Some proposals are poetic—La Radia shall be the pure organism of radiophonic sensation—but overall the choice of phrasing leans toward a technical language, as in "captazione, amplificazione e trasfigurazione" (reception or recording, amplification, and transformation). A sound signal, or vibration, could be captured in one medium and transferred to another, becoming transformed in the process. For example, sound waves are converted by microphones into electrical signals of fluctuating current. A radio transmitter joins these signals to high-frequency radio waves that it sends through space as radiant energy.[55] Recording technology creates a replica of these fluctuations of electrical current in a solid medium—wax, optical film, or magnetic particles. When read by special equipment, the replicated patterns are converted back into electrical current and sound waves. Sound film and magnetic media were nascent technologies in 1933, generally inaccessible to independent artists except through sponsorship by a corporate entity.

Silence

A predetermined length of broadcast silence was a common device used by early radio dramas to indicate a change of time or location. *La Radia*'s proposal to delimit silence is an attempt to artistically sculpt or give form to silence using radio technology. It recognizes and comments on the broadcasting industry's increasing dependence on sound enhancement through resonance adjustment.

Silence is impure; it is comprised of ambient sounds that are heard as sympathetic vibrations between two or more surfaces. When there are no sympathetic vibrations, a space is considered "dead," and the silence carries no information to the ear. To delimit silence one requires information about that silence, and this is conveyed by sympathetic vibrations between the solid or liquid surfaces dominating the space.[56]

The manifesto goes on to recommend differences in resonance for a voice or sound to render the size of a space acoustically. The logic of the statements, one following the other, is that a space of silence may be heard, but only by means of a referential noise that can reveal something more about the space. The resonance created by a voice or sound carries information about the relationships of surfaces within the space. This information is sufficient to approximate size. A variation in the resonance of a single voice or sound will change the impression of size because it will give an impression of different distances, different surfaces, or both. The isolated sound may decay, but the size of the "delimited silence" has been established.

The manifesto then inverts the proposal. Characteristics of a silent or semisilent atmosphere, that is, one with ambience, should be brought to bear on a voice (or sound) to give it a sense of place. Voice, normally shaped to some extent by qualities inherent to a certain space, can then be shaped by different qualities to suggest different spaces. The characteristics and size of a space are thereby revealed through the voice (or sound).

What has been described above was common, though sometimes controversial, radio practice. Naturally occurring resonance in broadcasting studios was deadened or canceled by the hanging of curtains that absorbed sound and prevented sympathetic vibrations. Various amounts of resonance were then added back into the sound artificially, leading to a new construction of space. The addition of resonance was achieved with sound reflectors, screens, tents, movable ceilings and walls (a later development), and special echo rooms or reverberent chambers, into which some of the sound was diverted via loudspeakers and then recaptured by microphones to be fed back and mixed with the original nonresonant sound to achieve the desired effect.[57] Resonance technique could be used to give the impression of a person traveling distances even while the speaker maintained the same distance from the microphone, standing still.[58] (See figure 1)

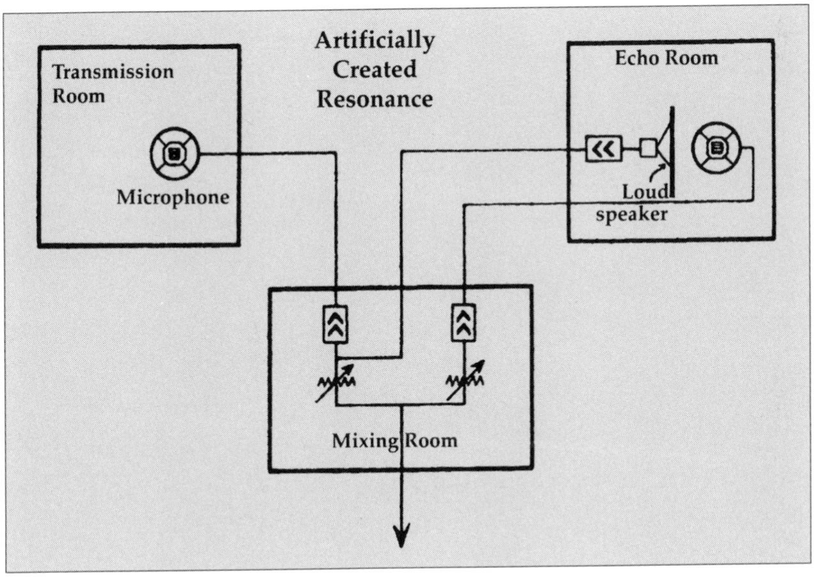

Figure 1 Artificially created resonance (from Rudolf Arnheim, *Radio*).
Courtesy Ayer Company Publishers

Arnheim wrote that sounds transmitted from a deadened space would be sensed as occupying the same space as that of the listener, and that sounds with resonance would be perceived to be external to the listener, a kind of "foreign space." He described the newly delimited space of silence not only as foreign, but as invisible, "It [the sound] is accompanied by a new, peculiar, invisible space; the broadcast is enacted on an 'aural stage' the character of whose resonance can be heard."[59] The aural stage was only invisible in theory; voices or sounds were to provide the listener with enough clues to conjure a familiar picture. Arnheim's description would be more perfectly realized through *La Radia*'s proposed sculpting of sound. If resonance were not the "pure color" of radio, it was the palette from which radio could freely choose to represent any part of the world.

At Berlin Radio the addition of resonance was called "space sound" (*Raumton*), and its application for artistic purpose in 1931 was controversial, particularly among musicians. The Austrian composer Arnold Schoenberg, whose music was performed widely on European radio in the 1930s, accused Berlin Radio of a ridiculous encroachment on the desired musical effect of vibrato and choral sound, which, he claimed, depended on a certain impurity of tone that required the ear to search for the "middle point of this 'simultaneous mass'—to extract the pitch." Schoenberg emphasized the importance of the naturally occurring resonance which "makes the tone 'living', 'interesting', 'lively', 'warm', and all the rest of it."[60] BBC Drama producers were sharply divided over the extent to which to apply resonance, some producers claiming the attention to technology was a distraction to the actor's art.[61]

La Radia recognized that the construction of space by means of radio was already a fact. Its contribution was to demand that these controversial techniques be made available to an audio art that would employ a process whereby radio technology would be exposed and could be enjoyed as radiophonic sensations (proposal no. 6). *La Radia* would cut through the industry-wide controversy of true and false sound. Marinetti and Masnata emphasized these new aspects of radio—the fact of radio fiction, the truth of a purely radio sound or sensation, and the transformative potential of radio freed from narrative.

La Radia also proposed the deliberate broadcast of interference between stations (no. 17). Continuous since radio's beginning in the 1920s, the broadcast of interference was assumed to be undesired and unintentional, an accepted part of a new technology that was susceptible to technical difficulties, static, the fading of signals, power failures, electrical storms, and the misuse of assigned frequencies. Further, radio receiving sets did not yet have noise reduction circuitry or automatic volume control.[62] Listeners in the early 1930s probably remembered electronic silences and broken-up sounds as integral to early radio experience.

On rare occasion, silence (with its component of ambient noise) and interference were shaped in unexpected ways. Because of the primitive state of receivers, ambient noise, static, and silence framed the singing of the before-mentioned broadcast of "I Love You Truly," adding to its angelic cast. Anthony Burgess recalled a revelation he had as a youth: the white noise of early radio yielding to the opening flute lines of Debussy's *Après-midi d'un faune.*[63] Incontrovertible truth took shape from the ether's hiss.

More remarkably, on the eve of the death of King George V, the BBC intentionally broadcast silent airtime. The corporation canceled all programs, substituting in their place a periodic update by BBC Chief Announcer Stuart Hibberd, "The King's life is moving peacefully towards its close."[64] The national presence at the bedside vigil was a participatory event that aspired to political unity by attempting to convey time and space in new ways. This royal silence, a technical simulation of the supposed quietude in the king's chambers and in his heart, forced the listener to imagine the true silence while recognizing the false as broadcast noise and as acceptable deception.[65] Here was consummate radio art, the height of elegiac invention. Far advanced from the ubiquitous revolutionary rhetoric yet arising from it, this isolated gesture by the BBC hints at the (still) unexplored potential of radio. (It is inconceivable that radio would repeat such an experiment today.)

Electricity

The most important demand of *La Radia* was its call for a new art to take over where literature, art, theater, cinema, and story could not proceed (nos. 1 and 2). Indeed, all of the ensuing entries can be considered subsets of this initial call for a new radio art that saw itself born of time and space, apart from materiality and, as becomes more evident, apart from the chisel, pen, typewriter, and printing press, all representative of tradition. The Italian phrase eventually coined for the invention of the typewriter, *macchina da scrivere,* can be said to literally encompass all four of these outmoded technologies. The elimination of the *macchina da scrivere* would make way for new electric machinery that records, amplifies, transfigures, and transmits newly discovered (through electricity) acoustic coordinates of space/time such as the acoustic dimension of space or the vibration of a diamond.

To summarize, *La Radia* reported as well as imagined the facts and potential of sonic experiments already being broadcast from radio studios and laboratories elsewhere in Europe and America. With an eye on controversy within the field of radio, and on generating a controversial new art of electricity, wavelength, and vibration, it accused nine avant-gardists of radio drama of an unnecessary and outmoded commitment to realism. Among the radio avant-gardists left unscathed, several will concern us in building a context for Pound's first radio works. I have selected for discussion the radio and film work of Walter Ruttmann, Alberto Cavalcanti, Bertolt Brecht, Lance Sieveking, and Archie Harding.

German Radio

The Weimar Republic voiced high expectations that state-controlled radio would prove to be a pedagogical and progressive tool that could politically and culturally educate the masses. Perusing the 1935 comparative study *Radio: The Fifth Estate,* we find that every major power in Europe voiced similar goals with the inauguration of their national broadcasting facilities.[66] It was not government policy that pushed Germany to the fore in acoustic art experiments in radio, but the implementation of that policy by dedicated directors and producers who were able to finance and promote such work at the regional stations of German radio.

Broadcast radio in Germany began in October 1923 with the opening of the Berlin "Voxhaus." The economic climate following World War I precluded the federal government from risking possible losses, so it retained ownership of the transmitters through the Post and Telegraph Administration and created a decentralized system of regional broadcasting organizations. Concessions were granted to private companies—for example, Die Deutsche Stunde for entertainment programs, Buch und Presse for news and interviews. These concessions formed their own program companies in German cities where stations were located, the controlling interest being retained by the concessions. In 1925 the program companies centralized for certain purposes, but in general, producers at the program companies were more independent than, for example, those at the BBC, a centralized corporation under one director-general.[67] Another difference was that artistic resources in England tended to be pooled in London, whereas Germany's artistic resources were distributed throughout the country. In Britain, where the pay for independent broadcasting material was not considered attractive, producers generated their own original material. The German economic depression made German radio drama very attractive to writers as a means of employment, especially as production and publication became increasingly difficult. As a result, the commissioning of artists by independent producers in cities like Berlin, Hamburg, Frankfurt, and Breslau evolved more quickly than in Britain.[68]

Each system had its advantages, to the degree that the resulting art sound experiments reflected the overall organization of the broadcasting entity. The fact that German engineers were separated from the program companies at least partly accounted for the bias for the single-stage broadcast. German producers preferred to assemble all their performing forces—cast, sound effects, and music—in one large room. The producer conducted the entire cast with a complicated system of body signals and a high dose of personal charisma. Performers were under great strain to react precisely or be utterly silent (precluding the noisy setup of effects or movement from one place to another within the room). The single-stage system undoubtedly had a relatively low threshold of complexity compared to a system like the BBC's that used many studios.

Mark Cory has identified three types of radio art from the 1920s in Germany: the radio presentation of drama without pictures, the drama written specifically for radio, and acoustical art, "a radical and short-lived breaking away from literary conventions."[69] The latter was called *Hörspiel,* or "sound play," and included any dramatized work with a radio-specific angle (for example, an adventure story might be built around the simulated news reportage of a disaster). Instances of acoustical art were few. A handful of German artists sought independence from the operatic studio model by experimenting with sound directly on film. The works' preservation since 1928 on the world's first recording-tape systems (manufactured in Germany), surviving documentation, and the focus of historians today on this period of German radio art have rescued this small and cogent genre. By 1929 a recognizable "congruity of form and content" in both dramatic and sound film works distinguished the new German *Hörspiel.*[70]

Ruttmann and Cavalcanti

Marinetti and Masnata could hardly include Walter Ruttmann in *La Radia*'s list critical of artists purported to be tied to realism. Ruttmann (1887–1941) created the first abstract films, a series of hand-tinted animations—*Lichtspiel* [Lightplay] *Opus I, II, III* and *IV*—between the years 1921 to 1925. Trained originally in music, architecture, and painting, he traversed the decade experimenting with the emergent technologies and adding to them with new inventions.[71] Perhaps *La Radia* had Ruttmann in mind when proposing entry no. 16: the art of painting would acquire new acoustic brushes made of noises, sounds, and harmonies. This is possible today by means of computers, and the term *brush* has even been carried over into digital tools. Ruttmann's transposition of the concerns of painting by means of light and time was astonishing for his day. His fulfillment of the previously untapped potential of the film medium was described by Leonhard Adelt for the *Berliner Tageblatt:* "He [Ruttmann] does it through the medium of the film, mind you, not through film per se. The film per se, which does nothing but photograph continuously, is totally without art; only by transcending its automatic naturalism will it become the servant of the arts, will it serve the poetic imagination, the dramatic mise-en-scène, the mimic presentation, and in animated film the graphic inspiration."[72]

Ruttmann's 1927 experimental documentary, *Berlin, Die Sinfonie der Großstadt* (Berlin, Symphony of a Great City), was acclaimed worldwide for its vibrant portrait of Berlin. The rich and poor, workers and bosses, factories, apartment buildings, streetcars, trains, rivers, restaurants, and Berlin's ubiquitous iron grillwork were strikingly montaged in a sixty-two-minute virtuosic display of cinematic collage, superimposition, and rhythmic cadence to portray the diversity of the city. Concealing his camera to shoot heroic portraits of ordinary people, Ruttmann democratized the demographics of the screen. He montaged his images to be provocative and suggestive, but stopped short of using the language of film for direct statement. The large number of images and the rhythmic emphasis of the editing insured that no one person, group, or ideology emerged supreme over the aesthetic of the filmmaker himself. Conceived by Carl Mayer as a "melody" of pictures, the film divides, like a melodrama, into five acts.[73] It depicts five segments of a single day in Berlin and concludes on a note of nighttime leisure, champagne, and fireworks—a satisfying and dazzling ending. Ruttmann's cityscape anticipated *La Radia*'s proposal (no. 10) for a soundscape made from an infinite variety of sounds—abstract, or even dreamed—and became the inspiration for a generation of radio producers who sought to do with radio what *Berlin* did with the camera, that is, aestheticize social commentary.[74]

Ruttmann went on to pioneer sound experiments on film. His work *Weekend* has been called the first truly acoustic art for radio. Before examining it, I want to return to the cinematic subject of the city and to another influential cinematographer, whose work was also tangential to Pound's BBC work.

Berlin was preceded by the 1926 portrait of Paris, *Rien que les heures* (Nothing but the Hours), a silent film by the Brazilian Alberto Cavalcanti (1897–1982). The two films formed the basis of the "symphonic" film movement of nonnarrative, protodocumentary work emerging from Europe. Based in Paris, Cavalcanti had created the first film work of highly personal social commentary. The film's point of view was highlighted rather than hidden by new camera and editing techniques to show the impact of industrial capitalism upon body and soul of the city, the contrast of lifestyles between wealthy and poor. The thirty-five-minute work has intertitles, but no divisions. It opens with scenes of fashionable women, dandies, and their chauffeurs. Employing startling filmic effects, Cavalcanti "rips" the women from the screen as if they were no more than an image out of a magazine, crumples them, and tosses them to the floor. He changes the chauffeur's elegant limousine into a donkey cart, the chauffeur into a peasant. The intertitle explains, "This is not the modish and elegant life." He turns the camera on the prostitutes, pimps, and the homeless of Paris, tracking them from the small hours of the night to high noon, day after day, in a string of candid and staged shots. The destitute die in the streets and under the piers of bridges; the working poor die at the hands of criminals. Not content to suggest that unemployment was ravaging the city, Cavalcanti used the visual language of film to present his evidence: a series of right-left-right film "wipes" that passed from rich restaurant fare to buckets of scraps; "insert" shots in the center of a restaurant's fancy steak platter to play the slaughterhouse routine back to the well-heeled diner; shop signs and advertising messages whose words testified to the wound that was Paris. Cavalcanti reacquainted the world with the Paris of Villon, five centuries later, with the new, powerful vernacular of film language that was shocking in its literalness. Using every word and visual technique at hand to make clear statements rather than suggestions, he inspired the French avant-garde between the wars to use the language of cinema to mount an assault on bourgeois decadence. Cavalcanti found great sympathy for his work in England where the documentary radio movement, as soon as it was officially formulated by the BBC in 1932, focused on the life of the worker and the unemployed.[75]

Sound film was a by-product of the radio industry's development of the photoelectric cell. Once it was generally available, the commercial film industry exploited the technological advances but were slow to develop an aesthetic, favoring a straightforward synchronization of sound to picture. In 1928 Ruttmann wrote that the invention of sound film had completed its laboratory phase and was available for production; the aesthetic of sound film could next enter the laboratory phase, to emerge in all probability as an optical-acoustic counterpoint.[76] When sound became available to independent filmmakers, Cavalcanti edited picture and sound to destroy synchronization, thereby creating a spatial and emotional displacement that would fit well within the guidelines of *La Radia*'s battlefront for the dramatization of sound and time. Cavalcanti's sound-editing techniques borrowed from those used for film collage: out of context, out of order, juxtaposed, fragmented, inverted, and applied in unexpected and sometimes humorous ways. When recombined with the screen image, the sounds transformed the spatial, psychological, and emotional depth of the picture, allowing several ideas to be expressed at once. The recurrent theme of simultaneity in art took on a cubist dimension, an almost chiseled aesthetic, in Cavalcanti's sound work in Britain in the mid-1930s.

Radio producers of drama conceived of radio as a specialized extension of theater, music, and literature with its own dynamic and were quick to understand the creative implications of the registration of sound onto film. It could be edited, projected, and recorded onto the new recording machines, and then broadcast. Until that time, radio had depended largely upon live performers and phonograph records already in distribution.

German radio and Tri-Ergon-Gesellschaft, the manufacturers of sound film equipment, engaged Ruttmann to direct the first feature-length sound film, *Deutscher Rundfunk* (German Radio), a portrait of diverse broadcasting stations in various German cities. The project was completed in little over a month, premiering on August 31, 1928. Ruttmann wrote afterward that sound was a new form of art.[77]

Ruttmann next created his single work for radio, *Weekend*. Edited on film stock, this eleven-minute sound piece was transmitted on June 13, 1930, by Berlin and Breslavia radio and represented a significant advance for broadcast art.[78] *Weekend* conveyed through natural sounds, voices, and music the cyclical journey through the work week—the approach, duration, and fading memory of a weekend, and the return to work. Of greatest concern to Ruttmann was the accurate articulation of space, as if photographed, and the differentiation of spaces. If a word was heard as close by, it would next be contrasted by a distant sound. The singing of a group of people moving into the distance would become fainter and fainter. Sonic dissolves between two sounds created a third, new sound that had never before existed, and between words, new words that had never before existed.[79] This musical approach to the detailed assembly of sound fragments into a larger rhythmic design depended on increments as small as a fifth of a second for its effect (the drive for precision recalls Pound and Antheil's efforts to notate *Testament*'s microrhythms).[80] *Weekend* has been championed as the first radio work born neither of the *macchina da scrivere* nor of the literary mind, the first radio work removed from theatrical concerns, and the first to employ sound film as an artistic medium.[81]

La Radia would exhibit an awareness of Ruttmann's significant contribution as well as an awareness that radio in Germany, unlike radio in Italy and Britain, had become, to quote Klaus Schöning, "a suitable agent of both production and patronage."[82] With hindsight we can establish a chain of influence from Ruttmann's art sound backward to futurism's "art of noises" as well as forward to futurism's 1933 updating of the "art of noises" for *La Radia* and *Sintesi radiofoniche.*

Brecht

Emboldened by the protective coating of a Machiavellian prologue of allegiances, the writers of *La Radia* closed their eyes to political reality and focused the acoustic lens of radio on the nervous system directly, ignoring the implications of a mass media and its promise of political education. Nevertheless, *La Radia*'s call for a new breed of listener-producer and the transmission of environmental sounds was aware of, if not sympathetic to, Brecht's earlier innovations for radio. Without eliminating the audience (*La Radia,* no. 20), Brecht marginalized their role and made them irrelevant.

Bertolt Brecht (1898–1956) proposed turning radio space into a megastage in *Der Lindberghflug* (The Flight of Lindbergh), a play ultimately destined for children's choruses, soloists, sound effects, and radio sets (microphones and loudspeakers to facilitate transmission and reception within the play). Brecht's libretto about the thirty-three-hour Atlantic crossing by the American hero Charles Lindbergh in 1927 emphasized the importance of collective responsibility, dedicated teamwork, and personal resolve. The work was conceived on two fronts—as radio *Hörspiel* and as *Lehrstück.*[83] The latter term refers to Brecht's experimental "learning play," in which he draws or structures the audience into the performance as student and participant. The character of Lindbergh (scored for tenor soloist), reflecting the dialectical structure of the play, was referred to both as "Flieger" (Flier) and "Hörer" ([radio] Listener).

In 1950 Brecht changed the title of the work to *Der Ozeanflug* (The Ocean Flight) to protest Lindbergh's support of Hitler's National Socialist agenda. In the revised work, the Flier states, "My name is of no importance. I was born in America. My grandfather was Swedish. I am twenty-five years old. For my oceanflight I've selected a monoplane which flies two hundred kilometers by the hour."[84] Another version of the play (titled *Der Flug der Lindberghs*) had the chorus sing the part of the Flier to encourage identification with the heroic traits of the masses rather than the individual. The work's fifteen movements include solo and choral passages of general commentary and character roles—the City of New York, Fog, Snow, Sleep, Scottish fisherman—and the incoming news reported by Ships-at-Sea and the American and French Press. (The interpolation of radio news reportage as if it were commenting on the dramatic action was a frequently employed technique in early radio plays.)

Invoking the alienation effect he was developing for epic theater, Brecht instructed that *Der Lindberghflug* be performed as a series of precisely styled mechanical exercises. The graphic layout of the first printing shows a text conducive to mechanical stylization—the repetition of simple phrases, unrhymed verse, and listing of supplies (the provisions Lindbergh stowed in his plane, *The Spirit of St. Louis*).[85] The choristers were to remain alert, follow the printed music in the score, and be mentally prepared to speak on cue. Brecht described this as "*concerted I-singing* (I am so and so, I am starting, I am starting forth, I am not tired, etc.)." The idea was to avoid "free-roaming feelings aroused by music."[86]

For an earlier broadcast of *Mann ist Mann,* Brecht made some prefatory remarks to prepare the listeners to recognize the source of the protagonist's strength, "That is to say he [Galy Gay] becomes the strongest once he has ceased to be a private person; he only becomes strong in the mass."[87] *Der Lindberghflug* was to impart a similar message to children by having them participate in all facets of testing, observing, and celebrating the pilot's strength. Two primary factors kept the elements of the work in flux from performance to performance: Lindbergh's fame, and the difficulty of the music. The reassignment of parts from soloist to chorus to diffuse the allure of the private person is mentioned above. The participation of young people was problematic. The music, scored for as many as one hundred voices, was too difficult for an amateur or children's choir. The work underwent numerous changes in the libretto, music, staging, and performance venue, seeking its balance of ideology with practice.

The staging of the dress rehearsal for its Baden-Baden Music Festival premiere could only suggest a radio broadcast by visual means. This has led to some confusion in published descriptions of the performance. The work was performed by professional adult musicians and choruses. Projected on the backdrop was a text about the proposed use of radio. The staging demonstrated how the sound effects, music, and some of the choral songs would, under ideal circumstances, be broadcast into the performance arena by means of a loudspeaker that acted as a receiver. The received broadcast was to include the introduction to the Flier, the challenges of the flight, and the anxiety about the Flier's survival. These sections established a situation that justified the learning exercise in the remaining sections, which comprised the Flier's response to the challenges. To combat passive listening, Brecht's goal was to create a dynamic tension between each imagined child assembled and the radio apparatus. The dynamic would arise from a self-awareness of occupying two distinct dramatic spaces—the physical stage space doubling as the invisible radio space of transmission and reception.

In fact, the performance was never literally divided between a radio space and a stage space, and Brecht's vision of radio as a two-way medium of communication did not materialize from this demonstration. Performances of the work thereafter were generally staged according to either concert hall or theater conventions, with the option of broadcast from the site functioning as concert entertainment rather than experiment. It is provocative to imagine Brecht's learning play enacted by children's choirs, particularly in public spaces, broadcasting to each other and tapping radio's potential to engage in local, national, or international dialogue.

Brecht used radio to advance an artistic technique that devalued the individual personality and the cultivation of the senses. In 1933, we find Masnata and Marinetti directing attention away from the use of radio as propaganda. Among other things, *La Radia* proposed that radio could be a quiet, private technology capable of enhancing sensory experience and awareness, outside a framework of communication.

Radio's ability to cut across class and literacy distinctions made it an indispensable medium for an ideology that located its strength in the masses. Brecht theorized that radio could only be the world's first "mass" form of communication if the masses had access to the means of production. When he understood that the National Socialists intended to monopolize broadcasting to develop it as the preferred medium of mass communication, he quickly ended this period of experimentation with radio. His willingness to politicize radio recognized and furthered the propagandistic propensities inherent in the medium. It would not be long before his ideas about radio, taken in a new context, would become the foundation of official Nazi policy, as is demonstrated in this 1935 retrospective assessment of radio by Horst Dressler-Andress, president of the Reichsrundfunkkammer (German Broadcasting Chamber) under Hitler.[88]

> Liberalism which centers in the well-being of the individual was replaced in Germany by a social philosophy [*Weltanschauung*] which calls upon every individual to stand unreservedly behind the commonweal. This maxim is expressed in the impressive slogan "The commonweal precedes the individual interest." This slogan had to

> become the life-rule for every German! The means of proclaiming it was the radio . . . The idea and the means of propagating these theses were thereby united in a unique system. In the new Germany, National Socialism and broadcasting have become one insoluble unit.[89]

At bottom, it was German radio's official policy of neutrality that was challenged by both Brecht and Dressler-Andress as a lie and obstacle to radio's potential for mass communication.[90] Brecht's utopian radio was a two-way street that would replace the existing institution with the "live broadcasting of law cases and Reichstag debates," as well as with listener's input, "interviews and discussion programs."[91] Brecht wrote in 1930 that *Der Lindberghflug* was justified artistically only if it were performed as a learning experience, and with the intention of altering radio by turning the listener into a producer.[92]

British Radio

The next section on British radio will introduce the organization that sponsored Ezra Pound's two art sound experiments, *Le Testament* and *Cavalcanti*. Pound remarked that he had anticipated radio well before its institutionalization. It is always compelling to regard technological invention as being as much a product of the literary mind as of the scientific mind. The radical act of Marinetti and Masnata was to propose cutting the literary umbilical. Ruttmann had done that, substituting a filmic soundscape for literature. Should Pound's aesthetic be heard as a conservative pole of radio art? The field of radio was too much in its formative state to make these distinctions. Its aural world without vision suggested a new path to the logic of unity, one that was still under construction. Radio offered the potential for a new unity of time and space, as well as a new unity of word and noise.

Pound came to radio to promulgate certain historic voices with uncounterfeitable traits. Marinetti found voice on radio a burden from the past and reduced it to generic sounds. Arnheim's analysis of radio sound offers a compelling reason why a literary mind might compose either music or soundscape:

> The meaning of the word and the significance of the noise are both transmitted through sound, and have only indirect effects. It is difficult at first for most people to realise that, in the work of art, the sound of the word, because it is more elemental, should be of more importance than the meaning. But it is so. In radio drama, even more forcibly than on the stage, the word is first revealed as sound, as expression, embedded in a world of expressive natural sounds which, so to speak, constitute the scenery. The separation of noise and word occurs only on a higher plane. Fundamentally, purely sensuously, both are first and foremost sounds, and it is just this sensuous unity that makes possible an aural art, by utilising word and noise simultaneously . . . It should be realised that the elemental force lies in the sound, which affects everyone more directly than the meaning of the word, and all radio art must make this fact its starting-point.[93]

The BBC

Since 1924 one woman and three men at London's British Broadcasting Corporation had been creating a small body of works that paralleled the development of radio art in the Weimar culture. These four producers were the British forerunners of the "radiasta" (engineer-artist) sought by Marinetti and Masnata. They employed cutting-edge technology to transmit an audio montage in the process of its coming into being; that is, sound dissolves and effects were "performed" live. At the BBC's Savoy Hill facility, as many as six studios were controlled from a producer's booth, where entrances, cuts, levels, and resonance were facilitated by means of an electronic fader and switcher. Communication to the studios was accomplished through headsets.[94] Quite different from the German system of broadcasting, which was modeled on the grand opera, the British system created a radio-specific environment that allowed producers to manipulate sound on the model of film shots and cuts.

The BBC's emphasis on radiophonic invention began with its first chief engineer, Peter Eckersley. Formerly an engineer for the Marconi Wireless Telegraph Company, Eckersley became one of the original staff members of the newly formed British Broadcasting Company, hand-picked in 1923 by John Reith, the company's first general manager.[95] Eckersley was a brilliant inventor and irrepressible entertainer who defined himself as "the inventor of mechanisms to serve ideas."[96] His legacy to the BBC at the time of his departure in 1929 included, in addition to the powerful long-wave transmitter at Daventry, a laboratory culture committed to realizing the technical and artistic vision of a new breed of engineer-artist and producer-artist. Called the "backroom boys in the Peter Eckersley tradition" by Andrew Boyle, the engineers and producers hired by Reith tended to be jacks-of-all-trades who solved issues in radio technology, technique, and program content as one large interdisciplinary job assignment.[97]

The BBC's centralized control was vested in a chairman, governors of the corporation (appointed by the prime minister and the postmaster-general), the director-general and controller, who directly supervised program policy, administration, and finances for all of the stations. Producers were at the bottom of a top-heavy hierarchy directly responsible to the assistant controller of programmes, who in turn was responsible to the assistant controller (finance) and the chief controller.

As noted, the sponsorship of experimentalism and art in German radio was not a matter of policy set at the top level of broadcasting administration, but of individual initiative by program builders in each regional program concession. At the BBC, partly because of Eckersley's enormous influence from the beginning of British broadcasting, it was both. Reith personally mandated the creation of an elite research unit within the institution to nurture the radio form as a unique medium of expressiveness: "The original Research Section was formed in 1928 . . . with an undefined roving commission to browse over the whole field of programmes, to initiate ideas, to experiment generally."[98] The specific assignment was to "prepare special programmes as occasional features and to build suitable programmes for broadcasting's special dates in its calendar."[99] The organization of such a unit fell to Lance Sieveking who, together with three of his colleagues—Mary Hope Allen, E. J. King-Bull, and Archie Harding—developed an independent laboratory of sound in the midst of an institution that was otherwise highly prescriptive and firmly controlled.

As part of his leadership style, Reith cultivated a culture of Calvinism, to which all BBC employees and listeners were subject.[100] A telling incident recounted by Andrew Boyle gives a picture of the intellectual strain created by Reith's firm hold on the corporation, and its effect on policy. At a meeting between Reith and members of the press, the latter were discussing how certain topics were offensive to a great number of citizens and were therefore unsuitable for broadcasting. The topics mentioned to Reith were betting, racing, and birth control. Reith was tacit on the first two, but insisted that birth control, because it was controversial, was the "stuff of broadcasting, no matter how delicate or dangerous."[101] When translated into program decisions, Reith's directorship advocated controversial acoustic art experiments (and contemporary serious music programs), and marshaled editorial policy to launch artistic offensives in the face of public complaint.

The staff were constrained from publicly discussing internal affairs while employed at the BBC, but many unburdened themselves through the publication of memoirs. Their comments and complaints receive clinical examination in Asa Briggs's multivolume *The History of Broadcasting in the United Kingdom,* but it is the personal opinions of individual staff that shed light on Agnes Bedford's summary judgment that "the savage mistrust of everyone else in the building" had a detrimental effect on the *Testament* broadcast.[102] Maurice Gorham, editor of *Radio Times,* did not hesitate to draw a picture in which "staff lived in a fantastic atmosphere of ambition, suspicion and intrigue," fueled by their own "confusion of values."[103] Raymonde Collignon, a singer in the 1931 *Testament* broadcast and occasional performer on the BBC, complained to Pound regarding the difficulty of access to producers, "tiresome young men" who first took care of their relatives and lovers.[104] Part of the discontent can be accounted for by Reith's quasi-dictatorship and part by the high level of unemployment in England, which put jobs at a premium.

The competition between departments for funds and the special privilege of the Research Section will be apparent in the discussion of the production budget. Internal strife also arose from within the Drama Department. In 1929 Research was placed under Drama, supervised by Val Gielgud, productions director.[105] Gielgud was often at odds with the members of Research over the issue of technical invention for its own sake, especially when it overshadowed the actors and actresses of radio drama. He could not tolerate staff preoccupation with the art of resonance, political views of the left, or producers who sought to combine literary with social issues, proposing instead that radio "art" with any news or journalistic content be placed under the News Division.[106] A new department, Features, headed by Laurence Gilliam, replaced Research in 1933, while Gielgud went on to head Drama, but matters between the departments did not improve. The friction between Gielgud and Features smoldered behind the scenes for the next thirty years, often kindling passionate, divisive debate among BBC producers. The factionalization at the BBC set the tone for the Research Section's rather renegade and controversial outpost of experimentation during its tenure.

Sieveking, Features, and the Dramatic Control Panel

Lance Sieveking (1896–1974) joined the BBC in 1924, commencing his acoustic experiments in 1926 with a one studio/one microphone dramatized documentary called *The Seven Ages of Mechanical Music.* His 1928 piece *First Kaleidoscope, a Rhythm, Representing the Life of Man from Cradle to Grave* straddles Cory's second and third categories of radio art being broadcast in Germany at the same time: a dramatic work for radio striving to be an acoustic art on its own terms. As Ruttmann would do for *Weekend,* Sieveking utilized jazz to signal changes from one psychological state to another. Val Gielgud refused to describe the work as a play or radio drama, and called it "a study in rhythm," its sounds "welded together" into a "music shape and rhythm" with an "original and compulsive effect."[107]

Sieveking coined the term *radiogenic* to describe the modern sound and experimental design of the new programs, billed as "features." These consisted of political soundscapes, literary events, special holiday programs, plays written for radio that benefited from the absence of visual stimuli, and forays into new documentary forms and interview techniques. Like all radio programs, they required scripts and producers. They also required a director but generally were works without plots. Features were a British counterpart to the German *Hörspiele.*

The technical key to the acoustic experiments emanating from the BBC was not film but the Dramatic Control Panel (DCP), an electronic device that coordinated microphone inputs for the singers, instrumentalists,

Figure 2 The dramatic control panel, a primitive audio mixer credited to BBC engineer A. G. West, installed in the BBC's Savoy Hill headquarters. Val Gielgud, Director of Drama, at left; Denis Freeman, independent music contractor for Pound's *Testament*, observing; Saunders Jacobs at the controls. © BBC, courtesy BBC Picture Archive

actors, and sound effects (figure 2). It also controlled the addition of resonance to these inputs to render the dimension of space. With its ability to mix inputs at discrete levels, switch signals, and control fade-ins and -outs, the DCP gave the producer great freedom to montage a work according to editing precepts established by film. A creation of the BBC engineering department, it evolved according to specific requirements of the program and technical staff, emerging in 1928 as an impressive technological addition to the radio studio: "It was no longer a small black box on a table in a cubicle. It had taken on something of the size and shape of an organ keyboard, and rated a room of its own for its accommodation. With its long row of control-knobs, its cue-light switches, its 'talk-back' key and microphone for the producer's use, it had all the fascination of a new and complex mechanical gadget."[108]

The DCP was placed in a "silent room" adjacent to the studio and occupied by the program's announcer and producer. They were connected to the studio by means of a window and a headset. There was also a telephone connection to engineers in the Control Room. By 1931 this prototype of our modern audio mixing board was indispensable for music and drama programs. It could process signals for up to ninety minutes, controlling the output of the music and actors' studios as well as the echo room and the effects and gramophone rooms. The number of actual pieces dedicated to a study of acoustic principles, such as Sieveking's study of rhythm, was small. The emphasis for production shifted to a new genre of radio productions, not all of which were dramas, organized around the capabilities of the panel. The conducting impulse of the German producer was not dormant in the British producer: "Some BBC producers prided themselves on simultaneous directing and operating microphone controls on elaborate dramatic productions in which cast, music, and sound effects were divided among a half-dozen studios of varying acoustical qualities."[109]

Harding, Actuality Programs and the Dramatic Control Panel

The volatile atmosphere of rarefied experimentation subject to internal institutional policy differences and personal intrigue had been building for some time at the BBC when in 1931 the most technically adventuresome and politically outspoken of Sieveking's corps, twenty-seven-year-old Archie Harding, proposed to mount Ezra Pound's opera *Le Testament* as an acoustic experiment wrapped around the DCP. Harding wrote to Pound that development of a radio script depended "largely upon one's knowledge of the devices we have developed here for making a drama immediately realizable to the ear alone." He concluded, "And that is why I must see you as soon as possible, to give you an idea of what these devices are."[110] That lesson on devices a month later would bring Pound up to date on modern radio equipment and theory.

Joining the BBC as an announcer in 1928, Harding produced his first feature program the following year. *Imperial Communications* was about the Post Office's duty to maintain a wireless network between the Admiralty, the War Office, Air Ministry, Treasury, India Office, Foreign Office,

Colonial Office, and Board of Trade.[111] The work was described as "groundbreaking" by Gielgud, who, by the time his memoirs appeared in 1959, had publicly reconciled his ideas with the more radical experimentalists.[112] Many of Harding's programs fell into a subcategory of features called "actuality programming." They were based on fact, written specifically for radio, and dramatically rendered for a sense of heightened realism. Harding focused, in particular, on the political hot spots in Europe—Germany, Austria, and Spain.

Actuality reports proposed to capture stories as they happened on the world stage, their outcomes unknown, realized by nonactors, and apart from all literary tradition. Brecht, long frustrated with the general quality of radio programming, was mining a similar vein when he offered this advice to German radio: "You must get closer to real events with your equipment and not allow yourself to be limited to reproduction or reports. . . . You must carry out real interviews in front of the microphone instead of dead reports."[113]

British and German radio concurrently developed the short-lived genre of actuality programs through their on-the-spot reporting and outside broadcasts. At the BBC, because development of actuality programming was fostered within the Research Section, the first such features on British radio tended to emphasize the montage effects made possible by the DCP, that is, features were part documentary and partly aestheticized and theatricalized.[114] *The Republic of Austria,* Harding's feature on the history of Austria since the eighteenth century, was promoted as a "Poster in Sound." To help the listener follow the German language, *Radio Times,* the BBC's weekly program guide, provided English translation and an outline for the narrative.[115] It was not unusual for instructive articles and prefatory remarks to accompany these programs. Because the printed material could be read during the actual broadcast, the approach was somewhat Brechtian, and one could argue that in the development of actuality programming Brecht's influence was palpable. When considered in the total framework of production, promotion, and presentation, we find the work of BBC features is not purely an acoustic art, but a blend of education, politics, and the aestheticization of sound.

This point can be demonstrated by a comparison of Harding's 1931 feature *Crisis in Spain* and Marinetti's 1933 *Dramma di distanze* (Drama of

Distances).[116] The choice of similar raw materials—geographical place sounds—warrants a direct comparison of the two methods used to compress space and time in ways that are unique to radio. This BBC feature, as an example of the kind of radio experimentation Harding introduced to Pound, and the subsequent work of Marinetti, as an example of the extension of acoustic principles to their conceptual and reductive extremes, provide a useful external reference for a study of Pound's portrayal of the simultaneity in history within his two radio operas.

Harding's actuality program, also a drama of distances, was a collage of dance and military music, speeches, street sounds, and voices from within Spain. He subjected these elements to interruption and commentary by the international and national press in their diverse languages. The program goal was to make the issues come alive just before a discussion program about the abdication of the Spanish monarchy, sponsored by Hilda Matheson's Talks Department.[117] By using filmic principles of montage (contrast, close-up and distance "shots," superimposition, juxtaposition, and interruption), Harding was able to create an impressionistic collage of sound that transpired in "altered" time. What kept the collage of sound focused on the civil war in Spain was his creation of two limited menus of sound. One contained the recognizable diurnal rhythms of life in Spain; the other was made up of the sound of news reports about Spain from around the world. The function of the news reports, which did not refer directly to the sounds heard, was to offer indirect commentary on the unfolding daily changes in the quality of life, as indicated by this production note from the script, "The following sequence expresses the irresistible advance of the revolutionary movement in terms of announcements from radio stations all over Spain, interrupting rather ironically the even tenor of daily commercial broadcasting of dance music."[118] Harding disappeared behind the controlling rhythms of the composited sound in order to promote the listener's own psychological involvement, so that the listener formed impressions as if he or she had experienced events directly rather than through a producer or a narrator.[119]

Features producers took pains to draw the listener into a new relationship with radio. The sounds entered the mental and emotional matrix of the listener at the same time that the listener's ordinary life continued to unfold in familiar surroundings, lending verisimilitude to the broadcast material. The impact of features programs hinged on the power of radio to give the illusion that the broadcast words and sounds were actual and immediate even though they had been prescripted and edited, often with prerecorded components.[120] The live "Talks" program that followed, having been prescripted, gave the listener a predigested point of view.[121]

Marinetti's script for *Dramma di distanze* is no more than a list of seven sound sources, eleven seconds selected from each, and each tied to a distinct geographic location—a military march in Rome, a tango from Santos (Brazil), Japanese religious music played in Tokyo, country dance music from Varese (northern Italy), sounds of a boxing match in New York, street sounds from Milan, and a Neapolitan song performed in Rio de Janeiro. The arbitrary and artificial time constraints subject the sounds to purely acoustic objectives, diminishing their literary and political meanings. The futurist objective for this work was something akin to the aforementioned expansion of experience, a change in the listener's psyche, something as direct as an impression on the nervous system. The script neglects to mention if the segments should be played in sequence or all at once. It also leaves unresolved whether prerecorded sounds are to be broadcast from one city, or from each of the cities, or if sounds should be live or prerecorded. Broadcast from each of the cities would require a special worldwide communications linkup, for which there had been a single historical precedent—a 1932 Christmas program produced by Archie Harding (see below).

In both works geographic space could be instantly signaled through the abstract and linguistic properties of sound. We can isolate the key difference between Harding's and Marinetti's radio works as the artists' montage of time. Harding's work employed rhythmic intercutting on the connotative, emotional, and rhythmic dynamic of his sound sources to inspire the listener to composite a corresponding narrative for the sounds. The two time frames, those of recent changes in Spanish daily life and a chronology of world perspective through the news, would theoretically be conjoined to the listener's present time and circumstances. The listener, drawing upon an imagination stimulated by radio's fictionalized representation of time, would have the illusion of being up to the minute, as if a nondramatized actuality had been broadcast.

Assuming that Marinetti proposed seven equal units of real time, that is, the content of each of the sonic items of his script list joined end to end, the result of the addition is a larger unit of time that encompasses undisturbed each of its component units. Because no apparent narrative, commentary, or cohering emotion is implied other than the concrete sounds, this drama of distances enhances realistic notions of the passage of time. Marinetti's rhythmic invention, unlike Harding's, reveals itself as nothing more than rhythm. If the list of sounds were to be performed simultaneously, that is, in a total of eleven seconds, and particularly if these were broadcast live from the seven cities in a world linkup, the superimposition of sounds would create a new sound in the unfictionalized presentation of real time.

Marinetti's work reduces radio space to an instantaneous act of cognitive perception. Aspiring toward global simultaneity, his script proposes to activate *La Radia*'s call to receive broadcasts from different time zones (no. 7). The reference to a time zone, rather than to a space that can be visualized, is highlighted by the absence in Marinetti's script of a need to render spatial dimension. Also absent, then, is the need to calculate a proper acoustic resonance to represent spatial dimension. The ear's quick identification of place-sounds, performed either in succession or contemporaneously, collapses distance and space altogether. The listening brain recognizes rhythm, sonic contour, texture, and words, which is all that is required to generate a specific and qualitative perception and cognition of distances. There is nothing but hearing and time. With the elimination of volumetric space, Marinetti dispensed with the pictorial imagination in favor of a "wireless imagination," expanding on the idea he first wrote about in the spring of 1913: "the absolute freedom of images or analogies, expressed by disconnected words and with no wire conductors of syntax and no punctuation."[122] Douglas Kahn has written that "Marinetti thought that all conventions of relationality . . . would break down . . . and that the new disposition to this transmissional reality, the *wireless imagination,* required a radical response from among the arts."[123] The convention of contrast is the one tradition of relationality Marinetti reserves for his *Dramma di distanze,* juxtaposing styles and places with a maximum of difference.

Harding's shifts of location employed a different approach to the problem of simultaneity, "a complex crosscutting between events," to invent, as did Ruttmann and Sieveking, new conventions of relationality.[124] Ruttmann, Sieveking, and Harding all directed their editorial prowess toward the presentation of place in the service of fictionalized ideals or constructions. *Weekend*'s eleven minutes referred to the larger narrative of the human cycle of work and repose, told through jazz, art song, and sound effects. *First Kaleidoscope* traversed the human life span in the duration of one program slot, pitting jazz against classical music in the conflict between Good and Evil (played by John Gielgud and Richard Harris). *Crisis in Spain* gathered voices from around the globe to impart the idea that the whole world was witness to the "inexorable march of events towards the proclamation of the republic" represented by parades and military bands.[125]

Harding's ability to manipulate the perception of volumetric space and geographic distances acoustically was of great import to the BBC. In December 1932, a year after his production of *Testament,* he was charged with producing a special program to promote public support for financial allocation to the recently inaugurated Empire Service, which broadcast to all parts of the British Empire (which at that time was also referred to as the Commonwealth). The result was the first of what would become a tradition of Christmas features, a state-of-the-art "radio hook-up" that circled the earth in sixty minutes. The broadcast's central event, a Christmas greeting by King George V, traversed the earth's time zones, stopping long enough in each place to be answered by the locals in, for example, Vancouver, Brisbane, and Cape Town. The event furnished the BBC with a successful end-of-the-year celebration of the new Empire Service as well as for the recently opened Broadcasting House, the new facility, which, on the basis of Harding's Christmas program, presented itself as the first "centre of world communications."[126]

Harding, whose career was on a meteoric rise, turned to other projects before his planned spring 1933 premiere of Pound's second radio opera, *Cavalcanti.* With affinities to Europe's "symphonic" film movement, Brecht's epic theater, and German *Hörspiel,* Harding's approach to programming at this stage in his career was guided above all by a commitment to the medium of radio. He was proving himself a jack-of-all-trades extraordinaire, upon whom Director-General Reith depended.

D. G. Bridson offered this character study of his first boss at the BBC: "Harding was the only Oxford intellectual Marxist that I had so far met. And nobody could possibly have been more Oxford than Archie Harding always remained . . . his background was impeccably Upper Class. It was just this background which Oxford and intellectual restiveness had taught him first to challenge, then finally to reject."[127] As Harding left no memoirs, it is from Bridson we learn that he believed all broadcasting was a form of propaganda. Harding wished to open the airwaves to the working classes, to combat the status quo of BBC radio—by default a form of propaganda that favored capitalism—and to overcome the economic hardships endured around the world. He hoped that popular access to the microphone would lead to a redistribution of wealth. Unlike Brecht, Harding believed the current system could be overhauled from the inside.[128]

If boosting the prestige of the BBC worldwide does not square with Bridson's portrait of a Marxist, it can be explained that Bridson encountered Harding, a political exile from the London office, at the new Manchester facility.[129] Harding had inserted political content into his work, a violation of the BBC's official policy of political neutrality. His production challenge for the New Year's Eve program a week after the successful world linkup had been to sonically unite all of Europe. Recalling the major events of the past year, he created radio portraits of the capital cities. His dramatized script depicted Poland as a country preparing for war. Reith was pressed by the government's Foreign Office to apologize to the Polish ambassador in London for Harding's gaffe.[130] The incident was considered very serious because it misled the public into believing that the BBC was speaking for the government when criticizing Poland. Reith's apology was intended to contradict that impression, but many persons abroad had trouble making the distinction and viewed the BBC as an arm of the government.[131]

In their account of the social, political, and cultural impact of British radio, Paddy Scannell and David Cardiff, recognizing Harding's contribution, remarked that his transfer to the BBC Manchester office at the end of the summer of 1933 signaled "the demise of the research group and of formalist experiments in 'pure radio.'"[132]

Plates

Plate 1
Ezra Pound, c. 1943. Courtesy AP Wide World Photos

Plate 2
E. A. F. Harding, BBC producer of *The Testament of François Villon,* shown here as Director of Staff Training, 1943. © BBC, courtesy BBC Picture Archive

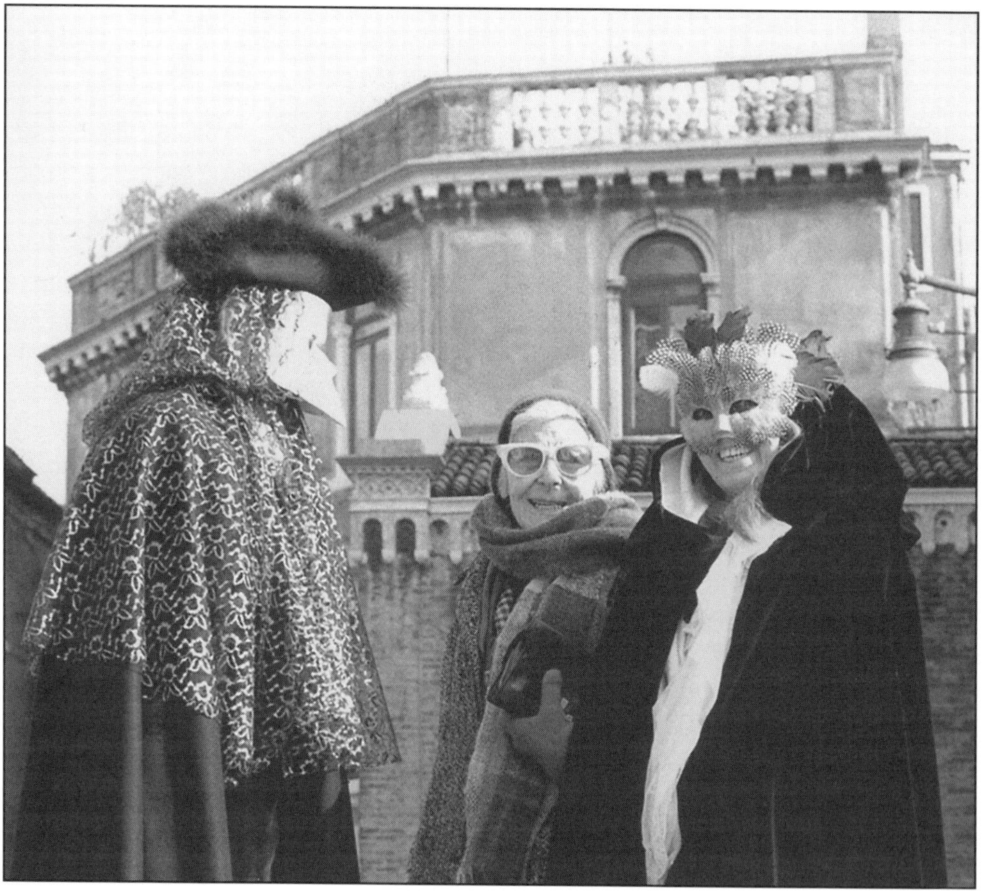

Plate 3

Olga Rudge, between two unidentified persons, during Carnevale in Venice, February 1987.

8.45 'The Testament of François Villon'

A Melodrama by EZRA POUND
Words by FRANÇOIS VILLON
Music by EZRA POUND
Presented and Produced by E. A. HARDING

Characters :

The Warrant—A Sergeant ; The Captain of the Watch.
The Victim's World—François Villon ; A Barman ; An Accomplice ; Ythier Marchand ; Rose ; La Belle Haulmière ; A Gallant ; Ganthière ; Villon's Mother ; A Priest.
The Gibbet—A Woman ; Six Gibbeted Corpses ; Two Halberdiers.

A Tribute to the Memory of François Villon (1431—1931)

(*An article on François Villon appears on p.* 262)

THE year of birth of François Villon is generally taken to be 1431, and it is in honour of the fifth centenary of that year that this 'melodrama' is being given. The play is an interesting experiment in a kind of impressionism that is only possible over the microphone or, perhaps, in a sound film. The music is by Ezra Pound, the distinguished American poet ; the libretto is taken from Villon's own poetry, interspersed with brief snatches of dialogue in 'hobo' language. These elements form a harmonious and interesting whole, depicting the life and character of the picturesque poet-drunkard-thief in the most vivid way. That the poetry is in French, and in old French at that, need not matter ; the musical setting is of such a kind as to give the right impression of the poetry, even without an understanding of the words.

9.45 'The Second News'

WEATHER FORECAST, SECOND GENERAL NEWS BULLETIN

10.0–4.0 *Daventry National Programme*

Plate 4
Radio Times listing for the October 27, 1931, London Regional Programme, evening broadcast of *The Testament of François Villon.*

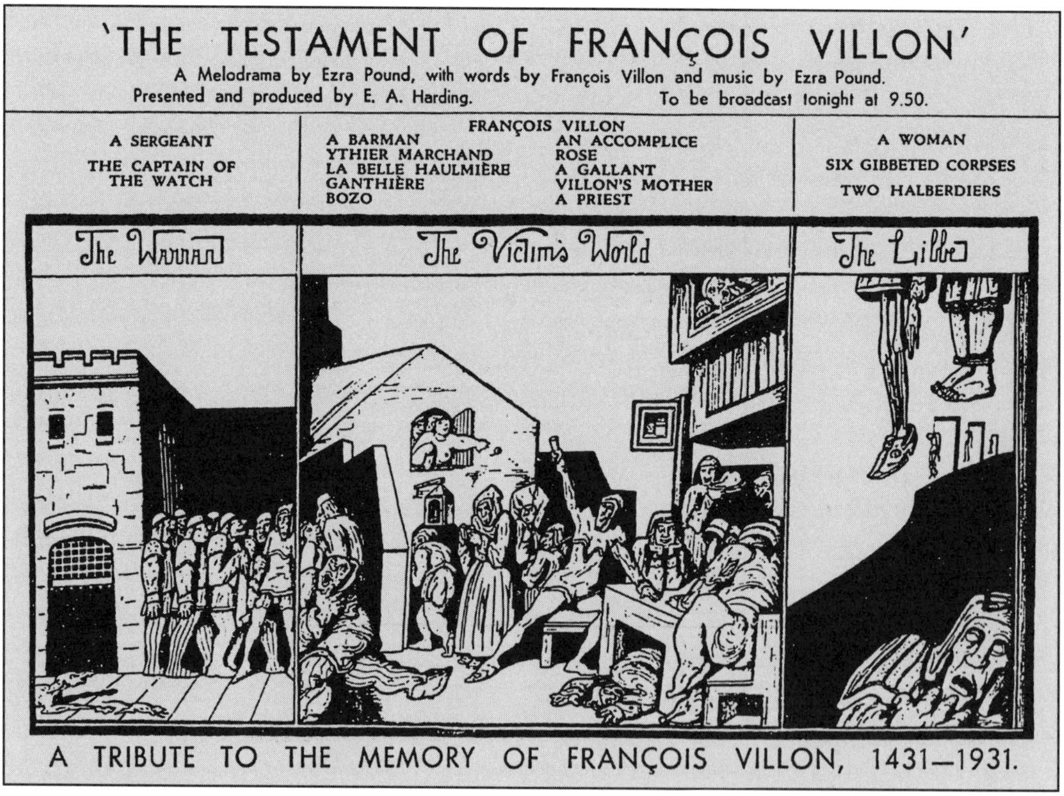
'THE TESTAMENT OF FRANÇOIS VILLON'
A Melodrama by Ezra Pound, with words by François Villon and music by Ezra Pound.
Presented and produced by E. A. Harding.
To be broadcast tonight at 9.50.
A SERGEANT
THE CAPTAIN OF THE WATCH
FRANÇOIS VILLON
A BARMAN
YTHIER MARCHAND
LA BELLE HAULMIÈRE
GANTHIÈRE
BOZO
AN ACCOMPLICE
ROSE
A GALLANT
VILLON'S MOTHER
A PRIEST
A WOMAN
SIX GIBBETED CORPSES
TWO HALBERDIERS
The Warrant
The Victim's World
The Gibbet
A TRIBUTE TO THE MEMORY OF FRANÇOIS VILLON, 1431—1931.

Plate 5
Woodcut by Alan Odle, of the *Radio Times* art room, for the *Radio Times* announcement of *The Testament of François Villon* for the October 26, 1931, Daventry National Programme. © *Radio Times,* courtesy BBC Written Archives Centre

Plate 6
Drawing of Heaulmière by Ariel for the San Francisco Opera Western Opera Theater poster announcement for the world stage premiere of the 1923 Pound/Antheil *Le Testament,* conducted by Robert Hughes, November 13, 1971, at Zellerbach Auditorium, Berkeley, California. © 1971 Ariel

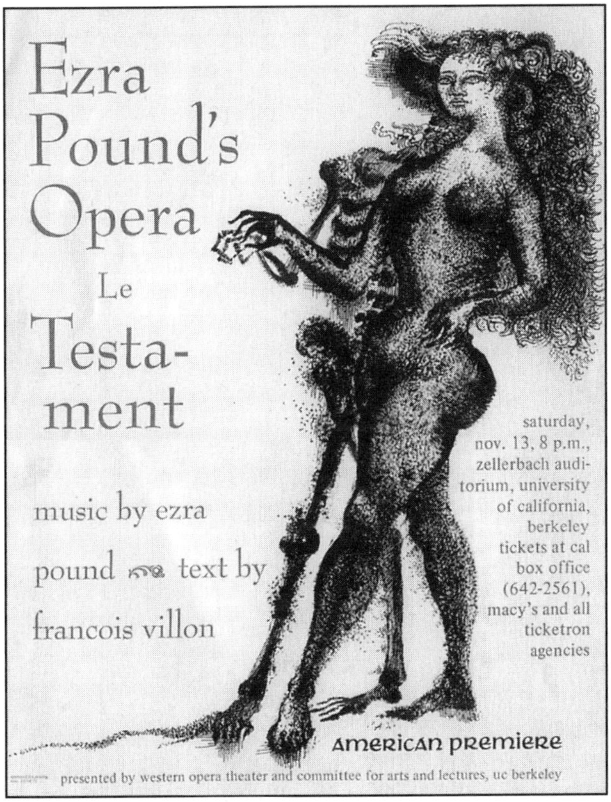

Plate 7
"Yvette Guilbert taking a curtain call," watercolor and crayon by Henri de Toulouse-Lautrec, 1894. Pound composed the "Heaulmière" aria with Guilbert in mind.
Courtesy of the Museum of Art, Rhode Island School of Design (Gift of Mrs. Murray S. Danforth)

Plate 8
Robert Hughes conducting The Arch Ensemble's world premiere of Pound's second radio opera, *Cavalcanti,* San Francisco Herbst Theatre, March 28, 1983. © 1983 Frank Wing

Plate 9
John Argue in the role of the radio announcer, *Cavalcanti,* San Francisco, March 28, 1983. The ribbon microphone seen here was introduced in 1931 but was not generally in use at the BBC until 1935. © 1983 Frank Wing

Broadcast of a Melodrama

3

Production Background

ONE OF HARDING'S GOALS for the Research Section was to bring the best English writers of the time to the BBC. Established poets were not particularly attracted to work for radio, given that the pay was insignificant and irregular and the value of the publicity dubious at that time.[1] One way to bring a poet on board was to use intellectual bait. Harding asked T. S. Eliot for a translation of two stanzas from François Villon's *Le petit testament* for a special New Year's Eve program in 1930, but Eliot turned him down for lack of time. With only two weeks before the scheduled broadcast, Harding telegrammed Pound for the translation.[2] Pleased with the quick response and hoping Pound would continue his relationship with the BBC, Harding cast his line anew: "Broadcasting is, after all, sooner or later going to free poetry from the limitations of print."[3]

Pound was interested and asked Agnes Bedford to help him secure a production of his opera *Le Testament,* which had previously only been performed in excerpts with reduced instrumentation.

> Mr Harding of the B.B.B.B.B.C having committed the initial imprudence of paying me for translating a bit of Villon is now interested in the opera.
>
> Needless to say anything you can do to maintain illuminate or otherwise etc/ this interest wd. be deeply appreciated.[4]

Pound also solicited help from his friend Olga Rudge, featured violinist of the 1926 Paris program of chamber music excerpts from *Le*

Testament. Working at the London BBC on a broadcast of another program, she arranged to play pieces from the Villon opera for Harding.[5] The audition prompted Harding to propose a performance of the opera that year, confident the work could fit into the programming goals of the Research Section. He thought *Testament* well suited to radio and foresaw only one problem, "to make it immediately intelligible, as drama, to people who do not know French."[6] The solution, he advised, would lie in the use of resonance and effects to convey changes in the action, scene, and time.

This strategy would require mounting the production in the studios of the BBC at its Savoy Hill headquarters as opposed to broadcasting a stage performance from an outside location. He built a case for the former by insinuating that the small stage was too precious for a man of Pound's reputation: "The alternative is to broadcast it from some 'klein Kunst' platform such as the Arts Theatre Club, but I, personally, have too great a respect for your and Villon's work to be satisfied with such a restricted audience for it; especially as I am certain that, properly presented, it would appeal to a general audience as opposed to one whose reactions are partly conditioned by the desire merely to be in the swim."[7] The Arts Theatre Club would have been a London counterpart to the Paris Salle Pleyel where the excerpts of *Le Testament* performed in 1926 had created a stir among art circles. The Pleyel was the kind of venue commonly booked for the premiere of new music, where audiences were small but informed and reputations were secured among critics and colleagues.[8] Part of the success of the Salle Pleyel performance depended on Pound's personal presence, by which he was able to maintain his accustomed stature and authority as a poet.

It was a big step from the salon atmosphere to a radio audience of tens of thousands of listeners. A studio performance had drawbacks as well: the isolation of composer and performers from their audience and the lack of interface with the specialized contemporary music and literary scenes. Perhaps sensing the difficulty of promoting Ezra Pound on the stage as a BBC-sponsored composer, or possibly having already received word that Pound would not come to London for the production, Harding steered the broadcast away from a staged performance. More importantly, the "klein Kunst" venue would have limited Harding's authority; he would have been second-in-command to a theater director, deprived of the opportunity to adapt the opera's script to radiogenic principles or explore new technical parameters.

It was decided that the *Testament* broadcast was to be a live mix. The coordination of effects and electronic modulation demanded the skilled direction of a features producer. Harding would control the microphone inputs from several locations within Savoy Hill—musicians, sound effects booth, echo chamber, and announcer's booth—and be responsible for blending them into a dramatic tapestry of sound on air by means of the audio mixing panel. In the end, the 1931 broadcast to a mass audience was barely noticed. It was fraught with technical problems and provoked a modicum of critical commentary that had little, if any, impact within the art world.

The question remains why the production did not fall under the auspices of the BBC Music Department. Unlike the experimentalists in Drama, the Music staff were described as "stiffly-starched."[9] Music was one of the largest and most prestigious of the BBC's departments; it hired the greatest number of professional musicians in England and patronized the arts on a large scale. The formation of the BBC Symphony Orchestra in 1930 under Adrian Boult was designed from the outset to be the world's greatest orchestra. From 1927 to 1935, Music broadcast eight contemporary chamber concerts a year, which included the music of Stravinsky, Webern, Hindemith, Schoenberg, Berg, and Bartók. (In 1931 two of the eight were all-Schoenberg programs.) Music prided itself on maintaining rigorous professional standards for program selection and commissions. Fighting an uphill battle against the conservative tastes of its audience, Music organized a commissioning program in 1930 on the model of German radio, aimed at developing a new repertory of text-based works for speaker, voice(s), and instruments written specifically for the microphone and palatable to their audience: "The subject of the text should be such as to appeal to the masses irrespective of the actual music. That is why the 'Lindberghflug', though perhaps doubtful on purely musical or artistic grounds, did make a sensational appeal in Germany to the masses."[10]

It is my guess that Ezra Pound, poet-composer of one vocal setting, was not someone Music was prepared to consider. Had they produced *Testament,* Pound would have played a more passive role in the actual production. An anomaly in music altogether, *Testament* was an anomaly in Harding's laboratory as well, where it was taken on as a feature. This led to Pound's personal involvement in many details of the production. Music's sole involvement was to loan the *Testament* production a conductor—Leslie Woodgate, organist and composer, who had joined the BBC in 1928 and was conductor of the BBC Theatre Orchestra by 1931.[11]

Harding procured £470, a sizable budget, for Drama's experimental branch to produce this unknown opera. A comparison with budgets proposed in 1938, when the BBC hoped to begin mounting its own opera productions, puts the 1931 *Testament* allocation for a one-hour broadcast closer to the cost of a 1938 full-scale opera (£600) than to a short opera (£250).[12] The funding seems particularly high in light of Director of Programmes Roger Eckersley's threat to cancel all contemporary music in the fall of 1931. He warned that it was not an "essential" part of Music programs, especially with the corporation on the brink of imminent financial constraints.[13] This threat certainly accounts for the hostile atmosphere that Bedford described.

Pound, like all authors and composers whose work was performed by the BBC, would receive a token sum. His first check for broadcasting—£50 for the two transmissions—was symbolic of his progress as a composer, "As to Villon/ . . . Am more concerned with its being . . . also with chq/ and fact of being paid for a musikal komposition . . . wod els/."[14] Pound had reason to be proud; his £50 was the same amount offered William Walton for a half-hour work in the BBC's first commissioning program.[15]

Harding linked Pound's opera to the quincentennial celebration of Villon. To help the listener navigate the medieval French of the songs, he scheduled preprogram talks, but these were canceled at the last moment due to hotly debated elections held that week.[16] A page-length preview article, "Paris Pickpocket Whose Poems Live" by Harry Richmond, appeared in the October 23, 1931, issue of *Radio Times.* The program listing in that issue introduced Pound's work as entirely new, yet listener-friendly.

> The year of birth of François Villon is generally taken to be 1431, and it is in honour of the fifth centenary of that year that this

> "melodrama" is being given. The play is an interesting experiment in a kind of impressionism that is only possible over the microphone or, perhaps, in a sound film. The music is by Ezra Pound, the distinguished American poet; the libretto is taken from Villon's own poetry, interspersed with brief snatches of dialogue in "hobo" language. These elements form a harmonious and interesting whole, depicting the life and character of the picturesque poet-drunkard thief in the most vivid way. That the poetry is in French, and in old French at that, need not matter; the musical setting is of such a kind as to give the right impression of the poetry, even without an understanding of the words.[17]

The sound film was something Pound himself had promoted in an interview for the *Chicago Tribune.* Pound made it clear he was aware and interested in radio as a technical first step for the filming of his opera. Like Harding, he saw advantages to rejecting the Arts Theatre Club as a venue, "Opera would be better on film than in theater."[18] Harding hoped to interest Alberto Cavalcanti in directing a film adaptation of *Le Testament:* "a friend of mine with films, who is in with Cavalcanti etc., might put it up to them, if he likes it."[19]

Testament's broadcast was to follow the evening news, a time of minimal radio interference and optimal reception on the continent. Even so, Dorothy Pound, writing to Pound from London almost daily about the opera's progress, conveyed Harding's worries about the quality of the radio signal: "Its not certain, about yr. hearing if the air is bad."[20] The air was good, and Pound received the broadcast, "Whatever the demerits of the work, this much is established: I sat in the electrician's kitchen in Rapallo when the Villon was broadcast from London, and I not only knew who was singing (so far as the singers were known to me), but I could distinguish the words, and the sense of the words."[21]

Production

THE TESTAMENT OF FRANÇOIS VILLON

A Melodrama by Ezra Pound
Words by François Villon
Music by Ezra Pound

The point of departure for the melodrama was the 1923 Pound/Antheil music score, referred to as a "graph" by Pound. The term is significant because it carries the original idea of traduction into the technical work of adaptation.[22] Harding's first tutorial in radio introduced Pound to the concept of a radio script: "Radio scripts, like cinema scenarios, are only notations of works which do not completely exist until they are performed."[23] At the BBC there would be no prior editing of cuts and effects on sound film; everything was to be coordinated electronically by the producer from a control room.

The 1923 score, or graph, included very few "joins," or short spoken transitions between arias. The finished radio script would eventually contain 665 words of dialogue for dramatic reading by actors in 21 different voices.[24] Harding counseled Pound but was reluctant to compose dialogue himself. The written correspondence between them documents the nature of the collaboration, the tone and progress of the letters consistently demonstrating Harding's deference to Pound.

Harding initiated the radio adaptation of the opera libretto by making a "skeleton scenario" for Pound to work from.[25] At their single *Testament* production meeting in Paris that spanned May 9–10, Pound marked his own notes for radio directly onto the 1923 master score in color pencil, so that we have a graphic document of decisions made on that date. Their working method included reciting the script aloud: "Hard 24 hours on libretto with Harding.// That part aloud// fixed."[26] The changes included additional music, additional dialogue and notes on its delivery, translations, notes to the copyist, and crossouts where prerecorded effects and music would be substituted.

Harding's initial suggestions rarely made the final script but were important catalysts that opened Pound's mind to the necessity of restructuring the opera as part of his essay in the world of radio. Counterinitiatives from both men surely inspired the "hard 24 hours," but the final form and substance of the libretto was determined by Pound. His authorship of the text is confirmed by Harding's request for clarification of dialogue lines when their meaning was not readily apparent, "It's stupid of me, but what exactly does V's Mother's line 'Ye aint got no choice' at end of 'Ganthière' refer to. & do you intend it to replace her 4 lines 'Fille, veuilles nous entremettre' or to follow it . . . or in addition to it?"[27]

As with *Crisis in Spain,* Harding planned to dispense with a narrator. At first he recommended that a song or soliloquy be added to the original opening of the 1923 Antheil edition to set the time and place:

> Villon could either sing (without further preamble) "Et meure Paris et Helaine!", or first speak a few lines of soliloquy, like those in the first stanza of the Petit Testament—or, for that matter, the Grand Testament—locating himself, temporally, spatially, and spiritually. The first stanza would'nt do, literally, because he puts himself indoors in it; but perhaps you could give him something along these lines; the more concrete the indication of time (in the year 14 ?) and space (Paris by St.Julien les Pauvres, or St.Benoist le Bientourné) the better, because the more evocatively vivid.[28]

The soliloquy proposed by Harding could have easily set up the expectation by listeners that they would be fed the opera's main points by means of evocative description. But descriptive passages could not be experienced firsthand by the listener; they could at best explain. The radio script that ultimately resulted from the Paris meeting contained very little visual detail. The following passage from Harding's second letter to Pound is quoted at length for its evaluation of techniques already attempted on features programs. Harding has by now dropped the idea of soliloquy or additional song to set the stage:

> Drama on the radio is generally more effective if one can do without such a figure, the existence of which tends to emhasise the disadvantages of the "blindness" of radio instead of exploiting its advantages. I have experimented in various works with narra-

> tors standing (mentally) in various relations to the body of the work they were compère-ing, but only in two instances did one feel that this device made the most, dramatically, of the work. In the others, they tended to destroy the illusion by going behind it and explaining it. In this respect, the least destructive were the ones given formalised utterances like those of a chorus: (this, incidentally, is a convention which modern listeners have learned to accept.) Anyway, in your work one could, I think, by slightly elaborating the dialogue and pointing it—or amplifying it by sound effects—(No! Not the sound of footsteps and wind-machines, but bells, and various degrees of echo on speech to get evocative resonances, etc.) make the drama self-explanatory. . . . To convey aurally the change of location from such a prologue to the main scene of the action could, probably, be done quite clearly by altering, artificially, the resonance of the voices, and by fading in a bell striking. . . . This would convey the proximity of the church which plays so important a part in the action.[29]

With rehearsals under way, Harding informed Pound when the listener needed some additional aid to follow the action in the absence of a narrator: "I think a line of dialogue is necessary in interval between stanzas of 'Je renie [sic] Amours' to indicate agglomeration of foule [crowd] dans la [word illegible] about to burst into [the drinking song] Père Noé. V's friend might say apprehensively, 'Say Frankie, there are too many folks around here for my likin' or something similar. Would you suggest a line?"[30] Harding made a very small number of last-minute changes to the script.

The cryptic style of the text gives the appearance of having been dashed off in a hurry, but Pound was neither given to turning out superficial works nor explaining his work. The addition of dialogue resulted in a serious major new work, a drama with music. It was Pound's first laboratory of sorts for experimentation with the juxtaposition of voices from past and present in a new and public medium.

With the addition of two introductory scenes, Pound added enough dramatic detail to suffice not only for radio but for the anticipated film production to follow. Promoting the work as a melodrama, he intended the formal meaning of the word, a dramatic use of spoken words interspersed with music. The dialogue was not to be a subordinate form of explanation or connective to the music but was a reworking of a number of substantial ideas that Pound had planned for the stage performance of *Le Testament,* "2 days rather stiff work with Harding to change visual libretto into an audible one."[31]

Significant alterations to the work were the use of two languages (one for the text of the songs, the other for speech); a choice of time and place for the writing of Villon's will, which deviated from Villon's own date given in the poem; and the consistent eye toward film evidenced in both dialogue and technical notes. Pound's shaping of colloquial speech is especially noteworthy because of his growing interest in communicating to a larger public and the potential of radio to disseminate his ideas. The new work was given an English title, *The Testament of François Villon,* and was essentially two scripts in one. A decade later when writing on art criticism for his World War II radio speech, "Continuity," he referred to the two-in-one script: "I am held up, enraged, by the delay needed to change a typing ribbon, so much is there that OUGHT to be put into the young American head. Don't know which, what to put down, can't write two scripts at once."[32]

The radio drama carries over into another medium some of the major techniques of *The Cantos*—shifts from prose to poetry, a unique perspective of time in art, inclusion of documents, and the honing of an ideogrammic, multilingual craft. The script furthers the theme of simultaneity that we have been following in Pound's work and in the radical art movements of the early century.

Two Languages

The freshly annotated 1923 Antheil score that Harding took with him to London from Paris contained dialogue in French and English. The lines were first written in "correct" modern French, then translated directly into colloquial English:

> Friend who has entered says: whispering,
> Il faut que tu quittes Paris!
> got ter clear[33]

The retention of Villon's text in French went unquestioned.[34] The use of English slang and archaic words next to the Old French was out of the ordinary. Archaic words presented no obstacle to Harding:

> To my mind, there is no objection to using archaic words either in dialogue or narrative, so long as they are not ineffective pastiche; which the ones you use would'nt be. The great point is to make the listener experience what he is hearing, and, to do this, one can't make a work, within its frame, too actual. If that is well done, the listener will accept anything; even long slabs of a language he does'nt understand. The combination of the voice with the instruments, and the rhythm of words and music, will make him feel what he can't constater intellectually. Set his imagination going, and he'll then dream the lot. At least, to work here, one has to assume so, even if it is'nt true.[35]

Archaisms aside, the dialogue fueled a controversy at the BBC. Harding described the debate that ensued over Pound's use of English: "There is a certain amount of argument going on here about the libretto. Some say they would prefer it all in French; others that the narrative method would have been better."[36] A remark by Lance Sieveking, writer-producer-director of numerous radio dramas as well as features, helps us to understand that the debate over *Testament*'s language in favor of either a French or English narrator was really a debate against English slang and dialect. We have Sieveking's published statement that he rejected on principle the use of a "vast auditory palette" of different dialects, claiming that, in a broadcasting facility in the heart of a large city, actors and actresses came from more or less of the same class and were likely to all sound alike.[37] Evidently the vocal range used by some, if not all, BBC Drama and Features producers at this time was limited to the "standard English" of the educated classes, even though the use of dialect could instantaneously signal information about the speaker's locality, class, and occupation to the listener, eliminating unnecessary words or the presence of a narrator.[38]

Three approaches to Pound's script were given serious consideration: connective dramatic text in English slang, connective dramatic text in French, and a narrator's text in standard English. Commenting from last to first, standard English narration would have been more instructive but less expressive. The argument for using French dialogue was in favor of consistency. Harding worried that British listeners who did not understand French would receive the false impression that the songs in French "must be 'pretty pretty,'" presumably because the sound of French to a nonspeaker was a pleasant sound, associated with agreeable sentiments.[39] Presumably, these listeners also would not comprehend the reason for the coarse tone of the English dialogue.[40]

The bureaucratic operation of the BBC would have insured that certain staff were involved in the decision: (in order of seniority) Assistant Controller/Director of Programmes Roger Eckersley, Productions Director Val Gielgud, Research Section Director Sieveking, and Harding. The Harding/Pound design eventually was approved: "For the libretto I have prevailed and it is going to stay in English."[41] The use of two languages, medieval French and contemporary English slang, each vitally expressive, was the most experimental method of the three. The idea of a narrator was buried.

Contrast: A Counterplay of Cadences

Pound, as noted, appears to have used his two radio operas as a laboratory to heighten the sense of hearing by constraining visual cues until his climactic scenes. Having examined to some extent the nature of the relationship between Pound's radio dramas and *The Cantos,* it will be helpful to further articulate the working method of the Pound/Harding sound montage by referring to Pound's prose statements, and augmenting these with Rudolf Arnheim's summary findings on the essential principles of counterplay in radio.

The Arnheim formulation of counterplay was a strategy of "parallel and contrasting sounds" leading to "a host of finely-graded plot-motifs."[42] Compare this to Pound's stated "main scheme" of *The Cantos:* "rather like, or unlike subject and response and countersubject in fugue."[43] While not interchangeable, "parallel and contrasting sounds" and "like and unlike subject" are similar enough in method to hypothesize that the point of interest of the radio dramas in relation to *The Cantos* is their attempted substitution of sounds for subjects. The subjects of each melodrama have already been delimited by Pound's choice of poet and poems. The main interest lies in the sound.

Arnheim concluded of radio drama that "contrast, which makes counterpoint possible, is notoriously the most important motif in composition. . . . [It could be achieved by the] counterplay of alternating voices . . . always determined by the content and yet recognisable as being tonally significant."[44] His method depended upon contrasting voices "so that the 'intellectual problem' itself implies an opposition of tonal feeling."[45] Following Arnheim, we may expect the dramatic function of the two languages in the Pound/Harding script to convey the intellectual problem, or conceptual focus, of the work.

Pound had already effectively interpolated dramatic voices speaking prose within his long poem, as well as passages in foreign languages. The radio operas would import these devices, bringing them into counterplay with each other and with Pound's music to develop dramatic motives in a move away from *The Cantos*' characteristic disjunction and nonlinear progression. The most basic dramatic motive of the radio version of *Testament* is the alternation of speech and song, an alternation made oppositional by the introduction of the cadence of a second language with its differing rhythms and rhetorical, colloquial accents.

The cadence of language is the rhythmical flow of words modulated by the rise and fall of the voice. When transposed to music, the term *cadence* carries two specific yet opposing meanings. It refers to the progression of notes (or chords) used to bring a musical phrase to an end—for example, with conclusive or inconclusive harmonic resolution, with strong or weak beats. A musical cadence also refers to the rhythmic character of the entire piece—for example, a march, estampie, or lament. Pound's song settings employ cadence in both senses of the term to highlight the musical qualities of the word phrases and the movement of the whole poem. By placing the prose speech in a different language, he could impart the basic action and meaning of events, while keeping the listener's ear tuned to the cadence of the poetry. The method illuminates his statement, "The perception of the intellect is given in the word, that of the emotions in the cadence."[46] His unpublished *Testament* press statement for the BBC explained that this is achieved by adhering to "the mediaeval insistance on absolute correspondence of words and notes, not only of the sound of individual syllables with individual notes, but the tone leadings inherent in the words, and in the large of the whole emotional movement and sonority of the words."[47]

Using Arnheim's work as a road map to the first radio opera, we can now identify parallel and contrasting elements of the fifteenth-century French and twentieth-century English voices of *Testament.* The BBC's policy of adding resonance to give spatial dimension to the sound created one kind of parallelism. Resonance was calculated by scenic considerations and was therefore applied to singing and speaking voices equally. Together these voices created the aural spaces of the melodrama, within which the two languages worked together, as they did in individual cantos of *The Cantos.* Within the shared aural space of radio, the dual-language voices create counterpoint through a contrast of their inherent tonal qualities. Because the music had a medieval flavor in a foreign language, and the spoken words a modern sound in a familiar language, Pound was able to bring past and present time together in one aural space, achieving simultaneity (but without the confusion of time, for example, that Pirandello aims for in his play *Enrico* IV).[48] Pound's intent was not to paint a picture of fifteenth- and twentieth-century lives, but an audiogram of one fifteenth-century voice cutting through numerous twentieth-century voices. The original intellectual exercise of *Testament,* the sung rhythmic dynamism of fifteenth-century strophe line development (and its impact on English writing), was made salient by the counterpoint of the pitch-driven, clipped, lilting cadence of Cockney-inflected speech. The use of English slang augmented the tension or drama of sound solely by means of sound, without relying on print or picture.

Testament characters spoke an English inflected with certain class and regional mannerisms. The stylistic delivery was variously described in promotional material and published reviews as "hobo," "racketeer," and "Cockney." The reference to "racketeer" language referred to Villon's use of the jargon of French brigands and pimps transposed to American gangsters. Words and phrases from American slang—"fetch," "dunno," "yer," "Gees!" "Git along!" "What ch'you doin'?" "You DAMN fool, you gotter git"—sounded British when spoken with a Cockney accent. They combined seamlessly with the British elements of the script—"Wot," "'ere," "a-comin," "lummie," "young hearty," "Mother love!" Pound's amalgam of American and British dialects would theoretically have blurred the distinction of locality. Geoffrey Bridson referred to the dialect as "Pound's particular brand of Brooklynese," a term favoring the idea of a linguistic melting pot.[49]

This technique had some basis in the contemporary issues preoccupying many BBC producers. Hilda Matheson, first director of Talk programs, and more liberal in her views of broadcast speech than others of her colleagues, wrote of the "hotch-potch of Cockney vowels, Midland burr, American slang and intonation" that could lead to a "universal hybrid speech."[50] She recognized that human migration across Europe and the global makeup of the British Commonwealth had already initiated this hybridization of language. Harding's program reference to *Testament*'s "hobo" language carries a hint of this human transience. Pound's choice to write a hybrid vernacular was apparently an informed and artistic one. He had used colloquial speech to more precisely identify individual characters in *The Cantos* by their psychology as well as their nationality and race ("you [can] tell who is talking by the noise they make").[51] Here it would be used to remove such indicators. The blurring of dialects would have created a very broad stereotype, preventing the listener from misinterpreting characters as specific persons from London's East End caught up in Villon's life as a fugitive in Paris.

Where Pound derived precise musical notation from the speech rhythms of Villon's words, the lower-class speech of the actors demonstrated a lack of rhythmic precision and indiscriminate pitch assignment. In this way the dramatic design of the Villon radio opera built upon the differing cadences of the Old French and the hybrid Cockney English to create melodrama.[52] The introduction of a narrator's cadence would have brought stability to the drama, defeating the necessary tension or conflict. When action is told, recounted, or analyzed by a narrator or by an actor's asides to the audience, the listener tends to gravitate toward this stabilizing force.

It is worth repeating here Pound's description of the language of melodrama, "The language of this or of any other melodrama is capable of exposing the course of events, and of giving 'character' in comic relief.

It is, however, utterly incapable of expressing emotion."[53] Having set his parameters a decade before, he created his melodrama with the cadence of speech set against the musical cadence, or emotion, of poetry.

That is to say, the counterplay of cadences built dramatic tension independently of theatrical emotion. By scenes three and four there is little spoken dialogue in proportion to song. What little there is sustains the lean narrative line with cryptic remarks that isolate what is important to the scene, but give few clues as to why. Pound's progression of songs, one right after the other, insured that his melodrama would be "utterly incapable of expressing emotion." His stage instructions for the action of *Testament* confirm this. His deliberate stylization and refusal to let action and dialogue build toward a single emotion allow each song of the opera to express its central emotion. The swell of the whole of his song progression is underwhelmed and unencumbered by the stray dramatic emotions that happen to surface from the characters and their circumstances. Those stray dramatic emotions and plot motives will not tie into a neat concluding bundle; they will be abandoned at the moment of the work's final image.

Because cadence or rhythm supplied dramatic tension, rather than narrative, we are able to account for the uncertainty of Villon's end. When charted by the Arnheim map, the ambiguity gives way to an internal logic of sound. Visually, the final tableau consists of six young lads; therefore, Villon is not among them. Sonically, however, Villon is present in each of their voices; therefore, he must be among them. The melodrama *Testament,* built on contrast, is revealed in its final tableau to be a ghost play, not unlike the Noh, where "the emotion is always fixed upon idea, not upon personality."[54]

How convincing can an ending be when based on idea or structure rather than narration, action, or theatrical emotion? Arnheim theorizes that a new kind of "formal unity" is made possible by the "pure aural world." This is achieved by what he calls the "acoustic bridge."[55] The theory states that in film, theater, and opera, sounds emanating from the stage, wings, balconies, audience seats, and orchestra pit are perceived and understood as separate entities possessing their own corporeality in a corporeal world known by the eye. The purely aural world permits a unity previously unknown:

> The laws of the sound-world only become effective and recognisable when one is aware of this sound-world quite alone, without any recollection of the "missing" corporeal world.
>
> The formal expedient, by whose aid the complete new unity of such varied sound-presentation is achieved, which hitherto could appear at most merely as a "combination" in the same work, we shall call the "acoustic bridge". The acoustic bridge which the sound builds is the only sensory quality common to all these different modes of representation.
>
> . . . What hitherto could exist only separately now fits organically together: the human being in the corporeal world talks with disembodied spirits, music meets speech on equal terms.[56]

The modernity of the idea is easily obscured by our distance from early radio and by Pound's use of older dramatic forms. Pound has left us this description of the classical Japanese play, "When a text seems to 'go off into nothing' at the end, the reader must remember 'that the vagueness or paleness of words is made good by the emotion of the final dance', for the Noh has its unity in emotion."[57] If the abrupt transition from his melodrama, incapable of emotion, to a ghost play, with its unity in emotion, is unthinkable because it appears to rupture the traditional time, space, and stylistic unities of drama, we also know that Pound has already dispensed with the traditional unities by mixing his centuries, languages, and dramatic idioms. Throughout the drama's aesthetic arc, the voice of Villon is always present in each song; it is his emotion that moves through each song's cadence.

Pound's Radio: Autonomy of the Individual Listener

Radio dramatists had to write for an audience trained by cinema and the modern stage to react emotionally and intellectually to a corporeal theater through the sense of vision. The first play written for the microphone, Richard Hughes's 1924 *A Comedy of Danger* attempted to solve the dilemma of entertaining a "blind" radio audience by situating its action in a coal mine. At the beginning of the play, an accident extinguishes all light. The audience's acceptance of darkness allowed the play to become a viable space for interior monologue and other devices that depended solely upon the live mix of sonic elements.[58] Tyrone Guthrie, author of the 1929 radio play *Squirrel's Cage,* came to the conclusion that the listener's experience was not "blind." Despite radio's unique aural world, he wrote, radio dramatists, their actors, and producers strived above all to create a visual world through a variety of auditory cues. "The mind of the listener shapes and expands these into pictures."[59] The radio play also specialized in evoking sounds of phenomena never actually visualized—the interior voice, the supernatural, allegorical figures, monsters, and new creatures—for which there was no general trend for the listener's imagination to follow.

Taking hearing and seeing as two poles of the listeners' experience, gradations between these approaches lean either toward psychology or poetry and music. Exploring the latter approach, Donald McWhinnie, former BBC drama director, speculated that "the radio performance works on the mind in the same way as poetry does, it liberates and evokes. It does not act as stimulus to direct scenic representation; that would be narrow and fruitless. It makes possible a universe of shape, detail, emotion and idea, which is bound by no inhibiting limitations of space and capacity."[60] Before radio drama took form, T. S. Eliot used the phrase "auditory imagination" to explain the "feeling for syllable and rhythm, penetrating far below the conscious levels of thought and feeling, invigorating every word."[61] Louise Cleveland's perspective on Samuel Beckett's radio plays applies equally to Pound's radio opera. Beckett, she writes, "exploits the power of the voice to evoke a transitory presence in a temporal universe antagonistic to that presence . . . [so that the] drama is in the struggle of the voice to mark time, whether time is silent or filled with competing rhythms and sounds."[62] Elissa Guralnick draws Cleveland's observations on Beckett into their full musical dimension: "Neither stage, nor film, nor television can effectively compete with the radio as a forum for words that make music. It is radio alone that yields appropriate conditions for releasing the music in language: namely, a performing space at once empty and dimensionless, from which words can emanate free of any material associations."[63]

Pound was neither a picture builder in the sense given above, nor a crisis-in-the-dark kind of dramatist. He sought to provoke his audience to heightened listening, which he believed would lead de facto to individual insight synonymous with self-edification. This could occur at any moment in the opera depending on the listener's power of perception: "It is not what a man says, but the part of it which his auditor considers important, that measures the quantity of his communication."[64] The presumption of the autonomy of the individual was a key operative in Pound's radio philosophy. He broadcast not to build an audience but to reach an existing audience, not to create sound that never existed before but to bring worthy sounds that existed in the past to the modern ear with modern means. Built into his operative was an implicit sense of responsibility on the part of the individual listener to pair up his or her listening with a consciousness that admitted, rather than proscribed, new experiences. The individual autonomy of the listener was quite controversial in early British radio, which managed (and also mismanaged) a precarious balance of ethics and patronage in an environment in which government interest often conflicted with public taste.

For the radio script, Pound considered an accessible approach to art that appealed to the popular ear: "You must get the meaning while the man sings it." And of "the other school [that] culminated in Dante Alighieri," with canzoni that were "not always intelligible at first hearing," he wrote, "They [the canzoni] are good art as the high mass is good art. . . . The second sort of *canzone* is a ritual. It must be conceived and approached as ritual. It has its purpose and its effect. These are different from those of simple song. They are perhaps subtler. They make their revelations to those who are already expert."[65] Just as he had divided the productive mind into the *phantastikon* and the germinal, he divided the receptive mind into the popular and the persistent, and assumed a cognitive and energetic reaction to sensory input on the part of both.

The *Testament* script catered to the spirit of both types of listener. It made a minimum of sense without a great deal of preknowledge and effort by offering immediate sensory stimulus and the requisite entertainment to hold its audience. Expertise and effort were to be rewarded with an experience of the work's structurally complex and intellectually coherent basis that would lead to deeper and more subtle insights. To achieve this scope, the script reserved certain standards of complexity for radio broadcast and others for film projection or the stage.

One can track Pound's changing attitude to his mass audience from the *Testament* broadcast to his wartime speeches. (I limit my remarks to comment on the progressive trend of his demands on his audience, and will abstain from comment on the construction of the speeches, a subject that naturally follows, but is outside the scope of this book.) He took pains with the Villon melodrama to not address the audience, save for two lines that announce the closing of the play. No overt demands were made on the British listener other than to follow the general action and the play of cadence, English against French. In *Cavalcanti,* the radio announcer addresses the listener directly, introduces the characters, gives a synopsis of the action of each act, and provides background to the play that mixes historical fact with dramatic fiction. In the second act, the dialogue of minor characters anticipates the listener's confusion with questions, skeptical asides and botched attempts to rationalize Cavalcanti's words. By the third act, the audience is asked to pay close attention—the music contains a cipher that has to be heard in order to be deciphered, and a final scene that has to be imagined visually. For the wartime broadcasts, Pound addressed an international audience directly and informally, with insistence and impatience, providing them with information that mixed personal and popular opinion with a wide range of documented and undocumented facts. His speeches presumed to diminish confusion by admonishing the listener to access reliable information about art and culture, history, economics, and health, often referenced in the talks. In this sense, the broadcasts by the 1940s had become a call to individual action, stopping short of a call to political action.

Dialogue

The melodrama opens with archaic speech made immediately recognizable by use of antiquated references to the French monarchy:

SERGEANT OF POLICE:	For violence against particular, for violence against the King's officers . . . that he did in the city of Paris . . .
CAPTAIN OF WATCH:	Stt! not so loud, now.[66]

The conversational idiom of the ensuing good-natured banter between Police and Men of the Watch characterized the dialogue of the opera until its closing lines. A line with certain tonal values would be contrasted with a line of differing value, as above. Characters whose name and rank were not part of the text had to be identified and subsequently recognized by tonal qualities. Though the characters were of an earlier time, the actors' casual speech rendered them more familiar to the listener, giving them currency in the present.

A casual greeting by the Barman becomes the occasion for Pound to channel his interest in the perception of time through an artless custom of speech:

BARMAN: Time o' day, Messir François.

Villon's rejoinder is thoroughly artful:

VILLON: Time, time . . .
(close to microphone, voice utterly weary)
(catching himself briskly) Time o'day, Joe.

After introducing the city of Paris, the script avoids further mention of place. This exchange between Villon and the Barman must convey place solely through dialogue and tone of voice. The intimacy called for in the notes for microphone placement will convey several things simultaneously to the listener: the place is indoors; that François permits himself to express his weariness indicates a safe place; the deference of "Messir" followed by "Joe" identifies the place as a tavern. A listener might have already assumed Villon would not be in confessional or at home, given that he had gained a reputation as a street thug. But drama on radio has to recreate the circumstance from raw materials. A study of early radio programming, *Psychology of Radio,* concluded in 1935 that a voice fulfilling a stereotype in the listener's mind, for example, that of a poet, politician, laborer, will evoke numerous personality characteristics attached to that stereotype.[67]

The scene unfolds exactly as Harding had counseled, "The great point is to make the listener *experience* what he is hearing."[68] The protagonist's first words reveal the source of that weariness: time has caught up with him; he is in trouble, he has not enough time to run for his life.[69] Villon's first words also refer to Pound's method of drawing Villon forward from the past into radio time. With great economy Pound tiers the meaning of the libretto's conversational lines into multilevel platforms for his characters, including an additional tangential platform for author's asides to his own melodrama.

The stray, never-to-be-resolved dramatic emotion here is Villon's preoccupation with death, played against the Barman's attempt to understand. Villon's obsession leads into the melodrama's first aria, "Et mourut Paris"—what could be called countersubject. Sung in fifteenth-century French, the aria introduces the "sound" of Villon, a long "slab of language" that the listener may not understand, but has had the privilege of experiencing (the illusion of) its inspiration.[70] Having left the room to "fetch" wine for Villon, the Barman catches only the second aria, "Ballade des dames du temps jadis." The Barman's response anticipates the listener's confusion: "I dunno." Pound also has him hint that the listener, if sharp, might hear some familiar bit to help orient their ear to the drama: ". . . I dunno where yer snows are gone, I dunno" refers to D. G. Rossetti's well-known translation of the poem's refrain, "Mais ou sont les neiges d'antan?" (But where are the snows of yester-year?) That the Barman understands French, without much attention drawn to the fact, was perhaps a subtle indication from Pound and Harding to the listener that he or she could also ease from one language to the next without much fuss, skipping what they did not understand, picking up the drama when they could.[71] The Barman's response in English mirrors a technique in *The Cantos,* whereby Pound's translation of foreign phrases, placed under or near the original language, sustains the afterglow of that language over what follows.

Villon's appearance in Paris in defiance of a court-ordered banishment provokes his friends to urge "Frankie" to "clear," to "git" out of Paris. His mother tells him he "ain't got no choice." The crude modern speech contrasts their individual arias in Old French, as if spirits of the past and spirits of the present alternate within each character. The words become less distinct as Villon's friends become drunk. When the clientele of the tavern break into the penultimate song "Père Noé," they sing *with*

Cockney inflection: We have only Pound's postperformance critique to alert us of this change in the characters, "Your actors were all right, and the cockney twang in Noe."[72] The twang in the voices mixed elements of the present with the past, signifying a subtle transformation within the collective psyche. The consciousness that views history as an ordered timeline of past irretrievable events has been altered.

The song "Père Noé" implores Noah, Lot, and Archetriclin, three biblical figures whose legacies are associated with drunkenness, to save the soul of Villon's recently deceased lawyer, Master Jean Cotart.[73] Pound inserted a short drunken scene in which Noah, Lot, and Archetriclin respond in person. Awakened from eternal slumber, the characters glance over the commotion of the crowd.

1ST VOICE: (hoarsely whispers)	It's a nose.[74]
2ND VOICE: (more or less drunk)	Back alley's half full 'er cops.
3RD VOICE: (burly)	Les flics![75] Ajh. They got nothin' on me.
4TH VOICE: (markedly drunk and blurred)	Yurr a nose.

The fourth voice would be that of Jean Cotart. Only recently buried, he resurfaces "markedly drunk." The dialogue was conceived as a self-contained bit of repartee among some of history's notorious drunks. Voice assignments in the final BBC script were reduced to three, distributed among members of the chorus and inserted between songlines of "Père Noé."[76]

~~1ST VOICE:~~ (hoarsely	It's a nose.
whispers) *2nd*	*Yurr a nose.*

2ND VOICE *[contd.]*: (boozy)	Back alley's half full 'er cops.
THE CROWD:	Jadis extraict il fut de vostre ligne. . . . L'ame du bon feu maistre Johan Cotart!
1ST VOICE: (burly)	~~Les flics!~~ *The cops!*
3RD VOICE:	Ajh. They got nothin' on me.
1ST VOICE:	~~Yurr a noze.~~

Harding's version takes on the more desperate edge of individual cries thrown out to no one in particular, as if they could be heard by others in the crowd.

The whisper of the first voice suggests that all four voices would be miked close-up for intimacy to contrast the crowd. Until this time the individual voices that were closely miked revealed little about their position in space other than the interior or exterior nature of that space; individual objects (door, window) are mentioned but in isolation. "Père Noé" unlocked the constrained spatial dimensionality of the opera. The many voices of the crowd were heard across as many points in space, a reflection of the actual distance of each actor/singer's voice from the microphone. Distance from the microphone diminished clarity as well as volume so that tonal differences alone provided information. The introduction of the drunks would have helped to fill in the many points of information needed for the mind to construct a spatial plan with coordinates drawn from the aural play itself.[77] I suspect this is the reason why closely miked voices were added to an already lively song with its own internal interest in the counterpoint of its rhythms. The consistent lack of visual cues until this moment enabled Pound to prepare the listener for the final scene. Prior to this, the listener would have visualized all or part of the melodrama with little external guidance. With the introduction of distance relationships, the listener's visual imagination would be guided by the work's sonic cues.

The final short scene emphasizes the distinction between seeing and hearing. A disembodied voice with no specific identity, asks Heaulmière "or any voice" what she sees.[78]

VOICE	What do you *see* there? [emphasis added]
HEAULMIÈRE	Six lads of the village, hung by the neck until dead. Did you ever *hear* a man sing on the gallows? [emphasis added]
VOICE	Hahj?
HEAULMIÈRE	I'm a-tellin' you. They're hung. They're hung by the necks. Can you HEAR 'em? [Pound's emphasis]

One knows a preternatural force is at work because Heaulmière says she can see that sounds cannot emanate from the throats of these particular dead. If one could not see, one could not be certain. The eeriness of the fourth scene, created by effects (sighing wind, creaking of the wooden gibbet, and silence) sets it apart geographically from the preceding scenes.[79] "Voice" could be interpreted as a rhetorical device to bypass the need for a narrator's explanation. Its identity could be Radio itself, speaking to the listener as well as to Heaulmière. A mental picture of the circumstances of the hanged men dominates the scene.[80]

Testament closed with three voices that signified yet another aural space, the space of multiple narrators whose French and English take on antiphonal dimension. Even as the role of narrator enters the work, it is not permitted a single perspective.

TWO HALBERDIERS: (sing)	Icy se clost le testament Et finist du povre Villon.
SPEAKER:	Here ends the will and testament, It's all up with poor Villon.

The sudden change to the halberdiers' simple unaccompanied unison melody cuts through the complexity of the "Frères humains" harmony (a diminished fifth in the instruments, open fifths and octaves in the voices) to conclude on a narrative and authoritative tone. The listener, caught in the act of identifying new figures and the new aural space, is simultaneously cast as eavesdropper. The halberdiers and speaker draw an invisible boundary around Villon's world, their task being to pull rather abruptly the (aural) curtain. The assignment to multiple speakers of the final lines further adds a theatrical decorum, so that the newly defined relationship between listener and radio cannot be understood as a personal communication from an objective narrator who stands outside the melodrama, but as part of the larger drama. The method of contrasting voices has been employed consistently from start to finish. The elaborate and thorough aural design of *Testament* was to transport the inner meaning or "intellectual problem" of the opera solely via the world of hearing.

Radiario (Radio Scenario)

Table 3 **Four scenes of Pound's 1931 *The Testament of François Villon***

Scene	Characters	Sound effects
1. "The Warrant" Outdoors: streets of Paris Time: Angelus	Sergeant of Police Captain of the Watch Private of the Watch Second Watch	echo church bell drum ostinato
2. "The Victim" Indoors: tavern earlier that day	Villon Barman	drum ostinato clock strikes nine
3. "His World" Indoors: tavern Outdoors: brothel, square Time: Angelus to compline	Villon Friend of Villon Ythier Beauty (woman in window) Heaulmière Gallant Gantiere, pupil of Heaulmière 2d pupil of Heaulmière	drum ostinato door slam echo church music tubular gongs[1] harmonium knock on door

1. Although the word *gongs* appears in the script, the correct term is *chimes*.

Table 3 ~ continued **Four scenes of Pound's 1931 *The Testament of François Villon***

Scene	Characters	Sound effects
3. "His World," *cont.*	Villon's mother Voice from the Church Priest Bozo, the brothel keeper Sergeant of Police Private of the Watch 3 Voices from the Crowd	noise of Bozo's fall noise of Gallant's fall
4. "The Gibbet" Outdoors: hill outside Paris Time: eternity	Voice Heaulmière The Corpses Two Halberdiers Speaker	sigh of wind creak of gibbet drum ostinato

For those familiar with the Bedford (1920–1921), Antheil (1923), Schafer (1962), and Hughes (1971) music editions of *Testament,* the Pound/Harding radiario differs significantly.[81] Where the staged one-act opera took place in two outdoor scenes, the 1931 radio melodrama was built upon two outdoor and two indoor scenes: "The Warrant" (outdoors), "The Victim" (indoors), "His World" (indoors), and "The Gibbet" (outdoors). The distinction between scenes was created through microphone placement and the adjustment of resonance levels.[82] The first three scenes are conveyed solely through aural means. The final scene brings forward the pictorial dimension to enhance the aural dimension.

Location

Pound's dialogue occasionally anchored a scene with a few nouns that, when combined with other nouns, sufficed for a set design—"St. Julian's" and the "jug" (the tavern); the church and back alleys; a skirt and a window. A review by John Rodker, editor of *Little Review,* claimed "there were few stage directions, but enough to call up clear pictures always."[83] The technique is that of the Noh theater, where a pine tree, a stick, a bundle, and a portal on an otherwise barren stage could produce the illusion of an encounter between the spirit world and the living. When comparing the Western stage with that of the Noh, Pound praised the latter, "where every subsidiary art is bent precisely upon holding the faintest shade of a difference."[84]

The setting for the melodrama was the square of the church St. Julien-le-Pauvre situated in rue St. Jacques on the left bank of Paris. A captioned photograph of the church was printed with the *Radio Times* preview article about Villon's life.[85] The melodrama itself offers no visual description; the church is experienced not through eyes but through ears and the mind. When Pound's dialogue refers to the church of St. Julien, it is as much a poetic as a place reference, intended less for the action of the radio play than for its tangential literary richness.

For the duration of his studies at the University of Paris, François (Montcorbier) Villon lived with his patron Master Guillaume de Villon, priest of Saint-Benoît-le-Bientourné, in a house located in the cloister of that church. A murder attributed to Villon took place on church grounds. After six months' flight from Paris and a pardon from the king, Villon returned to live with his patron. Why, then, does the *Testament* radio script set the scene elsewhere? As the seat of the University in Villon's time, St. Julien-le-Pauvre was a church Villon would have known well.

> It brings to mind all those superior personages who have come to seek divine inspiration within its walls . . . illustrious men like Dante and Petrarch, and the great theologians since Albert the Great and Duns Scotus, troubadour of liberty, quoted so often by the dogmatists of Protestantism. Its arches have sheltered the meditations of St. Bonaventure . . . and Thomas Aquinas, of Gerson and of Lefevres d'Etaples, master of the Reformation. Other, less commendable, "scholars" like Villon and Rabelais came here to seek pardon for their faults and to forget for a moment their escapades.[86]

The church is still standing. Its sixth-century foundation marks the crossroads of two important Roman roads known today as the rue St. Jacques, leading to Orléans, and the rue Galande to Italy. The Gothic structure, circa 1200, is one of the oldest in Paris. Located in a quaint corner of the

Left Bank, wedged behind the busy rue St. Jacques and Shakespeare & Co. bookstore, the church grounds open onto the square René Viviani and a spectacular view of Notre-Dame. Church and square retain their medieval aspect in the center of modern Paris. The city's oldest tree, an acacia brought from America in 1601, dominates the square.

The church has honored three saints in its long history. The most colorful of these was St. Julian the "Hospitaller," who, to atone for his accidental killing of his mother and father, devoted himself to helping the poor and assisting travelers. He is the patron saint of ferrymen, innkeepers, travelers, and traveling minstrels. A saint who committed murder and protected minstrels would fit, "ply over ply," with Pound's Villon (by association, the figure of the ferryman comes forward from the classical Noh play *Sumidagawa*). An early murder-for-hire by several thugs took place on the grounds of the earliest St. Julien-le-Pauvre (A.D. 582). The perpetrator of the murder was protected from harm by his patron, but his companions, taking refuge inside the church, were denied sanctuary and died. The incident reminds one of Villon's own pardon for the murder at St. Benoît. Yet another personage kept in motion around Pound's Villon is that of Julian the Apostate, a minor scholar in the church who became enamored of pagan gods. As emperor of Rome, he survives secular history an educated, just leader. Pound thought Julian's death in Assyria at age thirty-two significant and recorded it in Canto CII/751. Villon was a similar age when he wrote *Le grand testament*. In the radio drama Pound turns Villon's mind to the subject of greatness and early death, "The good die . . . [young]."[87] The historic frieze conjured in the mind by the multiple personae of the figure Julian creates a rich bas-relief for the mask of Villon.

Though the melodrama explained none of this, the site was an important detail for Pound and for those who would follow his train of thought. That thought extended to a hoped-for future film production of *Le Testament*.[88] The setting of St. Julien would have made an ideal shooting location. This hint of a filmic subscript nesting within the radio script will surface again in an analysis of the melodrama's time frame.

Also nested within the radio script is a play for stage modeled on Japanese classical drama. The acacia calls to mind the pine tree of the Noh stage, "a congratulatory symbol of unchanging green and strength."[89]

This icon of strength would stand amidst church, tavern, and brothel, bringing these elements together into one ideogram of Villon's time.

Time Frame

Pound avoided the documentary approach by setting the opera in a place and time not usually linked to the accepted historical events of Villon's life. This was Pound's Villon rather than history's Villon. Consider the problem of dates. The 1931 broadcast was an anniversary celebration of the fifth centenary of Villon's birth. The Pound/Harding collaboration produced two new scenes. In the second of these, Villon tells the Barman his age:

BARMAN:	Eh, you'd pay me before you cash in, sir.
VILLON:	How soon would that be?
BARMAN:	Young fellow like you.
VILLON:	Thirty-nine.
BARMAN:	Plenty of time, sir.

Whether or not it was intended that the listener do some quick calculations, the underlying mathematics illuminate Pound's approach, which built upon, but distinguished itself from, Harding's guiding rule, "The more concrete the indications of time . . . and space . . . the better."[90]

Many listeners had committed the opening lines of *Le grand testament* to memory in their school days: "In the thirtieth year of my age . . ." or learned verse eleven, "Written in the year [fourteen] sixty-one . . .". If Villon were age thirty-nine, the year would be 1470.[91] A comparison of Pound's earlier drafts, emendations, and the final libretto confirms that the age thirty-nine (also typed as "39") was not an error. Pound intended his drama to introduce a fiction—a *third Testament* being written in the course of the opera by Villon in the year 1470. This interpretation conforms to Pound's phrase, the "repeat in history."[92]

Scene two opens with a sound effect, "Let clock strike nine." The effect refers the listener to the nine bells with which Villon brings *Le lais* (*Le petit testament*) to its conclusion. Having established this first *Testament* through the bells, Pound refers to the second, *Le grand testament,* directly by having Villon sing verses 40 and 41 and conclude his interchange with the Barman with the familiar "Ballade des dames du temps jadis."

By scene three Villon is seated in the tavern where he begins a *new testament* in the presence of his mother and his friends.[93] This third *Testament* can be accounted for on purely dramatic grounds. *Testament* productions of 1962 and 1971 assumed that the verses Ythier, Heaulmière, the Gallant, and Villon's Mother sang from *Le grand testament* were the verses Villon was writing down. The assumption is based upon a willing suspension of disbelief. The verse was not ready to be sung because Villon was in the process of writing it. Harding's emphasis on making the script more "actual" pointed to the need to provide the radio audience with believable dramatic context for the musical settings.[94] Each dramatic gesture required justification for its being, that is, a believable subtext or motivation for Pound's characters to speak, sing, or act. For the action to revolve around his introspected central character Villon, Pound had to repair the cartoonlike situation of Villon's extroverted companions singing the text of a document in the process of being drafted.

Time within the Time Frame

The Villon melodrama appears to move with the easy momentum of simple storytelling. It delivers a viable though incorrect first impression of clockwise time from day to night.[95] A synopsis of events would unfold as follows: a warrant is issued for the arrest of an unnamed violent offender. Ignoring the imminent danger he is in, the wanted man makes an appearance at a bar. The bartender recognizes Villon. One by one, Villon's old friends and his mother arrive to warn him of the movements of the police, who are tracking him. The last religious service of the late afternoon takes place in the church across the square. The business of the brothel next door picks up. That night Villon and his companions are apprehended. They meet their end on the gibbet.

This interpretation offers no serious contradiction of Pound's overall purpose to broadcast the words of Villon to a large audience: "Popularisation in its decent and respectable sense means simply that the scholar's ultimate end is to put the greatest amount of the best literature (i.e., if that is his subject) within the easiest reach of the public; free literature as a whole, from the stultified taste of a particular generation."[96]

Upon detailed examination of the text, two events refuse to conform to chronological time. The first is the transition between the policemen's departure for St. Julien's and Villon's appearance at the bar next to the church. This should be read as a *flashback* to a previous hour of the same day to account for the time lag (and resulting loss of tension) between the police dragnet and the upcoming sting. The second event is the ballad of the hanged youths, the "Frères humains." The action occurs outside of time, in eternity. (The song from the church, "Mère au Saveur," is also a voice from outside of time meant to be heard as a response to the prayer of Villon's mother and therefore moving within present time.)

A convincing radio presentation of past and future events was problematic. Film was better suited to move outside the chronological order because of its visible divisions of "shots and cuts." Changes in time could be instantaneously detected by changes in light (shadows, moonlight, candlelight), picture (costume, out-of-focus effects, unusual color tints), or film speed (slow motion or fast motion). While the logic of the *Testament* libretto relied upon the pictorial "shots and cuts" editing techniques, the radio listener was exempt from the requirement to understand that logic. The listener was left to construct his or her own interpretation to support an aural perception enveloped by the inherent present-tenseness of radio. If the listener remained tuned in to the Villon, the melodrama would have served Pound's purpose. Given that his music was a form of literary criticism and Villon's poetry was in French, Pound's expectations of British radio and its audience may be judged unrealistic. The producer, for his part, could probably in the end do no more than eliminate unnecessary confusion.[97]

The passage of time in the *Testament* script is signaled by the sounds of a clock striking the hour, church bells, a drum theme.[98] Pound moved his drama forward, backward, or sideways in time with the device of the repeating drum theme. It could also indicate a change of pace or focus. Occurring sometimes as three and sometimes as six bars of music, the drum theme was prerecorded. The drum beaters were equivalent to a commonly used device in film, in which the hands of a clock are animated by an unseen force to move faster or in a direction contrary to their usual movement.[99] Between *Testament*'s first and second scenes, the drums are used three times to move from one action to another. At the end of scene one, the drum theme moves the action backward in time. The police, occupying the alleys, gaol, and St. Julien's, will remain in a state of suspended animation until the man they are chasing catches up with them. In time, that is. First, the listener must understand who the hunted man is and something of his art: flashback from the hunt to the hunted.

Part of the tension of the script arises from the sacrilegious juxtaposition of Villon's world against the background of the church. Villon's declaration that the good die young is the first indication of this tension, explored linguistically in a series of double entendres; sonically, in the dissonant harmonies of "Dame du ciel" set against the purity of the melodic line of "Mère au Sauveur"; and visually, in the final gibbet scene, which cries out in the imagination to be seen as a crucifixion with Mary Magdalene in the person of Heaulmière at the foot of the cross. By the drama's end, Christianity, with its promise of release from eternal damnation, comes into the foreground in a moment that transcends time. Villon's "Frères humains" has liturgical counterparts to psalms recited at dusk in the service of compline.[100] The last prayers of the day and the indication of dusk enveloping the corpses describe a scene of spiritual despair arising from the fading opportunity to confess, to redeem, to restore the light—an audiogram for the radio listener. Yet this is not evening. This is a sentiment for all time—past, present, future—underscored by the song's popular name "L'épitaphe Villon."

Synopsis

This is the last in a series of synopses that began with a tracing of the great aesthetic arc, investigated the function of language, and examined the chronology of events. This annotated presentation of sonic and subject matter concludes my reading of *The Testament of François Villon* with detail pertinent to the meaning of events and characters, future staging, or media productions.

Scene One The Warrant:
"Fade in church bell tolling, hold and stop; add drum theme; add full echo."

The Sergeant of Police reads the warrant still outstanding for the arrest of someone who wreaked violence and deception on the King's officers, someone who spoke with foul language. The Captain of the Watch suggests that he knows who this might be. Confident of concluding his arrest at "Miss Catherine's," to the right of the "jug" (the tavern) and "next to St. Julian's," the captain points out *which* window of "Miss Catherine's" should be watched, and orders his men to stake out the place from the alleys, gaol, and church. Snide comments on the part of the police preceding mention of "Miss Catherine's" hint that she runs a brothel.

The *Radio Times* preview article briefed the audience on Villon's relationship with Catherine de Vauxelles, "a bourgeoisie," upon his return to Paris around 1456 ("Katherine la Bourciere," vendor of purses, *Le grand testament*).[101] With the melodrama set in 1470, Pound has transported Miss Catherine from her bourgeois surroundings to a brothel. Villon would have been pleased by the insult. Catherine had discarded him for another. He sought revenge by sending her his ballad "Faulse beauté," a song linking his name with another woman, Marthe.[102]

Scene Two The Victim:
"Off echo, hold little drum theme and slow out.
Let clock strike 9."

The clue to the identity of the hunted man, who has not yet been identified by name, lies in the nine strikes of the church bell. If Pound preferred the arts to "hold the faintest shade of a difference," one must ask *which* nine bells on the clock?[103] In the Middle Ages there was the ninth hour, that of none (the death of Christ upon the cross, Luke 23:44). But Pound also has the Angelus prayers in mind in the first of several double entendres juxtaposing Villon with the Church.[104] The opera's inclusion of Villon's mother in a scene with Villon, whose "passion" was at hand, points to the significance of the Angelus theme throughout the opera:

Finablement, en escripvant,
Ce soir, . . .
J'oïs la cloche de Serbonne,
Qui tousjours a neuf heures sonne
Le Salut que l'Ange predit;
Si suspendis . . .
Pour prier comme le cuer dit.[105]

[Lastly, tonight, as always at the ninth hour,
I hear the bell of Sorbonne,
which rings the Salutation delivered by the Angel;
I pause from my writing to pray as the heart would wish.]

To pray as the heart would wish in an artist's atelier, "comme le cuer dit," is quite different from reciting the Angelus as the church prescribes: three Ave Marias with versicles, followed by a short concluding prayer. D. B. Wyndham Lewis's biography *François Villon* highlights the importance of the mix of the secular with the sacred by opening his book with the nine *Bomes* of the evening Angelus bell in Paris. By decree of Louis XI, "the first note of Angelus from Sorbonne [was] answered by a brazen salvo, *tintamarre,* and clangour from all the bells of Paris full volley."[106]

The Barman's greeting, "Time o'day, Messir François," swings the listener from the streets into the drama's main arena, the tavern by St. Julien's. The cinematic quality of the transition is secured by the script's request for a "close-up" of Villon's voice. The short interior scene between the Barman and Villon is a decompression chamber for the listener to adjust to two languages. Obsessed with thoughts of death's grip on life and on love, Villon sings "Et mourut Paris" and "Dictes moi." One must imagine the implied counterpoint to the citywide recitation of Angelus prayers commemorating the Incarnation.

Scene Three Victim's World:
"drum theme"

A continuation of the previous scene, the drums move the action forward in time to build the particular circumstance in which the paths of the hunters and hunted will converge. The drum theme narrows to a countdown in scene three, signaling the approach of the police. News of their proximity is passed to Villon by a friend. This first warning is interrupted by the arrival of Ythier who, like Villon, is fixated on the subject of death ("Mort, j'appelle de ta rigeur"), but, unlike Villon, believes in an everlasting love. A whore at the brothel amuses herself by mimicking Ythier's pathos. No one, it seems, would allow a man his thoughts of death. The Barman corrects Villon with polite naiveté. The whore fights Ythier with sarcasm. But Villon is in the mood for more rather than less. Ythier's despair over his lover's death provokes Villon. He regrets only his lost youth, "Je plains le temps." The first friend impatiently tries to bring the song to a close. Villon cannot be dissuaded. Ythier urges him to flee Paris, but Villon refuses. The old whore Heaulmière tries to take the men's minds off death by having them contemplate the definitive and irreversible ravages of fate upon one who has outlasted her body ("Ha, vieillesse felonne et fiere"). Men fuss over the evanescent love and youth they have lost, but a woman cries over the tangible goods before her own eyes—former lovers in the street, old-age in and under the skin. Her tale of woe pauses briefly when Villon's friend once again tries to move him out of town.

FRIEND: [to Villon]	You fool, don't you know they're a-trailin' yeh. You hadn't ought to set round.

Villon goes nowhere. Pound's stage notes call for "Villon completely immobile from start to finish."[107] Villon's immobility renders him an observer to his own drama, something the listener must glean from the repeated inducements to get him to move.

Heaulmière, warmed to her subject and Villon's interest, launches into a lengthy catalogue of her lost charms and mossy remains ("Ou'est devenu ce front poly"), filled to the bitter brim with impassioned, streaming complaints. Pound indicated in his 1926 "Heaulmière" music manuscript the dramatic nuances he wanted the singer to supply—"simple, tragique, implorant, pompeux, presque parli, douloureux, violent, scandé, déchirant, intense, snarl, aspro, dolce, doux, triste, elegiac, resigné lent."[108]

The inclusion of cabaret singing, which never mixed with "serious" song recitals, represents Pound's more catholic interest in the relationship of words and music as well as his desire to collect idioms of the Western stage for his melodrama. He originally composed this aria with the popular French singer and screen star Yvette Guilbert in mind.[109] His description of seamless movement from one mode of expression to another matches Guilbert's instructional handbook of acting for singers, *L'art de chanter une chanson*.[110]

During Heaulmière's long complaint, a wealthy Gallant sporting a mandolin approaches the tavern. Pound's instructions for film and stage are drawn from the final 1934 edition of the Villon opera, which incorporated changes made as a result of the BBC experience:

> Gallant from right preceded by mandolin players & torch bearers. He is in gold coat. Sings after preliminary fuss. Giving various things to servants to hold.[111]

The figure of Gallant is a vehicle for the rescue of yet another kind of theatrical idiom, the jongleur's art. The size of the entourage prevents the Gallant from encountering Villon in the tavern, an important detail to the evolution of the plot for stage and film. Gallant is naïve enough to cringe at Heaulmière's tales of hypocritical love, but nonetheless intent on securing an hour of love for himself. He serenades ("False beauté") Villon's ex-girlfriend Catherine at the brothel window—the one held under surveillance by the police. To underscore the significance of this moment, Gallant's presence is preceded and concluded by the drum theme, which doubles as a kind of heraldry to his street performance. Scene three has now caught up with the end of scene one. The police have positioned themselves in the square when Gallant goes in to visit Miss Catherine. Villon's nonchalance in both matters provokes disbelief:

YTHIER:	Wot the hell are you doin', Frankie?
VILLON:	Ajh! Gees! I'm makin' my will.
(sings)	Item, m'amour, ma chiere rose . . .

To Catherine, Villon bequeaths his most sarcastic wit, bitter remnants of unrequited love recycled for posterity.[112] Recapturing center stage, Heaulmière brings forward two pupils, *filles de joie,* to observe this quick lesson in life's hard knocks. Her song "Or y penser" is a catechism for young whores. Villon's mother arrives at the tavern in time to join them for the envoy.

This was a significant last-minute correction to the script. The importance of the envoy is to place Villon's mother in the tavern with the whores, not in the church where the police are staked out. Having spoken her mind to the women, Villon's mother peels off a bit of advice to her son, "Yeh ain't got no choice." Although her words suggest only one outcome, the statement comes across ambiguously. Villon has either to flee or to pray, as she is about to do. The crudeness of her speech and the words she sings link her to the whores. Perhaps she too once earned her living as a prostitute, but has since become a pious woman, though not a meek one. Surrounded by sinners in a low-life tavern, she upstages Heaulmière with the urgency of her voice in prayer, an appeal to the Virgin for the redemption of her soul. It is no small piece of proselytizing. Like a hammer driving nails into a coffin, "Dame du ciel" delivers each phrase on one pitch in the manner of psalm-tone recitation, and holds spellbound the rowdy crowd that has been collecting in the tavern and drinking over the course of the afternoon. Pound has rescued yet another idiom, liturgical plainchant, the earliest musical form to be carried over into church drama. The power with which she delivers, or drives, her words, and the dissonance of the music, however, possess a very modern, machinelike character.

The diverse styles of the melodrama's religious music, of which the mother's prayer is the first of three pieces, comprise a quick lesson in early sacred music of different centuries within the already dense scenario. In addition to three religious pieces, Gregorian chant was inserted as background music to introduce the character of Villon's mother. A recording of music by fifteenth-century Flemish composer Guillaume Dufay was chosen, almost certainly by Pound, to preface the mother's prayer.[113] The pleasantness of Dufay's flowing counterpoint of shifting thirds is then contrasted by the most dissonant of Pound's settings in the entire opera, the "Dame du ciel." The dissonant intervals never come to rest or resolution. The bass accompaniment to "Dame du ciel" is made up of four-note chords with a half and whole step inside the gamut of a diminished fifth, or tritone (the "devil in the scale" or forbidden interval). The time would appear now to be early evening, though Pound is not finished with the Angelus theme.[114]

In perhaps the most misunderstood aria of the melodrama, "Voice from Church" answers the mother's prayer with a thirteenth-century verse song, "Mère au Saveur," in the vein of the Angelus prayers. For the 1931 broadcast Raymonde Collignon sang the aria in the original *langue d'oc* so that a new counterplay of languages is invoked.[115] The intensity of the music has been so carefully funneled into this magic moment that the aria should beam like a ray of light upon a dark tragic corner of the "jug," while it subliminally mocks the Visitation of Mary by the angel Gabriel.

The assignment "Voice from Church" should be understood literally as a voice without a body or name, that is, a spirit presence. To create this impression, the melodic line was accompanied by tubular chimes (imprecisely notated as "gongs" in the script) and a "harmonium."[116] It was sung from the basement of the BBC in a compartment called a "tin bath" to add pronounced echo.[117] The assignment "voice" will be applied twice more before the melodrama's end.[118]

Melodies of Dufay, Pound, and li Viniers have for a moment in radio time crisscrossed a square that exists only in radio space. Villon triumphs, and mockery triumphs. To secure his transition, Pound briefly segues into Villon's "Suivez beauté." The melody, taken from the *Selection Yvette Guilbert,* was composed in a nineteenth-century style, possibly by Gustave Ferrari, arranger of the collection, or even Guilbert herself. The part, marked "Bass profondissimus" and "Very husky priest walks across stage bawling the four bars," was sung by an elderly Russian man named Lubinoff.[119]

With the sounds of someone "approaching, singing, jeering" outside the tavern, the melodramatic character of the "Suivez beauté" successfully breaks the pious mood established by the "Mère au Saveur," temporarily closes the philosophical exposition of Villon's world, and prepares the listener for the lively, upcoming "Père Noé."

The 1931 radio audience could not identify the character behind the jeering "Suivez beauté." His voice had not yet been heard, nor was there previous reference to him. But they had to catch the change of mood as the melodrama turned from tragedy to comedy. Enter the priest, apparent alter ego of the mother, with several free hours before the service of matins commences the night watch. Villon's friend announces him to the crowd (and to the radio audience).

FRIEND: (ironically)	The Reverend Father approaches. And the voice on him.

The radio audience cannot know if the priest arrives in secular or clerical garb. Without dramatic motivation and character development, the priest's role is mood-changing and symbolic. The brief scene is an example of Pound's using comedy to refer to the larger issues, in this case the violation of the sacrament of coition that had once been central to ancient religious rites like the Eleusinian mysteries.[120]

Bozo, manager of the brothel, refuses the Reverend Father, "To hell with you . . .". The reason is not immediately clear. Bozo's aria ("Se j'ayme") is a drunken sprawling display outside the brothel entrance—a ploy, it turns out, to distract attention from a disturbance brewing inside. It is no time for new or regular customers. Bozo attempts to temper the outrage of the priest by boasting of chivalrous service to Margot, his lady love. An inversion of values briefly overpowers the scene; the brothel keeper embodies the higher sentiments, albeit as part of a ruse; the priest, the lower. But Bozo cannot sustain his end. Succumbing to the attentions of the crowd gathering around him, his braggadocio turns to drunken indiscretions of domestic life in the whorehouse. He eventually collapses, to the crowd's delight, from his exertions.

Gallant emerges unsteadily from the door of the brothel behind Bozo. His hour of love met with unexpected violence, causing him to curse all love ("Je renye amours"). Bleeding, wobbling about, he gasps out his final words, "A dying man can speak his mind," and crashes to the ground mortally wounded. The crowd misunderstands Gallant to be drunk, "The little gentleman is emergin'! and a-wobblin' about on his pins," and breaks into Bacchanalian frenzy ("Père Noé").

"Père Noé" calls for humor and riotousness. Notes in the margin of Harding's score read, "work itself up to dancing pitch" and "orchestral acc. must indicate a dancer & a giggler."[121] Between the second and third strophes of "Père Noé," Pound inserted "Gaite de la tor," an anonymous *trouvère aube* from the thirteenth century.[122] The song was omitted from the 1931 broadcast despite Pound's insistence on its inclusion, conveyed along with other emendations to Harding's typescript.[123] The short verse warns that the bliss between man and woman will soon be interrupted by dawn, the "robber." In the case of the radio scenario, the danger was the approach of the police. The warning emanates not from Villon, but from a voice two centuries earlier.

The police have been observing the window and the door of the brothel for signs of Villon. When Gallant reappears partially obscured by Bozo and wobbling as if drunk, the police are confident they have their man, but they must work through the crowd to get to him. Only then do they discover it is not Villon but Gallant. "G. crashes into heap extreme left back at final bar [of music]."[124] Finding Gallant mortally wounded, the police realize they have a more serious case of murder on their hands. The plot has just taken yet another remarkable turn. The first of the three voices warns, "It's a nose" (a slang term from the 1920s and 1930s for a police informant or paid spy). The second sounds the alarm that police are in the back alley. Another warns, "The cops!" but the crowd pays no attention. Pound's original script introduced three drunks from history to unravel the mystery of Gallant's true identity and his death. Harding reassigned the voices to the chorus. (See the discussion of Noah, Lot, and Archetriclin above under "Dialogue.") A pattern emerges in which Pound uses voices from other centuries, including his own, to comment on Villon's century.

Though the words of "Je renye amours" are Villon's, Pound has cleverly suited them to Gallant's double identity. Gallant renounces women, blames them for precipitating his death, and determines to follow up on what he started out to do, to follow his intention, "poursuivre vueil mon entente." The brothel has proved a fatal distraction from the task of rounding up Villon. In this context Gallant's final words, "Qui meurt, a ses hoirs doit tout dire" (a dying man may speak the truth) were directed away from Villon's original meaning, that is, speaking candidly about women, and toward Gallant's imminent exposure as a spy. Pound dispensed with further details of Gallant's masquerade or death. One had to deduce that his job was to flush Villon out of the brothel and into the hands of the police.

Once Gallant's identity as an informant was known, the audience would need to mentally retrace the previous scene in which he appeared (perhaps to be aided in the future by filmic flashback). The significance of Gallant's initial entrance would have been lost on the radio audience but was held in reserve for future film or stage production. According to Pound's notes, Gallant, upon arrival, should remove his gloves and hand to his numerous servants various items to prepare for his playing of the mandolin.[125] Accompanying Gallant were the torchbearers, an indication of the evening hour. The darkness, the size of the entourage, and the bustling about of Gallant as he prepared to serenade Catherine prevented him from noticing Villon inside the tavern. The moment would have been a bit of commedia dell'arte, the informant unable to sniff out the prey right under his "nose," if the audience had previously been made aware that Gallant worked for the police. As film the scene lends itself naturally to parallel editing—Villon, the hunted, taking refuge inside the tavern; the spy in disguise, outside; each unaware of the true significance of the other's being.

But Pound chose a literary style, that of the "whodunit," for his unmasking scene. Gallant's true identity is revealed after his death. At the drama's close one still does not know who killed Gallant. Curiosity sends us back to sort out in retrospect the few clues we have been tossed. Certain he would find Villon inside the brothel, Gallant had proceeded there. Exiting the brothel without Villon, Gallant had shown signs of having suffered great bodily harm. The tension of the scene's orgiastic dancing and singing had continued to build after Gallant's collapse, suggesting the greater mystery had yet to be encountered. The scene had climaxed with the arrest of Villon, to be underplayed against the originally scripted drunken revelry of mortals (the crowd) and immortals (Noah, Lot, and Archetriclin).

Pound has another reason to bring three biblical voices (plus Cotart) forward into the dialogue. He will pump the "Père Noé" up to a fevered pitch in order to plunge the drama and its audience into the final tragic scene. The radio listener would again have no idea of the identity of the voices, but a film director could produce a hilarious scene with the drunkards, still schnockered after two-plus millennia, rising from their graves to look upon the revelry below (or above).

Pound carefully moves the drama away from a one-track ending by dividing perspective between action and observation. Commentary that began with the "Gaite de la tor" poet and the drunken patriarchs is taken up by Villon, calm before the storm:

VILLON: On ne les aime.

[the crowd sings the third strophe of "Père Noé"]

VILLON: Que pour l'heure.

Set apart from the general fray, Villon has oscillated between participant and observer throughout scene three. The introduction of voices from the "other side" allowed Pound to split Villon between the greater constellation of historic figures and the present action of the play. The crowd sings the third and fourth strophes to "Père Noé," oblivious to any danger. When the police spring upon the crowd, it is sudden, underscored by the drum theme. Villon is captured but the reference to his arrest is secondhand:

FRIEND: Gawd, they've pinched him.

Scene Four The Gibbet:
"*(with lots of echo)*
(*Slow in* drum theme, hold and slow out; pause; In a sighing of wind, *hold, down a little, add creak . . .*)"

"Six lads of the village" hung by their necks beg for absolution from beyond the grave. The scene is made more ghastly by the presence of the old Heaulmière, who survives them but cannot save them. Perhaps their crime was to shield Villon from arrest. Perhaps several of them attempted to rob Gallant inside the brothel, or scuffled with him, causing his death. These were young villagers; Villon, a Parisian, was old and worn out at thirty-nine. He has disappeared again, but his bequest continues.

Production History

Censorship of the Whore and Appropriation of the Brothel Music

The public airing of Heaulmière's breasts, vulva, buttocks, and thighs (Pound's song setting of lines 520 to 524 from Villon's *Le grand testament*) was evidently too much for the BBC in 1931, even in an antiquated foreign language. The only reference to an abridgment of the expansive whore's aria is in Harding's radio script. There does not appear to have been notification by letter or internal memo that the aria was to be cut. To minimize the impact of the excision, Harding reshaped the verse as a quatrain. He had Gustave Ferrari in the role of Villon sing the first line of the octrain (line 517) without echo. Maisie Seneschal, as Heaulmière, repeated the same line with echo and then sang the next two lines. The final five lines were omitted—a total of sixteen bars of music.

Harding's notes in the margin of what appears to be the penultimate script (now archived in the Beinecke Library) indicate there was also a question as to whether an earlier octrain (Pound's song setting of lines 501 to 508) would be sung at all ("Ces gentes epaulles menues . . ." [These small and delicate shoulders . . .]). The lines are not included among the typed verses of the script, but Harding's editorial notation between verses indicates the octrain was to have been reinstated. The final script (archived in the Lilly Library) appears to have also been Harding's, and contains cues for operation of the DCP. It does not bring forward the notation to reinstate the eight lines.

Musically, this cut would have been welcome to the musicians. The eight lines bear some of the more difficult mixed meter in the aria (bars 194–198: 15/32 to 5/8 to 7/16 to 6/16 to 2/8, and bars 203–213: 11/16 to 3/8 to 19/32 to 2/4 to 3/8 to 11/16 to 7/16 to 2/8 to 3/16 to 2/8).

The Pound/Antheil score called for the drum theme to enter at the end of this passage (lines 501–508), breaking up the long aria here and elsewhere from the midpoint of Heaulmière's song. The distinctive refrain of the drums, accompanied by nose flute, has been called "Brothel Music" because its purpose was to punctuate the whore's aria. It would have been a simple matter to bring in the drum theme twenty-eight bars earlier to shorten the song without anyone noticing save for the constant followers of Villon. However, notations in Harding's final script show that the drum theme was used consistently from the beginning of the melodrama to announce new characters and new time frames. It announced Heaulmière's entrance but was otherwise omitted from the interior of her aria. The next two entrances of the drum theme announced the arrival and departure of the gallant. These were all revisions to the Pound/Antheil score. Until recently, the thick crossouts over each drum theme in the score were thought to be a warning to the music copyist not to enter the drum music into the instrumental parts, because the short passage was prerecorded. This explanation is only partly accurate. The technical cues in Harding's final script confirm the redesigned purpose and placement of the drum theme for the 1931 broadcast.

A second instance of the BBC's prudery occurred when Alan Odle, staff artist for the *Radio Times,* submitted a triptych for the promotion of Pound's melodrama. The centerpiece depicted the nude Margot, Bozo's wife, leaning out of the brothel window. The illustration did not pass the editorial staff, and Odle was requested to tone down the picture. One bare breast was reported to have been within the allowable limits, but not two.[126]

Reviews and Postperformance Critique

The mixture of medieval French and modern English provoked considerable controversy. The *Manchester Guardian* came out favorably for the opera but questioned the connective text:

> "François Villon" was one of the best plays the BBC has given us. . . . There was only one small difficulty to be got over, and that was the modern idiom used by Mr. Pound for the conversations. ("Here comes your boy friend.") Taken in itself it was not wrong; but there was an incongruity with the poems of Villon, which were sung, and beautifully sung, in French.[127]

The Star's critic Eric Dunstan ran a negative piece of radio criticism, whose title, "Rubbish," was followed by the subline "The Bright Young Department Runs Riot":

> Thanks to the clear description of what was coming—given by Mr. E. A. Harding, the producer—I realised what was supposed to be happening, but I cannot believe that this sort of stuff is in any way suitable for broadcasting. It was the Bright Young Department run riot and getting very near to nonsense. . . .
>
> . . . As broadcast the only thing I really understood was his mother's prayer. The rest was a long procession of meaningless French—archaic French at that—sung either unaccompanied or

> to one violin with little or no tune and monotonously unmelodious.
>
> Occasionally someone shattered such 13th century atmosphere as was achieved by breaking into cockney or modern slang, such as "They ain't got nothing on me" or "What the hell are you doing, Frankie?"—Frankie being, if you please, François Villon, the poet.
>
> I hate to be unkind, but the truth is that I thought it all complete rubbish.[128]

The two reviews in combination tell us that the slang, recalled verbatim, stayed in the ear. It distracted both writers, and probably many other listeners, from Pound's intention to convey the beauty of Villon's verse. Compare the charge that the songs were "unmelodious" to Pound's own publicity statement written for the BBC, "The primary interest is a musical interest in the strength and firmness of the melodic line. . . . But a sustaining factor is the quality of the words actually to be sung. I.E. some of the greatest poetry in the world."[129]

Radio Times lauded the boldness of the venture, putting its listeners on notice that, in the case of the rare experiment in broadcasting, it would not cater to taste but to idea:

> The disagreement of critics, both public and private, as to the merits of the recent radio-play production, *The Testament of François Villon,* has been both prolonged and heated. That a play of this character, with music of so strange an order as Ezra Pound's and a convention so extraordinary as that of making the vagabonds of fourteenth-century Paris talk in the dialect of Chicago racketeers, should have met with whole-hearted approval from every listener was scarcely to be expected. He [the producer] knows that *The Testament of François Villon* was an experiment, that the path of the experimentalist is thorny, and that the first attempts at a novel technique are at best groping. . . . To rule out experiment in an art as greedy of new material as Broadcasting would be mere folly; the constant demand for programmes calls for adventure in programme-building.[130]

The editorial went on to compare the experimental producers of the BBC to cinema's "revolutionalists of imagination," who, with their "eccentric camera-angle, 'expressionist' photography of shifting and dissolving shapes, . . . have become serious rivals of the synthetic studio-picture." It recalled Sieveking's *Kaleidoscope* as "dramatically unsatisfying" but enriching to the industry on the whole. The editorial concluded, "Of the year's 60,000 hours of Broadcasting a mere dozen hours are devoted to experiments in drama."[131]

Pound's postbroadcast critique to Harding was concerned almost entirely with problems in music performance and radio reception, little with the actors' dialogue. The music required more preparation in the areas of precise rhythmic performance, enunciation of the lyrics, balance of instruments and timbre, and clarity of the strategically placed polyphony and homophony. On the whole Pound favored the performances by singers he himself had cast: Maitland, Collignon, and Marquesita. He raged over the performance of Gustave Ferrari in the part of Villon:

> The Villon role is difficult. All the parts done in Paris were better done. I mean better done in the Paris concert.
>
> Or no, I wont say that. The False Beauté was about even.
>
> The gallant sang a few notes wrong but not enough to matter.
>
> Your Villon sang absolutely NOTHING that was written for him. God damned drivveling mess that comes I suspect from liking the watered down duParc, Chausson post Debusy typical modern french puke. . . .
>
> The Villon was the only member of cast I wd. absolutely throw out.
>
> . . . The god damn bastard who sang Villon has no savagery whatsoever. Vegetarian.
>
> I don't believe my being in London wd. have helped. But I must be there before the next performance. . . . In fact it was very interesting to listen to.[132]

Despite the close working relationship and friendship that had developed between Bedford and Harding, she singled him out in a rare display of anger and indignation: "It grieves me to say that as a producer he is almost a complete idiot, & a high water mark of incompetence even in the BBC where no one is at all competent anywhere."[133]

That the work was compromised by musical and extramusical matters, in Pound's mind, merely paved the way for film, though he considered the benefit of staged performances: "It needs the wear (*engrenage*) of repeated performance even in theatre; EVEN before tone film. The film ought to be done AFTER it is worn smooth, I.E. engine run till there are no more stops hitches etc."[134]

While Dorothy Pound stayed in touch with the cast in London, Olga Rudge attempted to promote performances of *Testament* in Paris.[135] At the same time Denis Freeman, the BBC's independent music contractor for the Villon broadcast, was interested in producing *Testament* on a London stage. Dorothy Pound advised, "Continue with Villon: the singers are interested enough to go on, if it could be done without too much interval. Freeman has the idea of putting on 2. performances, with staging, at The Gate Theatre—(it's some small place.) It would I'm sure be a good plan if he could do it soon at all."[136]

Pound appears to have been torn between the possibility of perfecting the Villon and continuing work with Harding. Radio held a new fascination for him.[137] Pound would reassemble essentially the same team for his next feature, despite the harsh criticisms of Harding and Ferrari, and set aside the summer of 1932 to complete *Cavalcanti*. Before he finished the work he was already thinking ahead to the prospect of television: "The seneschal [of the last act] possessed by the spirit of the statue may lose something, or rather reserve something; it [may] be mislaid until we have television to help us. The rest of the work has been done with consideration of the radio from the beginning."[138]

By the publication of *Guide to Kulchur* (1938) Pound appears to have dropped his pursuit of film. The period of amateur and professional experimentalism in early film and radio had passed. In 1950 Richard Lambert, editor of *The Listener,* the BBC's weekly literary paper, included in his memoirs a post-mortem concerning Harding and the other pioneers of radio production. He quietly invoked class differences to accuse producers of abusing their access to listeners. Radio listeners formed the new mass audience that had yet to "see and hear it all." They were profoundly disturbed by program material they did not understand. Lambert dismissed the era of radio experimentation as so much amateurism: "No one supposes, for instance that the series of dreary 'Feature Programmes' put on for several years by the Production Department, with their antiphonal narrations like the strophes of an imitation Greek Chorus, had anything to do with pleasing the listener. No, they were the day-dreams of young amateurs in the Productions Department, 'trying it on the dog' to see if he would yap or no."[139] After all the inventions, debates, departmental infighting, editorials, and career shifts, features producers were reduced to what Gregory Whitehead has called the "nobodies of radio art."[140] The surest contributing factor to such ignominy was the sheltering institution itself.

Cast

The vocal magnetism of the Parisian chanteuse Yvette Guilbert was in Pound's ear during the early 1920s when he composed the Heaulmière aria. Pound asked Harding to negotiate with Guilbert to sing the role, perhaps counting on her familiarity with his name from 1912 when he had provided the English translations for the *Selection Yvette Guilbert,* an edition of her repertory of troubadour songs arranged by Gustave Ferrari. But by 1931 Guilbert commanded top price for her appearances. There appears to have been little career incentive for her to participate in a BBC experimental production by the Research Section despite Pound's own public stature at the time. An invitation from Drama, which had not yet built a reputation, rather than Music (the BBC Symphony Orchestra under Adrian Boult) may well have been perceived as an insult by a singer of Guilbert's fame. Had Guilbert seen the difficult Heaulmière aria in advance, she may have calculated the time required to learn it as part of her fee. When negotiations hovered around £600, Harding despaired of hiring her, warning Pound, "I can't tell you how difficult it is keeping the thing on at all, and I have only been able to do so by swearing I'd cut every penny."[141] Harding forwarded the address of Guilbert's manager to Pound, should Pound wish to try to procure her services for less.

To sing the part of Villon, Pound proposed the 1926 *Le Testament* performer Robert Maitland, the baritone who had sung "Si j'ayme et sers" and "Frères humains" at the Salle Pleyel. He also had sung arias from *Le Testament,* "Et mourut Paris," "Dictes moi," and "Je plains," at a private concert at the home of Mrs. Christian Gross (see Table 4). Pound and

Table 4 **Differences in the performing forces of Pound's *Testament,* 1923–1931**

1923 Antheil[1]	***1924 Salle Pleyel***[2]	***1926 Salle Pleyel***[3]
piccolo/flute	violin (Olga Rudge)	violin (Olga Rudge)
oboe	tenor (Yves Tinayre)	tenor trombone (Jean Dervaux)
clarinet		bass trombone (Edouard Dumoulin)
saxophone	"Mort j'appelle"	
bassoon	"Je renye amours"	cornet dessus (Paul Tinayre)
French horn		harpsichord (Paul Tinayre)
trumpet		kettle drums (Ezra Pound)[7]
2 trombones		
mandolins		*Voices*
piano		Yves Tinayre, Villon
violin		("Et mourut Paris," "Je plains,"
cello		"Mort j'appelle," "Heaulmière,"
double basses		"False beauté")
percussion, 3 players:		Robert Maitland, Bozo
bass bells,[9] tubular chimes,		("Si j'ayme et sers")
nose flute, tam tam, small		Tinayre and Maitland
African drum, side drum, snare		("Père Noé,"[10] "Frères humains")
drum, cymbal, tambourine,		
bones, triangle, sandpaper,		
whistle		
Voices		
Villon		
Heaulmière		
Villon's Mother		
Ythier		
Gallant		
Bozo		
Woman in Window		
Gantiere		
Blanche		
Priest		
Voice from Church		

1. R. Murray Schafer's 1962 score from the Antheil edition adjusted some of the meters and added a slight amount of newly composed connective music to hold the arias together dramatically. This edition was broadcast by Third Programme on June 28 and July 31, 1962, produced by Geoffrey Bridson. The 1923 Antheil edition received its world stage premiere on November 13, 1971, by San Francisco Opera's Wesern Opera Theater at Zellerbach Auditorium, University of California, Berkeley, conducted by Robert Hughes; recorded by Fantasy Records, LP #12001.
2. July 7, 1924, at 22, rue Rochechouart, Paris.
3. June 29, 1926.
4. July 12, 1926; at 1, avenue Charles Floquet, Paris.
5. Broadcast October 26, 1931, at 9:50 P.M., Daventry National Programme, and October 27, 1931 at 8:45 P.M., London Regional Programme (both programs went out on the Daventry transmitter, which was long-wave—1,500 m. at 30 kw). A set of parts is held in the BBC Music Library, catalogue number 27296. No complete score for the 1931 broadcast has been located.
6. It appears from the program that Pound intended a fourth song but did not have time to finish the arrangement.
7. Pound's playing on the kettle drums is confirmed in letters from EP to Agnes Bedford, June 29 and 30, 1926.
8. The only complete listing of the cast (E. A. F. Harding to EP, October 10, 1931). The singers were not credited in the *Radio Times* listing. Maisie

1926 home of Mrs. Christian Gross[4]
violin (Olga Rudge)
singer (Robert Maitland)

"Et mourut Paris"
"Je plains"
"Dictes moi"[6]

1931 BBC[5]
piccolo/flute
bassoon
2 trombones
violin
cello
2 double basses
guitar (or mandolin)
percussion (prerecorded)

Voices[8]
Gustave Ferrari, Villon
John Armstrong, Ythier
Maisie Seneschal, Heaulmière
Violetta Marquesita, Villon's Mother
Raymonde Collignon, Beauty
and Voice from Church
Jan van der Gucht, Gallant
Lubinoff, Priest
Robert Maitland, Bozo
(Voices for envoy: Collignon, Gantiere;
Marquesita, Blanche)

Connective text
665 words for 22–24 voices

Electronic enhancement
Dramatic Control Panel, Echo,
Microphones, Resonance

Sound effects (see table 3)

Additional music
"Mère au Saveur," by Wm. li Viniers
"Suivez beauté," arr. Ferrari (?)
Gregorian chant
music by Dufay

Seneschal was a pupil of Ferrari, hired by Harding in September (E. A. F. Harding to EP, September 25, 1931). Lubinoff is described as "an elderly & décavé Russian"; Armstrong and van der Gucht are referred to as tenors "who are probably the weakest links but intelligent & hard working" (E. A. F. Harding to EP, October 10, 1931). Lubinoff may be the Russian referred to in a piece of prebroadcast promotion: "His [Pound's] melodies are founded on twelfth-century troubadour music, and their aptness as settings for Villon's poems can be judged by the following true story. When the producer of the melodrama was hunting for a cast, he tested a Russian, who brought along a tattered copy of his only song, a Victorian ballad with words by Elizabeth Browning. This was hardly the sort of thing wanted, so he was asked simply to read some of Villon's poetry. He chanted it quite spontaneously, with exactly the same rhythm, and almost the melody, of Pound's setting—which he had never seen!" (*Radio Times,* October 16, 1931: 175.)

9. Antheil notated unobtainably low pitches for the bells. For the Fantasy recording, a prepared piano played the part of bass bells.

10. In the printed program this number was referred to as "Motifs de la foule" performed by violin, harpsichord, and two trombones. Although no separate music part survives for voices, Olga Rudge, who supervised and attended the March 28, 1983, recreation of this concert in San Francisco, remembered that the voices also sang. See also note 72 to the text above, regarding the substitution of the name Jean Cocteau for Jean Cotard; this is another indication that the performance included voices.

Harding continued to look for stronger singers and eventually Maitland was transferred to the role of Bozo, the brothel keeper.

Raymonde Collignon, singer and diseuse, had been a longtime friend of Pound's since he had reviewed her 1917 London concert for *The New Age.*[142] She had sung "Mère au Saveur" as early as 1918, and it seemed natural for Pound to propose to Harding that she sing the "Mère" for the BBC *Testament.*[143] In addition to the "Voice from Church," Collignon would also sing the roles of Beauty and Gantiere.

Violetta Marquesita was to sing the role of Villon's mother and the small part of Blanche. Pound favorably reviewed her singing in London in 1919, but with reservations regarding musical taste and gesture.[144] She became known for her roles in musicals and light opera, particularly that of Lucy Lockit in *The Beggar's Opera,* which enjoyed a London run of 1,463 performances in the early 1920s.[145] Harding wrote that her voice was reputed to have weakened, but he admitted that it would be in line with the character of Villon's mother.[146] Both Collignon and Marquesita had been coached by and performed with Agnes Bedford.

Pound's recommendations appear to have so dominated the casting of the opera that Harding was pressed to find replacements a month before the show when the preferred singers, and then Pound's recommended substitutes for them, could not be booked. Yves Tinayre had sung the 1924 and 1926 performances, but due to a conflict of dates had to decline Harding's offer. Harding's September 25, 1931, letter to Pound was filled with angst over the matter and threw the casting back into Pound's hands, "Can you suggest a good, intelligent tenor who knows French and is generally in England?" A month before the broadcast, Gustave Ferrari, "a Frenchman, a light baritone of great personality," was hired for the leading role.[147] Pound was essentially coproducing the opera from Rapallo.

Music and Orchestral Balance

Harding set out to produce the 1923 Antheil edition of *Le Testament* but because of its difficulty was forced to switch to earlier versions of the opera following a plan volunteered by Pound: "The reinforcement of words by instruments is technically difficult. = when it can not be well done. — it would be better to rely on the simple violin accompaniment indicated in ms. used for concert in 1926."[148] Harding proposed ample rehearsal time. "Twenty first-class solo" instrumentalists were to share £225 for two performances and twelve rehearsals.[149] Six weeks before the broadcast, Pound was notified by Harding that it was necessary to reduce the orchestra by half.[150] At this point Pound lost control over the music: "Until I know exactly what notation was used I can't make any useful constructive crit."[151]

Emotions sometimes reached the straining point between the Engineering Department and the more independent producers like Harding who preferred to work the electronic controls themselves. The signal had to be strong, stable, and balanced to survive the requirements of transmission and the variable conditions of reception.

Dorothy Pound attended the October 26 broadcast at the BBC. When she listened to the radio for the October 27 broadcast, she made note that she could scarcely hear the orchestra.[152] Pound also had difficulty hearing some of the instrumentation: "As to the histkrumenks. I cd. hear the double basses , damn fine on Monday ; less on tuesday. Not a bloody trace of the trombones." The mandolins, sounding in the middle to upper audio frequency range, came through very well: "The mandolins sounded like a regiment of cavalry or at least 20 mandolins; that's O.K." When he heard the basses, he liked the effect, described as a "wide even strip like back of a frieze."[153] The optimal reception of the bass frequencies would influence his composition of *Cavalcanti*.

Reliance on radio operators to make necessary orchestral adjustments would not fix a sound that was not correctly notated in the first place. "Evidently one has to put in EVERY phrase mark/ am evolving a set of marks that OUGHT to be fool proof /// mah !!"[154] Pound further realized that no one from Drama or Engineering was going to solve the problem of orchestral balance. If the Music Department had produced *Testament,* orchestral balance would have been a primary concern. Lacking Music's sponsorship, Pound was forced to delve more deeply into the mechanics and politics of radio production.

His response to the mixing and balancing problems of *Testament* was to acknowledge the transmission characteristics and propensity for distortion by the microphones, transmitters, and receivers and to make accommodations for them as he composed the *Cavalcanti* score. An indication of his grasp of the technical challenge can be found in Pound's recommendation that an isolated percussion cue would be better assigned to the singer, who could be given a drum just for that purpose. It shows Pound conceiving the work in terms of the BBC practice of placing instrumentalists and singers in different studios to maintain balance through separation in the microphones.[155]

Radiophonic Effects

Effects in the early 1930s were produced by a designated Effects team. Studio 2, the drama room, was adjoined by 2E, the Effects Studio, sometimes called "the noise room."[156] In addition to manually produced sounds, prerecorded sounds from wax mastering discs, 16-inch aluminum transcription discs for professional sound effects, and commercial 78 rpm shellac records were also employed. These were played on electrically powered gramophone turntables wired for mixing and fading. A system of color pencil marks on wax discs achieved relatively precise needle cueing. Undoubtedly briefed by Harding on the state of radio effects, Pound proposed the use of prerecorded sounds for the Villon. These included the music of Guillaume Dufay, Gregorian chant, the drum ostinato that returned frequently throughout the program, and possibly the tubular chimes and harmonium.

Most prerecorded sounds were inferior in quality. They distracted listeners from the realistic ambience obtained from the live voices, music, and manually produced sound effects.[157] Poorly produced electronic effects led to a general prejudice against all electronic effects. The producer who used prerecorded material tried to give the impression when possible that everything was live, or "actual."

Artificial echo was the technique most frequently employed to add resonance to sound at the BBC. It was achieved in the following way: "A loudspeaker and a microphone were mounted on the staircase outside Studio I at Savoy Hill. As the staircase was spacious and constructed of stone, it was admirably suited to the purpose, the loudspeaker being placed at the bottom and the microphone at the top. The reverberant sound was superimposed on the main output by means of the two-channel mixer."[158] The unusual echo designed for "Mère au Saveur" required that the singer perform inside a special chamber called the "tin bath." "The Mère au Sauveur [sic] was sung in a tin bath—to give church effect!! . . . Everybody thought Marchese [Violetta Marquesita] sang the prayer most beautifully. I dunno, because I was in the tin bath in the basement."[159] The echo for "Mère au Saveur" had to suggest, in addition to the church's stone interior, the heavenly sound of a voice tonally distinct from the sound of the melodrama's corporeal characters.

Echo was also used to create movement. As the priest left the stone church to approach the brothel, echo lessened while a cross-fade brought the priest's song almost side by side with the voices of the tavern. This use of effects reinforced the alignment of voices alternately with the tavern, brothel, and church (the aural stage).

Given the creation of several types of echo, it is very likely that *Testament* was broadcast from four or five of the nine studios at Savoy Hill to accommodate the orchestra and singers, actors, effects, tin bath, and echo. With performers in separate and even remote locations, the chances of delayed or imprecise cueing increased. The cueing of effects, switching of microphones, and the addition of echo for resonance were notated in Harding's script. The work had its emotional toll, which Bedford described to Pound: "As to Harding, he was nearly in tears the second night, as he felt he was mis-timing all the effects & also felt psychic about you, & could see you sitting in an arm-chair at home through both performances, & making no attempt to listen, which nearly broke his heart!"[160]

Recording Devices

Pound's interest in developments in technology led him to suggest prerecording the drum theme, a three- to six-bar ostinato for African drum, tam tam, side drum, and nose flute. The advantage of having two to three fewer performers in the recording studio was to simplify the production. A recording insured precision in the performance of the ostinato, which, difficult today, was even more formidable in the 1930s. The proximity of drums to the other instruments could have wreaked havoc on the separation of sound obtained by diverse microphones, requiring a separate studio and up to three dedicated channels on the DCP. The sharp attack and decay of the drum sound would have recorded more cleanly than, for example, the complex, steady sound of a string instrument. If the recording successfully matched the live acoustics of the ensemble, its use would have resulted in the seamless blending of sound sources, a "trick" of the modern radio producer. If the recording differed acoustically from the live instruments, it could have been used impressionistically; that is, the difference in sound would have conveyed the desired scene change. As stated, the practice of mixing live and mechanical sound was ideologically controversial.

Pound must have also lobbied for a recording of "Frères humains," possibly as a commercial venture. Harding appeared eager to please: "Then, also, I will bestir myself about trying to find a good place for you to listen in on the French Riviera; also, the gramophone companies for recording the 'Freres Humains'. The idea of recording the drum theme is a good one, and I think we will have that done. It will simplify production, and should cut down the cost."[161]

"Frères humains" was a good choice for recording because it lacked instrumental accompaniment. Voices recorded better than most instruments. The singers could stand right up to the horn and transmit enough vibration directly to the recording diaphragm to register sound, whereas instrumentalists required some distance from the diaphragm. Two versions of the music existed, but neither was right for radio. Pound, preferring the polyphony of the 1923 Antheil edition and the metrics of the 1926 Salle Pleyel performance, probably hoped to finalize this combination in recording. The music was the right length for a 78 rpm recording and showed a mature compositional process, its rich harmonies capable of demonstrating Pound's ability with dissonance—an important consideration in modern music in the 1930s.[162]

Recording techniques by 1925 were "all electric," but there was still a lag time between the recording and the manufacture of a disc for playback. In May 1931 the BBC acquired the Stille system Blattnerphone, which featured steel tape that could be rewound for immediate playback after recording (figure 3).[163] BBC engineer Edward Pawley reported that the quality of the Blattnerphone was not up to reproducing music but was useful for rehearsal. One of Harding's earliest letters to Pound bemoaned the fact that broadcast programs were not preserved.[164] The technical advances in film and audio were so rapid that within a few months he had access to sound recording. He communicated his excitement to Pound at

Figure 3 The Stille system Blattnerphone, an English adaptation of the German steel tape sound-recording machine, developed with assistance from BBC Research and Engineering. Harding recorded the penultimate rehearsal of *Testament* on the BBC's Savoy Hill Blattnerphone. Courtesy CBC Still Photo Collection

their Paris preproduction meeting, and Pound enthused to his wife, "They've a new recording machine—wonders of science ETC."[165] The "wonder of science" was put to use at the penultimate rehearsal of the *Testament* musicians and singers: "The Stille system of recording on magnetised steel tape is, electrically, very good, but mechanically at present rather clumsy. We use it for recording rehearsals as well and then play back the record to the cast, showing them how bad they are in a way they can't but believe. You should have seen the faces of the Villon cast after hearing the record of the penultimate rehearsal. Its a great weapon in the hands of the producer."[166]

Microphones

At the time of the *Testament* production the Reisz carbon granule microphones were used at Savoy Hill (figure 4).[167] The microphones were more

Figure 4 Microphones in use at the BBC in 1931. *Top, left:* The Marconi Reisz carbon granule microphone developed by the BBC, shown here on a side-by-side theater stand. *Top, right:* RCA condenser microphone with suspension mount. *Bottom, left:* Western Electric double button carbon microphone. *Bottom, right:* STC 4017 moving coil microphone.
Photographs courtesy Robert Paquette, Sr.

sensitive than the popular condenser microphone because of their comparative tenfold potential for amplitude of diaphragmatic movement, but the transmitter was not accurate, tending to misrepresent various intensities and frequencies.[168] Directional characteristics were also inferior and "sound reflected from the walls was not reproduced with the same 'brilliance' as that coming from the front, and this tended to make the acoustic sound 'dead'."[169] As a result all BBC musical productions were treated with resonance. This explains Harding's preoccupation with resonance, not only to convey spatial dimension, but to bring life into the sound.

Dramedy

4

Futurism, Continued

ENGLAND'S VORTICIST MOVEMENT of painters, sculptors, and writers, known for its artistic and vigorous embrace of the new energy, rhythm, and aesthetic of industrial culture, was frequently paired in the public mind with Italian futurism. The central figure of vorticism was the English poet, novelist, and painter Wyndham Lewis (1882–1957), joined by Pound and by sculptors Henri Gaudier-Brzeska and Jacob Epstein, among others. Lewis's literary journal *Blast* was originally conceived to promote cubism, futurism, and vorticism, but the first issue in 1914 promoted only vorticism, and at the expense of futurism. The perception that survives in print is one of antagonism and rivalry.

Pound's own use of vorticism was to improve upon the poetry movement imagism (founded in 1912 by Pound, Hilda Doolittle, and Richard Aldington) in order to distinguish himself from the many imitators.[1] A vortex is a whirl of atoms, fluid, or vapor in constant motion around an axis. Pound called it "the point of maximum energy."[2] The renovated Image became "that which presents an intellectual and emotional complex in an instant of time."[3] The main tenet of vorticism asserted that an Image should be energized by the artistic elements from which it was constructed.

Pound's writing for *Blast* about futurism does much to obfuscate a comparison to vorticist thought, though elsewhere he clearly articulated one of the key differences between the two ideologies as the vorticist interest in history: "We [the vorticists] do not desire to evade comparison with the past. We prefer that the comparison be made by some intelligent person whose idea of 'the tradition' is not limited by the conventional taste of four or five centuries and one continent."[4] Pound's desire to bring forward and revitalize the "repeat in history" across national and cultural boundaries was an expression that was ultimately proprietarian in its reserve and centripetal force, apart from futurism's international grandstanding, declamatory aggression, and shifting interests. Although Pound shared the futurists' impatience with stultified tradition and praised their desire to "make it new," he refused to be identified with the movement or with Marinetti's "aesthetic principles."[5] In an article for the short-lived *Blast,* he buried the futurist connection: "Futurism is the disgorging spray of a vortex with no drive behind it, DISPERSAL. . . . CORPSES OF VORTICES. Marinetti is a corpse."[6]

Marinetti's promotion of *parole in libertà* (words in freedom) was itself an attempt to improve upon vers libre and to prevent words from perpetuating a poet's foolish sentiments, sounds, and rhythms. This was achieved by a futurist typography that freed the word upon the page from grammar and syntax. Though *parole in libertà* is listed among the demands of *La Radia* (in its most extensive passage, no. 12), broadcasting was not the essential and originating medium.[7] This proposed extension of *parole in libertà* to radio required a rethinking of the vocal projection of words, something for which Marinetti had already been criticized after a 1914 Petersburg performance of *Zang Tumb Tuuum* (his letter to Luigi Russolo from the Bulgarian trenches during the Balkan War). Marinetti's "mistake" was to have restored syntax and grammar, by means of the performance conventions of "gesture, mime, intonation and onomatopoeia," to words that had supposedly been set free of syntax and grammar on the page.[8] His five *Sintesi radiofoniche* would abandon words entirely.

Conversely, Pound's promotion of the specific and unique sentiments, sounds, and rhythms of poets was the great motivating force behind his composition. He explained his binding of words with music in this way: "The HOLE point of my moosik bein that the moosik fits the WORDS and not some OTHER words."[9] These two differences—a regard for the past within the present, and a conformation and transposition of words into systematized musical notation (another kind of grammar)—are fundamental to the unfolding relationship between Pound's vorticism and Marinetti's futurism.

Surrealism

Pound's forceful and frequent attacks against futurism and dada for their lack of structure were never turned against the third and youngest of the three art movements we have set out for discussion. He welcomed the development of surrealism: "After Dada there came a totally different constructive movement . . . utterly unconscious (as far as one cd. see) of ancestry and tradition."[10] Pound's reference to a prefiguration of surrealism was a quiet promotion of his own independent research in the troubadour and lyric poetry of southern Europe as the hidden tradition or ancestral stirrings of surrealism's quest for "reality outside the scholastic logic."[11] "Anyone who has for a quarter of a century held to an admiration for thirteenth-century poetry and fifteenth-century painting," he wrote, "has very little difficulty in adjusting himself to surrealism."[12]

In his 1928 essay "Mediaevalism and Mediaevalism," written for the American serial publication *Dial,* Pound had whimsically caught a medieval intellectual in the act of imagining form within radio transmission as "current hidden in air."[13] Pound attempted to rescue the medieval mind for the modern world by proposing that a "medieval 'natural philosopher' would find this modern world full of enchantments, not only the light in the electric bulb, but the thought of the current hidden in air and in wire would give him a mind full of forms, '*Fuor di color*' or having their hyper-colours."[14] Electricity connotes cyclical motion (the repeat in history). Air is one of the mediums through which the people, gods, and places of *The Cantos* make their qualities known ("Gods in the Azure air"). Electricity in the air became Pound's vorticist key to unlock medieval "forms," by-products of mental powers so highly charged that they ventured beyond, or existed outside (I'm not sure which, nor, presumably, is anyone else), the everyday mentality to become the cultural engines that powered a society: love, and *virtù.*[15]

Surrealists, in search of the essential inner forces of people, places, and things—inner forces, that is, that lay beyond the powers of human reason—did, in fact, reach back into their histories, acting as "archeologists of the intellect, unearthing and revitalizing theories and ideas that had long since been forgotten or discarded but that still held the potential for significant revolution."[16] Pound's interest in the movement lay in this potential of modern art to interact with history, and in the movement's ability to arouse a kind of religious fervor and moral discipline.[17] He had little patience with the focus on psychoanalysis by the French surrealists, whose investigations led to a certain cynicism or doubt that anything could be free of contradiction or embody one true nature.[18] The French surrealists' application of automatic writing and stream of consciousness techniques was quickly picked up by radio dramatists who found the resulting intimacy in the expression of self particularly suited to an aural medium. Pound instead used pithy expression, slang, and sound bites as a shorthand for personality (also used by radio dramatists), reserving music for the transmission of the deep-rooted psyches of his main characters.

The Italian and German surrealist sensibilities (the latter falling under the name "magical realism") possessed a propensity for the heroic voice. German magical realism eschewed humor or chance, favoring the weightier moral and social obligations that had transferred to the province of the writer. The goal was to create social awareness with "biting ridicule . . . a necessary part of this austere, strict, and heroic art."[19]

None of the surrealisms was entirely consistent with the goals of Pound's poetics. When measured by his timetable of transient, durable, and recurrent, these two poles of surrealism—art of the unknown and art with a social agenda—come together as transient expressions of sects that would eventually fade out, leaving behind only a record of the recurring human impulse to make a supreme intelligence perceptible in art.[20] Pound's impulse to same was schooled in the epic tradition and shaped by formidable predecessors—Homer and Dante. Dante's vision of a government tempered by philosophy, organized and authorized by words that master human reason and perfect moral science (*Convivio* IV.6), was taken up by Pound in a number of ways in his prose and poetry. The supreme intelligence perceptible in art and intelligence in government would become in his mind inseparable. As we saw in Canto IV, he married civic responsibility—the codification of human relations and social order—to the art of luminous perception, the most elusive, ephemeral, and episodic of human efforts. In partnership they would generate the earthly paradise, object of *The Cantos.*

Pound later recalled that the collective thinking, or the "life of the mind," of Europe in the 1920s was occupied by the question of civic order.[21] Citing this as his reason for moving to Rapallo, Italy, in 1924, he terminated his brief immersion in the Parisian artistic circles to draw closer to the Mediterranean, so that the qualities of place—and the new civic order—could enter the long poem.

Cavalcanti

A "sung dramedy" in three acts
Words by Guido Cavalcanti
Additional words by Sordello
Music by Ezra Pound
Narrator's text and spoken dialogue by Ezra Pound

The poet to whom Pound turned most often to investigate the "mind full of forms" was Guido Cavalcanti (c. 1250–1300). Florentine nobleman, natural philosopher and doctor, and writer of some of the finest lyric poetry in the vernacular tongue, Cavalcanti was an older friend and mentor to Dante Alighieri. "Guido came, let us admit, into a world that seems to us very highly conventionalized. His wildest statements, let us say concerning the emergence of spirits one from another, seem perhaps orderly in comparison with surrealist expression, but they probably did not seem so in A.D. 1284."[22]

Cavalcanti would be both title and principal character of Pound's second radio work, a "dramedy," Pound's term for a melodrama free to invent its own rules.[23] Pound must have dedicated this new work, for Harding sent back a rather stilted expression of gratitude, "Please let me know, in due course, how your new opera is getting on. I feel sensible of the honour of the proposed dedicace."[24] From Pound's perspective Harding may have appeared partly if not fully autonomous at the BBC. The intense collaboration at their first Paris meeting, the confident tone of his letters, and the unique mandate of the elite Research Section probably combined to form the impression that radio was inventing its own rules at the end of its first decade. Harding was obviously a brilliant talent in radio, but young and inexperienced in practical matters. Given the difficulties of the *Testament* broadcast, Pound strove to make *Cavalcanti* both radiogenic and Harding-proof. When Pound met Harding a second time in Paris, May 1933, his libretto was already scripted. The music bears no evidence of that meeting, nor is it clear that Harding was ever given the music. The letters indicate that Bedford was to retain all the music until the work went into actual production, at which time Pound would travel to London to supervise preparations.[25]

Introduction to the Work

As it has been recovered by Robert Hughes, *Cavalcanti* is comprised of two to five drafts of each of thirteen arias, a radio announcer's script for each act in English and in Italian, and untitled, uncatalogued pages of dialogue in English and Italian. Without a fully assembled radio script we lack indication of the kind of contrast that might have been achieved among the voices through special instructions or the addition of effects, although the presence of an Italian libretto does suggest that the contrast of two languages was no longer of principal interest. Pound was more confident as a composer and would now rely upon his setting of the individual numbers to achieve contrast and counterplay.

The *Cavalcanti* music is more melodically challenging while being rhythmically simpler than the *Villon*. The scoring for eight instruments is also in a simpler idiom and the numbers are through-composed. Though the orchestral parts are spare, the vocal parts are difficult both in their extended range and interpretive requirements. Dialogue is at a minimum. An announcer's part seems to have been agreed upon by Pound and Harding at a date earlier than August 1932.[26] Believing he had attained a level of compositional self-sufficiency, Pound independently drafted the opera's music in the spring and summer of 1932, adding finishing touches the following summer. He sent finished drafts to Bedford for her comments.[27]

The *Cavalcanti* opera had points in common with *Testament*. The *Villon* plot opens with the King's police seeking Villon in Paris. *Cavalcanti* draws its initial energy from the protagonist's desire to rout out the "gang of eleven" from Florence. The two poets are exiled from their native cities, Villon as a common criminal, Cavalcanti as a political prisoner with privileges—a castle, castelan, and page. Both works are concerned with the importance of a poet's legacy. Villon is quite capable of bequeathing his poetry; Cavalcanti appears incapable of direct bequest because of an excessive sensitivity and temperamental personality rendering him unable to overcome his circumstances. Cavalcanti dies in a remote outpost, consigned to remain in the shadows of Villon and Dante. The moral is offered for the taking by those positioned, even if accidentally, to tend the flame of great poets.

The larger dramatic interest of *Cavalcanti* is the poet's attempt to negotiate a position for himself within a poetic lineage. Pound tackles the question through both sound and narrative content, an approach that structurally differentiates the work from the *Villon.* The drama's final scene will be understood by the popular audience as: "Cavalcanti dies; and the poem ends" because Rico, the page, failed to learn it.[28] Pound's sophisticated audience will reflect not on the action but on the sound of the drama's end as it is presented in the next song, that of Fortune. Cavalcanti's voice after his death is literally and sonically carried forward into history within Fortuna's aria "Io son la donna," which Pound believed contained one strophe by Cavalcanti, the rest being completed by Machiavelli.[29]

The dramatic interest of the *Villon,* as guided by Harding to exploit the tools and effects of radio, hinged on the "intellectual problem" of the counterplay of two languages. The "intellectual problem" of *Cavalcanti,* posed independently of Harding, turned on the larger conception of radio's potential to cultivate and disseminate the voices of great poets. The Latin verb *radiare* (to beam), from which our word *radio* is derived, would become the ultimate metaphor for a poet's legacy. Drawing upon two decades of immersion in Guido Cavalcanti and his poetry, Pound created such a dense music of representative outline, filled with literary commentary and accompanied by narrative aside, that his newly formulated working method of multiple-scripts-in-one strained under the weight of external references and internal clues. An Atlas in the form of a radio announcer was required to shore up the work. To understand the logic of Pound's conceptual and practical construction, it is necessary to examine the poetry in more detail than was done for the *Villon,* and to organize the analysis slightly differently.

Guido Cavalcanti

The figure of Guido Cavalcanti looms large in Pound's total output; he is "the man who taught Dante his job," a reference to Cavalcanti's mastery of the Italian vernacular to render sonic contours and rhymes unrivaled in his time.[30] In 1912 Pound published his bilingual edition, *Sonnets and Ballate of Guido Cavalcanti,* and wrote in *Spirit of Romance,* "No man has written better ballate, and his individuality is unquestionable."[31] He identified Cavalcanti's era as one when "the most profound perceptions were those of the poets, the great condensers of words and the most efficacious communicators of spiritual knowledge." Pound defined "spiritual" as a summation of the meanings of "intelligence, intuition, knowledge."[32]

In 1932, after a spate of unfortunate incidents and delays with publishers, Pound issued a philological edition of the poetry with translations and photographs of the manuscripts in state archives, *Guido Cavalcanti Rime.* Pound's introduction does not mention surrealism but concludes, "These are no sonnets for an idle hour. It is only when the emotions illumine the perceptive powers that we see the reality. It is in the light born of this double current that we look upon the face of the mystery unveiled."[33] This volume included for the first time Pound's translation of Cavalcanti's philosophical canzone "Donna mi prega," a poem highly regarded as one of the most superbly crafted (and enigmatic) poems in the Italian language.

Pound had come lately to the view that the canzone was, to use Jacqueline Kaye's term, a "watershed" in the history of European thought.[34] Its philosophical discourse on refined sexual love—a topic outside the ken of the philosophers of Cavalcanti's time—may possibly have disguised a more heretical and dangerous discourse based on radical interpretations of Aristotle's divisions of the soul and their functions. One of these strains of interpretation, called "Averroism" after the Arabic philosopher Averroës of Spain (1126–1198), ran counter to the Christian doctrine of the immortality of the individual soul. Averroism is a highly technical, still not fully recovered, line of medieval thought. That Pound concerned himself with it through Cavalcanti complicates an exposition and analysis of the radio drama, whose form and content hinge on the unstated assumption of Guido's Averroism.

In a nutshell, Averroës claimed that at death, the individual intellect of the soul, known as the "possible intellect," was reunited with a "universal intellect."[35] Pound's contemporary Étienne Gilson explained the possible intellect by way of the figure of an angel: "Averroes conceived the possible intellect as a single entity, an intellectual substance wholly independent of the body—in short, what Christians call an angel—and he taught that, to an individual man, knowing means simply sharing in some part or other of the knowledge possessed by this intellect."[36] For a study of Pound's radio play, it will be sufficient to say that Pound believed Cavalcanti, writing not of angels but of spirits, edged very close to this idea in a number of his poems. Pound identified other trends in medieval philosophy in Cavalcanti's writing (such as Neoplatonic light mysticism) that particularly interested him for the writing of an earthly paradise.[37] I will examine the way in which Pound brings these medieval philosophies together in his setting of "Donna mi prega."

The *Canzone d'Amore:* "Donna mi prega"

The music's more intense, intellectual interest resides in Guido's aria, "Donna mi prega." Dante's *De vulgari eloquentia* twice mentions the "Donna mi prega" as exemplar of technical and artistic excellence in vernacular poetry.[38] Its eleven-syllable lines hold absolute privilege over poetry of other line lengths. The poem deploys single and double internal rhymes as well as end rhymes in its five stanzas. One third of its syllables are woven into this rhyme pattern, a technique that creates undertow in the poem's internal movement as the poem's cadence folds the line endings back into the poem's interior. The canzone is an inquiry into the nature of Love, based on Aristotle's *De anima* and written to resemble the technical form of a thirteenth-century *quaestio.* Stanza one presents the questions that will be answered in the poem: Where does Love reside? Who brings it into being? What is its virtue and what is its potency? What is its essence? What are its effects? What is its pleasure? and, Is it visible?

To the poem's critical line, "Love is not a virtue," in stanza three, Cavalcanti adds a qualifier below it that reads something like a credo: "Non razionale ma che si sente, dico" ([Known] not by reasoning but by experience, I say). Overall the stanza uses the scholastics' technical language to reason whether Love is good or bad: Love cannot be a virtue because it is an appetite, informed by the experience of the senses and not by reason. But why does Cavalcanti insert his personal voice, "dico," at this point? In his Latin commentary on the canzone (c. 1320), Dino del Garbo says that Cavalcanti is pointing to the difficulty of speaking of Love as a perfection, or virtue, when in fact it must be operative—in action and in verb—to realize perfection, and then its perfection is subject to appetites that are not regulated by reason.[39] This was problematic in the thirteenth century because reason was the only allowable authority for perfection outside of God. Guido's contribution in this tricky, and by no means resolved, passage is to negotiate a two-part perfection of Love: the ideal, formed in the intellect (which includes memory), and the experience of the senses, which, unregulated by reason, were susceptible to unsound judgment. The claim registered by "dico" transfers the authority to himself, the psalmist amidst the philosophers, something Cavalcanti establishes from the poem's opening lines, "Donna mi prega, perch'io voglio dire . . ." (A woman asks me, therefore I will tell . . .).

The canzone contains three voices that, excepting Guido's occasional self-reference, protectively cloud Cavalcanti's authorial position in relation to the philosophy expressed: experienced lover, weaver of philosophic reason, and commentator on the dialectic between experience and reason.[40] The authorial plan, briefly, is to establish that the possible intellect of the human soul receives its "forms" (angels, concepts, or intelligences) from a universal intellect.[41] This becomes the probable model for the two-part perfection of Guido's theory of love—the ideal (represented by the noun *amore*) must be received in its abstract form from the "universal intellect" and stored in the memory, which is part of the sensitive soul; it is then brought into being with the aid of the senses, to culminate in the individual physicalized experience (represented in the poem by the verb *amare*). Breaking with *fin'amors* Cavalcanti insists that Love must be consummated, but instead of rejoicing in that consummation, he warns that the result leads to suffering, a loss of will, and a substantially changed individual, the dark themes that dominate his oeuvre of lyric love poetry.[42]

If we glimpse Aristotle's reasoning about the origin of sound (*De anima,* section 419b), here we find a less controversial source for the process of two-part perfection, one grounded in the physical world: "Sound exists in two ways, in actuality and in potentiality. Sound that occurs in actuality is always the sound of something, against something, and in something: for what makes it is an impact. Hence it is impossible for a sound to occur when there is just one thing, for the striker and the thing struck are different."[43] Aristotle's passage helps to clarify why the model of a two-part perfection of love was of interest to Cavalcanti and his immediate circle, poets of the *dolce stil novo* (sweet new style): the lived experience of love cannot occur without a physical partner, whereas the refined idea of love may exist within just one person.

For the BBC *Cavalcanti,* this model of love is reflected back onto the medium itself. Radio is also a two-part process of perfection: transmission and reception. The lineage, as read earlier in the quote above ("the thought of the current hidden in air and in wire would give him a mind full of forms"), had been turned backward from radio to the medieval philosopher. With the proposed broadcast of "Donna mi prega," Pound reversed this vector so that radio would now become the natural beneficiary (as surrealism had been) of Guido's two-part love.

The "Donna mi prega" aria will be interesting to Pound scholars for its rich commentary on poem and poet, embedded within the music. Because that commentary requires the technical language of music theory and notation for its presentation, I have limited my comments to the symbolism carried by the music's shape, and the musical device used to answer Guido's last question, Is Love visible?

Pound referred to the philosophical canzone as "Guido's triumph of melodic symmetry."[44] His song setting is built upon short melodic cells that build to a representative outline that refers to the troubadour *canso* tradition. Pound had written that shape into Canto XX:

> In air, strong, the bright flames, V shaped;
> Nel fuoco
> D'amore mi mise, nel fuoco d'amore mi mise . . .[45]

The early *canso* form relied upon repetition to create the illusion of indefinite time. Poetic movement was more circular and, with a return to the same word, could even mark time, "The *canso,* like . . . organized speech, is linear and must unfold word by word through time; the uniqueness of poetry, however, lies in its capacity to draw attention away from its horizontal development and thus, in effect, to transcend its own temporality."[46] Pound uses melodic repetition to portray the troubadour ethos as the lineage from which Cavalcanti's very individual thought emerges. The scalar melodies of "Donna mi prega" ascend and descend, flamelike in their rise and fall, occasionally licking up to the octave. The melody of the canzone returns to the same note too often for a modern, thoroughly trained musician to abide, even allowing for the medieval mode, but Pound seems inclined toward a medieval rhetoric of music that seeks "analogies between the musical and verbal structures."[47] His musical setting of Guido's words (that reflect the technical language of the academicians) into a repetitious flamelike pattern conflates the language of philosophy with a nostalgia for a troubadour past. Guido's singular perceptions rise from a pattern of consensus as a spark rises from the flame: the tritone or *diabolus* in the scale that Pound employs to signal his voice, an awkward leap, or (as a rash of sparks) a sustained dissonance that mildly disturbs the harmony.

Pound folds back the devotional metaphor of lineage, "tending the flame" (of poets and philosophers), into the troubadour mystical flame of love in Guido's canzone, allowing Guido's word rhythms and intonations to give new shape to the symbol of the flame:

> I said in the preface to my Guido Cavalcanti that I believed in an absolute rhythm. I believe that every emotion and every phase of emotion has some toneless phrase, some rhythm-phrase to express it. (This belief leads to *vers libre* and to experiments in quantitative verse.) To hold a like belief in a sort of permanent metaphor is, as I understand it, "symbolism" in its profounder sense. It is not necessarily a belief in a permanent world, but it is a belief in that direction.[48]

Cavalcanti insisted on an idea that was slightly different from Pound's own, yet important, Pound thought, to retain in a medieval canon of lyric love poetry dominated by Dante: physical experience of love was essential to complete the knowledge of a greater love held in the mind (steeped, that is, in concepts formed by the possible intellect). Pound believed physical experience of love was essential to knowledge otherwise unobtainable or unformulable: "Coition, the sacrament, not the talk and registration. . . . The door to knowledge of nature. Not simple impregnation . . . but the awakening to knowledge of nature, the modus of entering into knowledge."[49] The knowledge referred to here is epiphanic, not a result of cognitive effort, or something held in the mind, but instantaneous, like light, and fleeting. In distinguishing himself from Cavalcanti, Pound aligns himself closer to Dante on a different front; neither poet could support the loss of will that so plagued Cavalcanti.[50] Pound chose to make these distinctions within music composition and a drama modeled partly on the Noh, rather than in the black and white of discourse in order to draw "the faintest shade of a difference."[51]

The operas began to take shape as a love trilogy, probably not as early as 1920, but certainly by the summer of 1932. Following on the heels of the carefully scripted social world of Villon's love-by-the-hour was a new, elaborate script about the vibrant "life" of Cavalcanti's Mediterranean mind, undone by love's mortal wound. Because Cavalcanti was the lyric love poet par excellence, we might expect the climactic vision to open onto Aphrodite or Venus, bringing the two operas to a satisfying conclusion in combination. But Pound's design is more than an economic seesaw of desire, cheap versus dear. To end *Cavalcanti,* Pound introduces Fortuna at her wheel and not Aphrodite. To understand Fortuna's appearance, and the contribution that a third opera could make to Pound's search for a "symbolism in its profounder sense," we need Cavalcanti's answer to Donna's question, Is love visible?

We have Pound's answer, as he worked it out on paper (figure 5): There is no likeness or image. Referring to the canzone's adoption of the scientific language of medieval color theory, J. E. Shaw's exegesis of "Donna mi prega" concludes, "Far from being visible like a material thing, which is visible because of its colour and an illuminated diaphanous medium, Love is an invisible light submerged in a dark medium."[52] What are visible are the effects of love in the lover and in the person desired, the "Donna." Pound sequences the musical numbers of his opera so that the next Cavalcanti poem to follow this idea, "Quando di morte," explains that desire formed from Love in its turn forms a new person: "Formando di desio nova persona" (Pound used this line to begin Canto XXVII). Referring again to Pound's notes for the "Donna mi prega," we find Pound clarifying the word *accidente* from the canzone's opening lines, which he translates as "affect."[53] He writes that neither "accident" nor "affect" is due to "chance"; that is, Love, being an affect, is not due to chance. Pound withholds Love and presents Fortuna, goddess of fate and arbiter of chance, as the final image of his drama. Pound's seemingly transparent intention re-

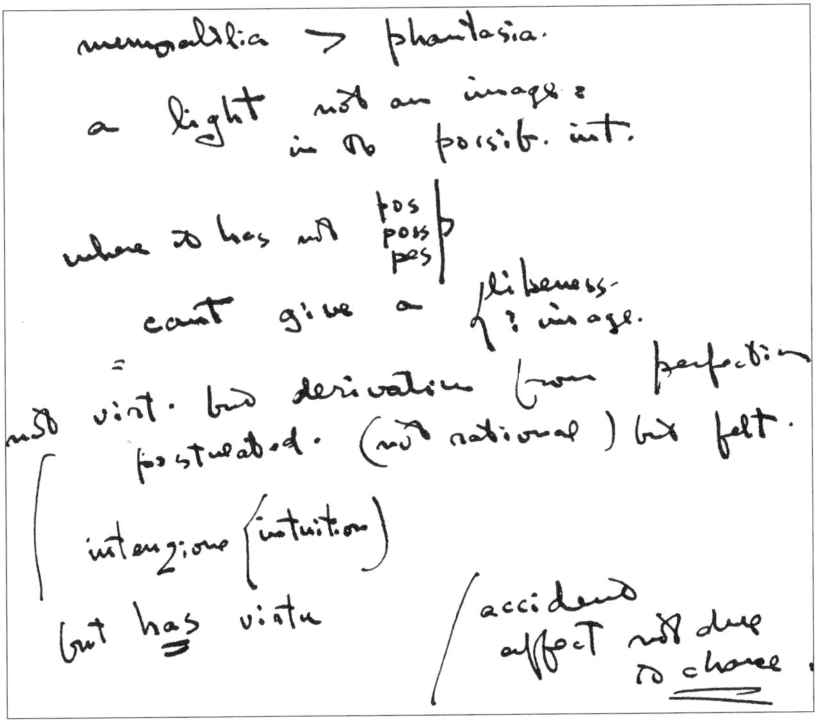

Figure 5 Pound's working notes for "Donna mi prega" by Guido Cavalcanti.
© 2002 Mary de Rachewiltz and Omar S. Pound; courtesy Beinecke Library

garding the appearance of Fortuna at Cavalcanti's death is complicated by this exclusion (doubly underscored) of Fortuna as a potential cause of love. The image is a dense one that builds, ply upon ply, Pound's theories of passion, prosody, and the pantheon of gods about him. Meanwhile, Pound holds in reserve the goddess of Love, Aphrodite, and the god of marriage, Hymen, for his nascent "Catullus" opera, *Collis O Heliconii* (figure 6).[54]

Cantabile Values

When Pound placed the canzone in the central position of his radio dramedy, he was forced to articulate the voices on terms quite different from his elaborate design of the published poem. The type face for the "Donna mi prega" in the 1932 *Rime* had emphasized other aspects of the canzone.

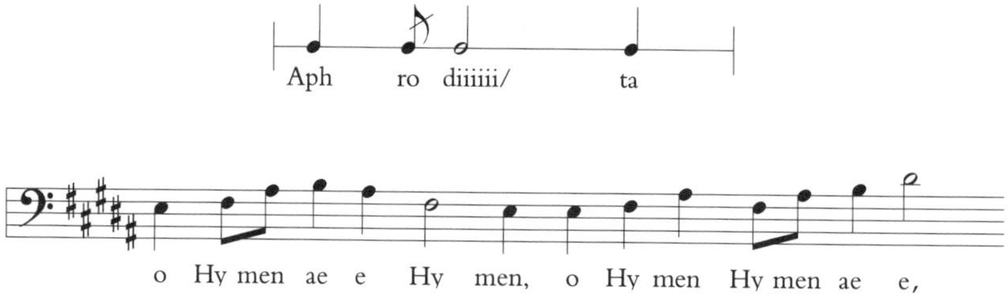

Figure 6 Pound's musical motifs, "Aphrodite" for Sappho's ode "Poikilothron," and "Hymen O Hymenaee" for Catullus's Carmen LXI, destined for the (unfinished) third opera *Collis O Heliconii.*

Sources: EP to Agnes Bedford, June 7, 1933 (Lilly); Ezra Pound Papers—Addition (Beinecke)

Pound visually reinforced the rhymes, phrasings, and inwardly directed movement of the verses by dividing each strophe into four parts: "I trust I have managed to print the Donna mi prega in such a way that its articulations strike the eye without need of a rhyme table."[55] Because he had attempted a philological study of source manuscripts with the aim of producing a critical edition of the poetry, his choices of spelling, punctuation, and phrasing hinged upon exact meaning and were therefore of considerable importance. Radio, especially for an English audience, would erase all such delicate delineation drawn from and between words. It could best convey the gross structure of the poem, its internal contours, the presence of rhyme, and the tone of the poet. The latter would further depend on the quality of Pound's song setting, which, composed for an ensemble of eight instruments, was even further dependent on the quality of the microphones and radio signal.

Radio, in other words, was not an ideal medium for poetry meant to stimulate a specific range of thoughts. Pound's term for such poetry was *logopoeia,* poems in which the interest is "in words and their usage as words" or the meaning of words.[56] Radio could better represent the kind of poetry that Pound termed *melopoeia,* in which "the interest and intent of the author . . . largely centres in the sound," in which the poet uses "words as a melodic stimulus" and relies almost entirely on sound for "conveyance of emotion."[57] Pound clarified *melopoeia* as dependent on "the actual beat, rhythm, and timbre of [the] words for the emotional effect of [the] work."[58] Because this type of lyric poem was made to be "delivered with varying pitch," he called it "cantabile" to distinguish it from poems intended to be spoken or half-chanted, and noted that the word sounds would be joined quite differently for *melopoeia cantabile* than for all other types of poetry.[59] Pound set only poems that were *melopoeia cantabile,* explaining that, even if such poetry were built upon complex ideas, this kind of poetry made its major contribution through sonic values alone.

For Pound, cantabile values of the thirteenth century communicate feeling as structural form and, therefore, as an expression of the thirteenth-century mind. Different from feeling as immediate sensation or feeling as word significance, Pound's interest in having one voice come through another, cantabile, was put to the test in the radio dramas. Rather than discuss, sympathize with, or analyze his dramatic characters, we are to hear them. And in hearing them, we attain a more incisive knowledge of them through the comparisons and contrasts that Pound provides.

Two Languages and the Language of Cunizza

Pound sent Harding a "tentative lay out" of the *Cavalcanti,* praising it over the *Villon* but apologizing there was "more stage [than radio] in it."[60] Harding replied, "The only way of making it dramatically intelligible will, I think, be to put into the mouth of the narrator a running commentary."[61] The two-language formula of the radio *Testament* was expanded to include contrast between the announcer's proper English and the medieval Italian of the singers. Occasional English dialogue between characters joined or even interrupted the arias with several varieties of humor—dry, witty, sardonic, parodic, and slapstick. The Provençal of Sordello was added for further musical contrast, and to bolster the narrative outline. Though the contrast of languages operates as a secondary interest, the use of English as commentary also retains its structural function to contrast, the thorough design for which had been tested in the *Villon.*

The spoken texts also survive in an Italian dialect that appears to have been partly coined by Pound. Pages with a mixture of English and Italian were probably first drafts, though Pound may have been experimenting with a new combination—movement between two languages even within the dialogue. We do not know if Pound intended the Italian texts for a particular venue, or if he was employing a language of less contrast to ensure that the listener would remember snippets of song over colloquial speech. The dialect in both languages has zest and rhythmic articulation, though some of the wordier Italian lines tend to flatten out dramatically, for example, "Non ze bisogno che tutto sia a porto dei bambini."[62]

The Italian dialect sounds Venetian, with Spanish or Provençal influence: "Una vez io ti coja" (I'll get you someday); "Non oggi S'oré" (Not today, Sir). Pound's Italian slang includes a few neologisms: "porco acidempopumpili" (porco accidente! or Damn pig!) and "scrofanino" (piglet of a breeding sow).[63] The significance of dialect is apparent only in the narrative in act III when Guido scolds Rico for incorrect pronunciation. Less apparent is the use of dialect to tie the elusive figure of Cunizza da Romano (1198–1279) to the drama in a way that Pound could otherwise not fully realize in the narrative, though he made a number of tries.

Harding's comment, "I think the action less viable over the radio than that of the Villon," is justified at least in part by Pound's insertion of oblique references to the romantic persona of Cunizza.[64] Married to Count San Bonifazio of the Veneto, she eloped with the Provençal-language troubadour Sordello. She is offered as a figure in the memory of Cavalcanti, a model for ideal love in its first perfection. Pound summed up Cunizza's beauty, compassion, and sense of social justice in his Italian script for the dramedy, a mixture of legend and history:

> Nostra racconta come stava in case dei Cavalcanti a Firenze donna Cunizza degli Exxzilini da Romano, figura quasi imperiale, conservando ancora a sessanta anni la leggiadrìa di portamento, la grande amoureuse; di donna che bella fù, con memorie del suo passato romantico destando l'immaginazione di Guido quindicenne, ricordando le canzoni del gran trovator Sordello, qua anche Dante putino piccolini avrebbe potuto guardarla, senza in anni teneri comprender gran che della sua storia, più tarde eternizzata nelle sue cantiche.[65]
> [Our story of how it came about that Cunizza da Romano, an almost imperial figure conserving even at age sixty a lightness of being, the great lover, a woman whose beauty, with memories of

a romantic past, stayed in the house of Cavalcanti, awakening the imagination of fifteen-year-old Guido, as she remembered the songs of the great troubadour Sordello. Here, too, the young Dante would have seen her, without enough years yet to understand her story, only later eternalizing her in his cantos.]

Pound presents Cunizza as a symbol of the refined love held in the mind of Cavalcanti, counterpoised to Dante's Beatrice. She does not enter the action of the dramedy directly; neither does she appear as subject in the words of song. Cunizza's former maid Vanna simply remembers that Cunizza taught her the song she now sings to Cavalcanti.

By insisting on Cunizza's inclusion as a memory only, without voice, Pound created a dramatic conundrum. She stands in the announcer's script as some of Pound's subject rhymes stand in *The Cantos.* Listeners acquainted with *The Cantos* would recognize that Pound's continual return to Cunizza was to invoke her as the symbolic crux of his ideas of love and politics. Her social and political accomplishment is documented by a legal act that freed her brothers' slaves (related in Canto VI). For this, she would come to represent to Dante the concept of noble generosity in love, for which she was rewarded a place in *Paradiso* (IX.33). An English draft of the announcer's script recounts Cunizza's elopement with Sordello, Dante's interest in her, the wars between pope and emperor, Sordello's legend, Robert Browning's *Sordello,* and concludes, "In the play that follows Cunizza and Sordello need mean no more than the princess of a fallen house and an adventurer, an adventurer of the grand line who joked and spoke his mind among princes."[66]

The radio drama was becoming a personal bulletin board. Left to his own devices, Pound's tendency was to fill *Cavalcanti* with fragments of ideas indexed from the narrator's platform. Pound cannot refrain from recalling in the announcer's script for act II that Dante was in some squabbles with a mule driver and a blacksmith, and in act III, that many people believed there were ciphers in troubadour songs. The announcer warns the listeners that Guido's cipher is "not in the words but in the music where only another musician can find it."[67] Pound disables his first kind of listener from grasping what is essential to the work, offering instead a radio shorthand that few could understand.

Dialogue

The announcer provides a summary of the characters, action, and location before each act. Each of his three texts is written for a different medium—stage, radio, film. Sounding like an impresario from the grand stage of a bygone era, the announcer begins, "Milords, Miladies, et cetera! You shall now see, or rather hear the voice of, Guido Cavalcanti, th' famous eyetalyan, the man that taught Dante his job. . . . God help the music, now first the orchester."[68] The sword fight, high jinks, balcony scene, and slapstick of act I are well suited to the traditional stage. Though the work is written specifically for radio, the script nods to the earliest radio dramas of staged events. For act II the announcer tones down his address to an intimate scale for radio listening: "Gentlemen, and ladies, if you still have your ear at the mouse hole . . .".[69] The intimacy among friends, Guido's extended "Donna mi prega" aria, a knock at the door, and reading of a document, conventions from a stage tradition, would be well served by radio, the concentration now centering on exact meaning as well as sonic contours of song and dialogue. By act III the announcer's script reads like a film treatment, "accent no longer marked":[70] "Evening at Sarzana, a sort of terrace or porch under the wall of the fortress, Guido in exile and on his death bed, in the garden an image of FORTUNE not very clearly seen."[71] The filmic style of presentation and the hint that one must strain for a clear picture prepares the listener for the shift the dramedy is about to take, from hearing to seeing. Only film (or the promise of television) could fulfill the demands of this act.

The libretto's connective dialogue in English provides just enough information to keep the audience informed about the main shifts of the "story," as in act I, when the Cobbler tells Guido his enemies have gone and his friends have arrived. The dialogue could be spoken by the singers themselves, actors who double the singers' roles, or by a narrator responsible for all of the spoken parts.

Pound channeled more of his own critical remarks into the conversation between characters, occasionally resorting to the more cryptic one-liners found in the *Villon*. The *Cavalcanti* characters engage in critical discourse about the song settings, permitting populist entrée into a sophisticated criticism. An example of this occurs right away in act I when

Cavalcanti opens with the dark "Poi che di doglia," a song requiring great virtuosity in its extended range. The enemy, Betto, taunts him by singing Cavalcanti's earlier poem "Sol per pietà" in a grand confident manner. Guido retorts that the poem is "derivative . . . showing the influence of earlier and inferior authors AND badly sung. Why don't you pronounce the words?"[72] Would listeners compare the first and second songs to infer that the first was superior? Probably not, but with a push in that direction, Pound's ideal listener from "the other school [that] culminated in Dante Alighieri" would not only get the emotion "as the man sings it," but return to examine the poetry at greater leisure to understand its full scope and significance.[73]

The unorthodox plot of *Cavalcanti* depends upon its secondary characters, those who do not fully understand the poetry, to keep alive inadvertently a tradition of poetry that might otherwise be lost. Guido is surrounded from beginning to end by enemies and friends who are unable to understand him. The questions, explanations, and scoldings given the "non-understanders" are equally directed to the listener. The banter was inserted to set the listener at ease, especially during the difficult "Donna mi prega." At several points, Cavalcanti's friends interrupt the song:

BIANCO 1:	Frankly, I DO not understand . . .
BIANCO 2:	Shut up.
BIANCO 3:	Not necessary that every animal should understand.[74]

The "Bianchi" interrupt Cavalcanti a second time to discuss the canzone in a more serious tone, but, after a fruitless attempt by Bianco 3 to pinpoint the difference between an "accident" and an "affect," the group is hushed by Bianco 2 so that the song may continue. When Guido's song moves in an unexpected direction, the comment is directed to the music and underscores Pound's intentional and unusual modulation.

BIANCO 3:	. . . eh . . . well, perhaps on a second hearing, hmh![75]

The words Pound put into the mouth of Bianco 3 were those he undoubtedly hoped were in the mouths of all who heard the *Testament* broadcast, which could not be fully absorbed on a first hearing.

Speech written for Cavalcanti and the Bianchi attempts to reproduce casual talk among friends who come from the best families of Florence. The colloquialisms sound awkward because they are purposefully prevented from rolling toward the easier cadences of slang, reserved for Cavalcanti's enemies. When Guido is handed a proclamation of exile signed by his close friend, the young Dante Alighieri, he appears to vent his emotions under a lid of self-imposed control:

GUIDO:	That runty little pig's fledgeling![76]

By contrast, Cavalcanti's enemies, the members of the Black faction of the Guelph party, are permitted slang. Note here the same contrast in tonal qualities found in scenes one and two of *Villon*.

BUENDELMONTI FOLLOWER:	The son of a bastard . . .
BUENDELMONTE:	Pthh—pth—Gahd!! The stinker!! I'll make this town too hot to hold him.
COBBLER:	Guarda ben, dico.
BUENDELMONTE:	Shut your trap.
COBBLER:	Now sir, now.
BUENDELMONTE:	What are you?
COBBLER:	A cobbler, sir, not much of a Guelph, sir.[77]

When Guido resorts to crude language, he is at the end of his tether, literally. He tells Rico, his page, he need not understand, but learn "the damn thing" (the song) to get back into Florence. A value is placed on the consequences of Rico's failure—the possible loss of a brilliant poetic career (Guido's):

> DON'T buzz up your z's. Don't pronounce a G like a Z. JeeZuss a man spends half a lifetime trying to shine up the language, and his own page in his own family pronounces it like a butcher.
>
> For God's sake try to remember that if you don't learn this song you'll never be let back into Tuscany. And don't ask me to explain it. You've not got to understand it, you've got to learn the damn thing.[78]

Guido's annoyance is Pound's annoyance inserted directly into the fabric of the work.

Returning to the second act, just after the "Donna mi prega," Vanna, former maid to Cunizza, sings a song of Sordello's, "Tos temps serai." The bit of dialogue following the very short aria allows Pound to comment on the relationship of Cavalcanti to Sordello. Anxious to grasp the unique clarity of "Tos temps serai," Guido presses Vanna for the source. Note that Vanna, like all the other characters except the cobbler, does not know.

GUIDO (as if to himself):	Damn, damn, damn, I ought to simplify.
GUIDO [to Vanna]:	What is it? (Voice quiet but eager, and with surprise.)
VANNA:	The song? One of Madame Cunizza's, that she used to sing.
GUIDO:	Sordello's!
VANNA:	I don't know at all.
GUIDO:	But I do. I'm telling you.[79]

Vanna sings an exquisite song (less than a minute in length) of an earlier period in poetry at a critical moment when Cavalcanti needs mental refreshment. Cavalcanti's brisk interrogation of her is the only textual key to the significance of her unannounced performance, and it is withheld until after she sings. The announcer's introduction to the act—already fifteen minutes past—made sidelong reference to Vanna as one of Cunizza's maids who remembered a song of Sordello's that her mistress used to sing. Vanna's speech reasserts her subordinate status—the deferential "Madame Cunizza" is followed by "I don't know at all." Vanna is most certainly not placed on a pedestal in the tradition of *fin'amors.* The text is unflattering, and the audience, pressed to find something in her other than mere theatrical device, must construct her merits on the basis of her splendid song.

Pound's radiario strains against traditional lore. To Love's gallery of famous valentines—Antony and Cleopatra, Paolo and Francesca, Dante and Beatrice, Romeo and Juliet—Italians will add the names Cavalcanti and Giovanna (nickname Vanna). Dante was the source of this otherwise unduplicated gossip that identified a Lady named Giovanna as one who formerly ruled the heart of his "first friend," Guido Cavalcanti (*La vita nuova,* XXIV). Thereafter, Cavalcanti has been amorously and irrevocably linked to a woman named Giovanna, or Vanna, a figure whose existence remains questionable. Though I will argue that Pound's Vanna is not meant to be Guido's Lady, I do so at the risk of merely snagging at the durable cloth spun by Dante.

Even audience members unschooled in Dante's early work will assume without hesitation that Vanna, if sung by an attractive performer in a staged production, is Cavalcanti's lover. Lacking guidance from the text, they will instinctively understand that: Guido is a famous love poet; a famous love poet needs a woman to rule his heart; Vanna, the first woman to appear in an opera of love poetry, will rule his heart; she does so by singing the light, flawless verse of Sordello; the song is a magnet to Guido, who discerns excellence because he is a love poet. The chain of logic is insidious and cyclical, so that the last idea finds its effect in the first.

Regardless of whether Vanna is a maid or lover, both designations are tropes, and as such, do not rise to the ambition of Pound's desire to mark this scene as the moment when Cavalcanti experiences a certain insight that is crucial to Pound's account of our poet, an account that begins to exhibit a revisionist trend. Pound removes Cavalcanti from the long shadow of Dante's fame by aligning him with Sordello. Cavalcanti's remark, "I must simplify," signals the poet's intention to distance himself from the implied figure of Dante, whose poetry was complex. Pound borrows the lightness of Sordello's verse to "backlight" Guido's dark verse, gaining the advantage for Guido of accenting the contours, or movement, of his poetry—the cantabile values—while at the same time, pairing his name with that of Sordello, and making him a direct heir to the tradition of *motz el son*.

With the brief "Tos temps serai," Pound attempts a vortex of sound in one voiceprint that compounds Vanna's presence, the memory of Cunizza, and the poetry of Sordello. Pound's essential point is that Vanna is unaware of the importance of her role. In theory, he extends this lack of self-awareness to the audience's lack of awareness of who she really is (and even to who the audience might be in relation to great poets). Leaving a character unnamed in a radio drama is a serious business if the character's role significantly impacts the protagonist. Pound intends that we ask, "Who is she?" I believe he forces the question in order to echo the opening line of one of Cavalcanti's best sonnets:

> Chi è questa che vien, ch'ogni uom la mira,
> Che fa di clarità l'aer tremare!
> [Who is she who comes, that every man sets eye on her,
> She who cuts cleanly through the air she stirs!][80]

The lines remark on a woman of extraordinary presence. Cavalcanti's impatient questions and imperious retort discredit Vanna as the kind of woman possessing the necessary radiant charm of the lady of "Chi è questa," though Sordello's song can radiate through her, like music through a radio receiver.

Vanna's singing parallels the singing of the "Voice from Church" in *Testament*'s "Mère au Saveur." Both songs are of an earlier period, meant to contrast the protagonist's verse. On radio, Vanna is likewise no more than a voice, but unlike the ethereal presence in *Testament,* her voice should be precisely incised, despite the "floating" nature of her character in the drama. *Testament* introduces irony in the priest's song "Suivez beauté"

(Follow Beauty), which leads the priest to knock at the brothel door. *Cavalcanti* introduces a more subtle irony in Vanna's song: "Tos temps serai" (Constancy in Love) is followed by a short exchange of dialogue (quoted above) and a knock at Cavalcanti's door. A messenger delivers a proclamation of Cavalcanti's exile from Florence, signed by the newly elected prior of the Florentine Commune, Dante Alighieri. The mood of *Cavalcanti,* like *Testament,* makes a 180-degree turnabout. With a change of act, *Cavalcanti* begins its descent into darkness with a very different poem by Sordello—"Ailas."

The complexity of the pivotal "Vanna" scene at the end of act II offers a glimpse into Pound's proposed use of music and the media for historical and literary criticism. Pound mixed imagination with fact to provide a new aural perspective of northern Italian poetic influence through the voice of one hollowed-out character, for whom there are no notes or stage instructions. We must look for the larger significance in the music itself: Pound's assertion that the mastery of Cavalcanti's verse may be better illuminated by verse of Sordello than of Dante. When Pound shelved (or stored) the opera after the BBC did not produce it, he concluded that the setting of words to music was a form of criticism ("Dateline," 1934). By the time of the composition of *Cavalcanti,* he had come to rely on dialogic joins between the songs as a part of that criticism.

Gender and Enmity: Fictional Constructs of Pound's Legacy Formation

In the *Villon,* Pound scored the music for a diversity of female personalities distinguished by tonal qualities: the mocking by Beauty of Ythier, the ranting of Heaulmière, the soothing tones of Gantiere and Blanche, the proselytism of Villon's mother, and the ethereal voice from the church. The *Cavalcanti* contains two short songs for female voice, one for the undeveloped character role of Vanna at the end of act II, and the other for Fortuna at the end of act III. The overriding theme of a poet's legacy rationalizes the absence of women as lovers in an opera of lyric love poetry. The opera's subject is the lyric poet and his poetry; the drama takes place in the soul of the poet. Love's first perfection, the feminine ideal formed in the mind and retained in the memory, is never seen.[81] The physical presence of a woman would be a distraction to the themes in circulation, for love in this opera is always unfulfilled, always straining. Pound's portrayal of the feminine has a specific alternative function: woman is a vessel for the poet's work, protecting it for posterity.

Pound's use of vocal ranges to signify primary and secondary characters, a staple technique of nineteenth-century opera, carries additional significance in this opera where vocal sound carries the primary content, twentieth-century criticism of Cavalcanti's poetry, and where the story line is of secondary importance. Pound partly constructs the psychology of a difficult poet on the poet's response to hearing his own poems sung out loud. Each act of the opera challenges Guido to reconcile the sound of his poetry as he hears it in his own ear with the sound of his poetry as it is sung by others. By and large, he is incapable of suffering the inevitable offense, betrayal, and corruption of his poetry. Pound's assignments of Guido's poetry to the opera's secondary characters always reflect back on Guido to explain his irascible nature and point to his own undoing.

In act I, Betto, the high tenor from the enemy camp, willingly perpetuates Cavalcanti's poetry by singing it loudly and grandly. Cavalcanti tells Betto the poem is inferior and he has sung it badly. In act II, another unwanted source of promulgation is the greater population of Florence, and perhaps points beyond: "One of his [Cavalcanti's] lighter songs is in the mouths of the populace, and his friends annoy him by singing it."[82] That would be the rowdy trio "In un boschetto." Some will conclude that it is arrogance that causes Cavalcanti to denounce his own poetry and undercut his fame. Others will praise him for holding to a higher standard than public taste.

In act III, Sordello's poem is remembered not by the trustworthy Vanna but by a French soldier in Italy who will eventually carry Sordello's song back to France: "From beyond the wall the tired voice of one of the stragglers of the French army singing yet another song of Sordello's" ("Ailas").[83] If lyric poetry is good enough, Pound seems to be saying, it is cantabile, people will set it to music, and it will survive, despite the protest of the poet, because people who do not understand the words will nevertheless understand its worth—enemies, friends, servants, and mendicant soldiers will disseminate the poetry. Once out in the world, it will be subject to corruption through popularization and linguistic differences.

The octave in *Cavalcanti* is the symbol of the natural order and resonance of Cavalcanti's personal relationships—their fixed alignment, like that of the overtone series that so fascinated Pound, was portrayed not as a matter of will but as a matter of destiny.[84] To strengthen the idea of order within the unchanging relationships that will determine Cavalcanti's fate, Pound scored the work's final act to span the operatic range from basso to boy soprano, with Guido's baritone range, the soldier's tenor voice, and the ethereal voice of Fortuna filling out the act.

Had he wished, Pound would have been able to cite Aristotle as his authority on the link between voice range and character, subject of an anatomical tract that received new circulation in Guido's time. Around 1260, the Flemish Dominican William of Moerbeke translated Aristotle's *De generatione animalium* from Greek into Latin. The relevant passage reads (in English), "It is believed that a low-pitched voice belongs to a nobler nature, and that in melodies the low-pitched is better than those that are tense: for being better consists in superiority, and low pitch is a kind of superiority."[85]

Testament's protagonist, Villon, is a baritone, while Bozo, the bass voice in the opera, is a delightfully ridiculous drunk who can only pretend to a noble bearing. Pound had not yet formulated his theory on harmony and "great base" that would consider the constant influence of the lower octaves on the upper in terms of tempo. The theory is outside the scope of this book, but suffice to say that the use of octaves are one application of Pound's theory in the *Cavalcanti* (see note 84). The symbolic values Pound instilled within *Cavalcanti* through the variety and assignment of vocal registers also agree with Aristotle's categorical equivalences. Cavalcanti's voice, scored in Pound's favored baritone range, must communicate authority, not only to color his role as protagonist, but to lend support to his dangerous opinion that experience, rather than reason, is a source of truth—a view shared by the very different character of Villon. (The baritone register for Villon can thus be rationalized in retrospect.) The bass voice in the second opera represents the rare person who somewhat understands the protagonist. It is used to exhibit two kinds of wisdom: that acquired through experience (Cobbler) and that which comes in a flash or instant of enlightenment, the character being merely a medium for that wisdom (Seneschal).

Tenor voice assignments are placed with the friend who annoys Cavalcanti and can not understand him (one of the Bianchi), Cavalcanti's enemy (Betto), and the French soldier. In 1300, the French soldier in Italy would have been an enemy to the White Guelph faction in Florence.

Pound's radio opera approaches the vocal design of character from a theoretical and anatomical perspective out of an unusual necessity. Each vocal range must represent a defining character trait of the role because the verses sung represent the words of only one character, the protagonist. At least Pound wants us to believe the verses are all by Cavalcanti, with two exceptions—the songs of Sordello. (But see the section "Synopsis and Analysis" below.) Save for the role of Vanna, the dialogue augments the listener's understanding of character at best, or provides clues to be followed up later.

Pound asked Harding to find a "high tenor or boy soprano" to sing Rico's part in act III's "Perch'io non spero," to insure that vocal quality alone would convey the futility of Guido's desperate attempt to teach the page a song.[86] Rico's voice would be two octaves above Cavalcanti's, the contrast further emphasized by the preceding "Quando di morte" in which Guido sings at the lower end of the baritone range. The distance Cavalcanti's song must travel to reach from its lower tessitura into Rico's head seems unreasonable and insurmountable compared to the vocal ease of Betto and the soldier. Rico's sobs and general emotional distress add to the drama: "Rico, almost tearfilly and very nervous begins Perch'io non spero di tornar giammai."[87]

Psychological justification, the underpinning of twentieth-century productions of narrative drama, would be sought by a twentieth-century audience to explain, without pictures, the page's inability to learn the technical demands of the song. The assumption of inadequacy as a feminine quality could provide a quick substitute for substantive explanation, a practical and efficacious solution to the construction of radio drama: The source of Rico's inadequacy lies in his feminine nature. But this interpretation of Rico's failure contradicts the successful feminine nurturing principle already established. Pound consistently builds upon medieval forms rather than twentieth-century ones. His use of symbolism essentially frees him from any but the most expedient commitment to psychological realism, an expediency necessary for his popular audience.

History's Cavalcanti and Pound's Cavalcanti

Information about Cavalcanti comes directly from his peers and succeeding generations. In addition to an anecdote from the "Ninth Tale of the Sixth Day" of the *Decameron* by Giovanni Boccaccio (1313–1375), source for the action of act I, and an anecdote from "Novella LXVIII" of *Trecentonovelle* by Franco Sacchetti (c. 1330–c. 1400), source for act II, Pound draws on two chroniclers whose accounts are considered reliable. From Giovanni Villani's history of Florence we have the details of Cavalcanti's death, and from Dino Compagni's *Cronaca,* details of Cavalcanti's character, his visit to Toulouse, and an encounter with his enemy Corso Donati, in which Guido was injured.[88] Dante, as close friend and younger colleague of Cavalcanti, holds pride of place. Dante's ghost permeates the work as Cavalcanti's ghost presence has been said to inhabit the *Commedia.*[89] Listeners who take their information off the top will hear loosely bound anecdotes from a life, as if that life had one maker. Listeners who dig deeper will come to understand, if not through recognition, then through research, that Pound's Cavalcanti has at least five makers. Pound effectively assembles these particular writers and historians into a cohesive unit for the first time, not hesitating to add himself to the group.[90] So that the single figure the listener is to become acquainted with, through accumulation, revision, invention, and technology, is Pound's Cavalcanti.

Time Frame

An early draft of the announcer's script reads, "We have caught up with time and you will now hear Guido Cavalcanti, the famous Italian . . .".[91] It is difficult to know exactly what is meant by this line, and whether it is related to the Villon line, "Time, time . . .".[92] Possible meanings could be "We have caught up with the past," or "The past is ahead of us." Pound's original impulse, even if not precisely understood, alerts us to the possibility of nonchronological time.[93]

The phrase could be Pound's disclaimer of responsibility for the ensuing chronological outline of Cavalcanti's life over two decades. The life is divided into time periods that register the poet's psychological progression: the young firebrand in act I; the mature nobleman, poet, and natural philosopher at the height of his mental powers in act II; and the political exile who undergoes a crisis of will in act III. If this is not Pound's time frame, then whose is it?

The measure is that of Dante, writing in *De vulgari eloquentia* (II.2) of the development of the three souls of man—the vegetative, the animal, and the rational—and their corresponding most worthy pursuits in life. The primal pursuit is self-preservation, represented by the subject of arms. The combative arts were considered an important stage in man's development. The second worthy pursuit is the enjoyment of love. The third is virtue, or the direction of the will. Each act of the drama will follow these themes, Pound's conceit being to tie the action to Cavalcanti's poems.

Selection: A Critical Endeavor

For the radio opera Pound selected eleven poems from among the *canzone* and *ballate* of Cavalcanti's total oeuvre. Of these, only one carries the

Table 5 **Pound's selections from the poetry of Cavalcanti and Sordello**

Act I	
	Poi che di doglia
	Sol per pietà (attribution questionable)
	Gianni, quel Guido
	Guarda ben dico[1]
	Era in pensier
Act II	
	Se m'hai del tutto
	In un boschetto
	Donna mi prega
	Tos temps serai (by Sordello)
Act III	
	Ailas (by Sordello)
	Quando di morte
	Perch'io non spero
	Io son la donna[2]

1. Since attributed to Antonio di Matteo di Meglio, 1384–1448.
2. Pound believed that the first strophe was by Cavalcanti, the remaining strophes by Niccolò Machiavelli, 1469–1527.

specific type of surrealistic effect Pound identified in Cavalcanti's poetry.[94] Pound inserted two poems by Sordello, in whose work "there is nothing but the perfection of the movement, nothing salient in the thought or the rhyme scheme."[95] All of the selections fall under Pound's category of *melopoeia,* with the exception of "Donna mi prega," which is constructed upon a rare balance of *logopoeia* and *melopoeia.*

The curatorial act of selecting and ordering poems for these dramatic works was itself a step toward realizing criticism through composition and the setting of words to music. On a list of songs provided Harding, Pound called the qualitative differences or acoustic contrasts between arias "the structure of the show."[96] Pound's selection has been almost completely purged of Cavalcanti's surrealistic effects, the entire body of sonnets, and the poems of mockery.[97] The Poundian themes the librettist wants us to consider are the poet's lineage, philosophic leanings (as contrasted to the transient surrealist impulse), the presence of gods, and the comparative sounds of the songs themselves. The assignment of the various poems to certain characters also carries critical significance. With the exception of "Io son la donna," discussed above, the poems of questionable attribution and the lighter poems are always given to secondary characters.

Synopsis and Analysis

Act I

After a short overture drawn from the *Ghuidonis Sonate* (the selection of violin pieces that carry the themes of the opera), the agile, witty Guido Cavalcanti, leader of a fiery group of young nobles of the White Guelph party in Florence, commences the somber "Poi che di doglia." Pound here defers to Dante's estimation of the work as Cavalcanti's most illustrious canzone.[98] "Poi che di doglia" posits an irreconcilable tension between love and virtue.[99] Pound noted, "Guido serious," and demanded a virtuosic agility to manage the intervallic challenges.[100] In this case, musical virtuosity and poetic virtuosity are one. Pound gives the singer the option to go to "head tone" and "falsetto" to meet the range required.[101] This is the first instance of vocal strain that will color the voices throughout the opera.

Pound opens act I in a cemetary, where Guido suddenly finds himself cornered by his enemies, the Black Guelphs, led by the equally powerful

Corso Donati. Donati's man Betto welcomes Guido into their company, informing him there is no exit, and launches into one of Guido's youthful poems with exceptional bravura. It is no coincidence that it is a song of pity for the poet's soul, the poet having been defeated in battle by his enemies (even if the battle is a metaphor for love). "Sol per pietà," builds to a high C#, a thrilling sound reminiscent of nineteenth-century opera. Pound noted: "VERY tenor."[102] The competition between baritone and tenor will be easily distinguished. The opera asserts a greater intellectual basis for the "Poi che di doglia," signified by Guido's baritone range and darker tone. For the listener who has not grasped the details, a few dialogic remarks ensue, as noted above. Within the first two numbers Pound has provided an appealing song for each of two kinds of listeners.

After an exchange of songs, Cavalcanti politely insults Donati's men: "You are gentlemen, in your own house. I should hate to insert an incongruous element," and leaps over a tomb, a "large sculptural monymint," to escape.[103] Watching the commotion at the edge of the graveyard, an old cobbler is called on to explain the insult to the noblemen, as recorded in Boccaccio: "[Your own house] means you're dead up here, from the neck, sir, up to your bald spot." The reference is to the men's intellect as well as to their habitat—monuments to the dead. Betto assembles a gang of eleven, but Guido and his friends rout them out of town, Guido injuring his hand in the fray. With his friends he manages to topple a large flowerpot onto Betto's head.

Pound uses the humor of Betto's situation as an excuse to insert one of Guido's lighter poems. "Gianni, quel Guido," a trio for tenor, baritone, and bass, is pure silliness, with delightful asymmetric rhythms that tease and tantalize with their clever wit. The shift to a giddy ensemble following a heated exchange of words accomplishes solely through aural means a change of action and mood.

The Cobbler, still watching the scene, warns, "Tin hat against bombard/Is no protection."[104] His song that follows, "Guarda ben dico," has since been identified as a fifteenth-century frottola by Antonio di Matteo di Meglio (1384–1448), and not a work by Cavalcanti. The word *frottola* denotes a tall tale, or nonsense, and the fifteenth-century music of the same name refers to a light song, often for several voices, and with repeating musical verses for each strophe of the poem. The date of the poem alters the progression of chronological time in *Cavalcanti,* if we want to be absolutely literal about Pound's libretto.[105] Pound was undoubtedly aware this was not a Cavalcanti poem, as is heard in the rhythmic emphasis of his music (discussed at length in the Pound-Bedford correspondence). The song stretches the truth twice as far when it is inserted by Pound to quietly introduce a character from the future to advise Cavalcanti, with the benefit of hindsight, that a hard head against good advice is no defense. Like Gallant in *Testament,* the Cobbler is an entertaining figure out of step with the others. The warning from another century is now a formula, whose origins lie in *Testament*'s warnings from the poet of the *Alba* and the trio of drunkards.

Pound employs the frottola to comment on the internecine warfare between Guelph and Guelph, Guelph and Ghibelline, in Florence in the latter part of the thirteenth century. The cobbler sings of the dangerous consequences of rival factions among men, to befall even the most courageous. A string of animal metaphors (lion, loon, colt, wolf, and frogs) colorfully illustrate the admonition that "good bands of men in disunion" are shameful and wasteful.[106] When the Cobbler states that he himself is "not much of a Guelf" the line is quite literal, as the two factions had more or less disappeared by his time.

This fourth number, scored for "basso satirico," has the Cobbler beat on his stomach to the *marcato* rhythms of his song.[107] If Pound has effectively set the words according to their tonal leanings and rhythmic nuance, this entertaining song should take on a different cadence from the poems of Cavalcanti. Following the trio, it serves to contrast two styles and periods of entertainment (a continuation of the trend by Pound to rescue the different idioms of theater).

Guido, "serene and lyric," interrupts the Cobbler's song with "Era in pensier."[108] The listener has been well prepared for the verbal and musical contrast that continues from "Guarda ben dico" into the fifth number. Moving along at a quick tempo, Guido's second song is the most sustained number of the first act.

"Era in pensier" fits the pastourelle genre in which the poet-narrator tells of a passionate encounter with a shepherdess. Pound appears to think Cavalcanti is after something more profound in this poem, and assigns it to Guido rather than to his friends. The poem departs from common pastourelle themes by stating that the poet has been felled by the lovely eyes of Mandetta, whom he encountered in Toulouse (this infatuation is commonly accepted as autobiographical fact). He is in no condition to woo another. When he happens upon two *forosette* singing "E piove gioco d'Amore in nui" (The play of Love rains within us), the poet beseeches them not for love but for a diagnosis and a cure.[109] After looking into his heart and testing his memory of Mandetta, they recommend that Guido appeal to Love directly.

The poem's descriptions of three kinds of vision should not be overlooked. The most complex of the three is that of extramission, which states that something is emitted from the eyes of one person to enter through the eyes of another.[110] The discovery by one of the women that Mandetta's gaze has pierced the poet-narrator's heart, leaving behind a light of unendurable, unquenchable intensity, moves the poem closer to a Neoplatonic mystical creation of internal light through the contemplation of Love.[111]

The Cobbler is irrepressible and resumes his song as soon as Guido finishes. He chides Guido who "would bite in the whole pie/Show greed in wolf pack and then feel injured." He boldly accuses Guido of losing time with words, "Even though I now speak to a mute that heareth and speaketh/Lost time 'tis to call frog from frog wallow."[112]

The Cobbler is one of two persons in the drama who somewhat understand Guido. Pound refers to him as the "most acute" of characters, a signal we should not ignore: "Nel atto pr[imo] . . . Guido d[']ingegno svelo. . . . Incompresa, dai quasi tutti, e compresa parzialmente dai piu acuti" (In the first act . . . Guido's brilliance unveiled. . . . Misunderstood by almost everyone, and understood partly by the most acute).[113]

Guido's question to the Cobbler shows he is in the dark about the Cobbler's true identity: "Com'è stai ancora qua . . . che pensi?" (What, you're still here . . . what do you think?).[114] There follows some conversational punning on Guido's singing abilities, and Pound closes the act with a guffaw and a musical riff played by the instrument most associated with humor, the bassoon. Pound has done all he can to entertain—an ambush and escape, armed battle, differences in voice and tempi, a bit of slapstick at the end, but, with all due respect, the opera has turned serious.

Act II

Guido, "serious," sings once more of unrequited love.[115] Instead of an irreconcilable tension between love and virtue, he is now reconciled to devoting himself to his Lady unto death, even if it must be a faithful service to a pitiless heart ("Se m'hai del tutto"). Despair vanishes. Taking up the song of the two *forosette* of "Era in pensier," he, too, is now able to rejoice in the rains of love upon his heart, "Par che nel cor mi piova/Un dolce amor si buono" (It seems the sweetest love rains into my heart).[116]

Guido's friends continue the pastourelle motif with their rendition of "In un boschetto," a tale in which there is no rejection, only fulfillment of youthful desire. As stated, the performance annoys Guido because his verse has been turned into a popular song. Guido's voice, no longer a "frog's wallow," now stands in relief to his juvenilia, and to the group.

The mature Cavalcanti, "at the height of his powers," is once more pinned down, this time by his friends who insist he recite his best, most serious work, though they confess they do not understand it. The "Donna mi prega" has been examined above. Pound's notes for the canzone read, "main aria, the capo lavoro, tour de force."[117] Guido is to sing it with his coattails nailed to a bench (a scene recalled by Sacchetti), or what his friends laughingly refer to as "cantus firmus." Guido's voice must strain against cantus firmus and the repetition of the music (the tradition), as well as the nail. Compagni's description of Guido's character, "too sensitive and irascible," is captured by Pound in "a music of representative outline."[118]

When Guido hears Vanna sing a verse of Sordello's, he compares his own technique and concludes, "Damn, I must simplify!" The act closes with the proclamation signed by Dante Alighieri ordering the expulsion of Cavalcanti from Florence for the sake of restoring peace to the city. As in *Villon,* a direct quotation from a legal document is placed at the center of the work.

Act III

Act III's contrasts, no longer kept lively by humor, draw upon voice range. The tempi of all four songs will hold steady at quarter note = 88 or 84 beats per minute. The listener's ear must become attuned to a development of style rather than a contrast of styles. A French soldier passes the castle where Cavalcanti remains in exile, deathly ill. Sordello's "Ailas" is scored by Pound for the soldier as "Tenor, melancholy, different voice from that used in other acts."[119] One of the few songs with a refrain ("What use are eyes that see not my desire?"), its distrust of the eyes and lovely melancholic questing reach a poignancy that seems subliminally to say, Radio is really sufficient if this must be my lot.

Hearing Sordello's song in transport to France, Guido finally yields to the impulse to salvage his own poetry for posterity: "That I must drag life out of death." The line is a translation of the first line of "Quando di morte," Guido's slow song of death, dark and filled with bass. The voices of soldier and poet are an octave apart, continuing the acoustic contrast of baritone and tenor begun in act I, but with new meaning: The figures go their different ways rather than enter battle. The soldier's passage across the aural stage repeats that of the priest in the *Villon,* and would undoubtedly have received special treatment by Harding to render the distance traversed as an acoustic effect.

Should questions remain about whose story is presented in the previous scene between Guido and Vanna, Pound takes firm control of Cavalcanti's story at the third song of act III. "Perch'io non spero" will be quite literal: "Because no hope is left me, Ballatetta, Of return to Tuscany." Pound leaves behind the Cavalcanti of Dante and the historians, the Cavalcanti we have "caught up to." From this point we most definitively have Pound's Cavalcanti, "Morto che fui a Sarzana" (I who died at Sarzana).[120] Pound changes historical fact, overruling the meticulous documentation by Villani: Cavalcanti will die in exile rather than in Florence.

Guido attempts to teach Rico a song to regain entry into Tuscany. A message to his party is concealed within the music, but Rico fails to learn the tune before Guido expires. It is not that Rico is tone-deaf or incapable; he is too young. His voice strains to achieve the proper range but he has not the power. The vocal strain erupts into sobbing at Guido's death.

The opera's focus inexplicably shifts from Rico's grief to the metamorphosis of the Seneschal. Pound dispenses with the sentimentality most operas attach to the death of their heroes and the suffering of those who loved them.

The surrealist effect of the boy soprano magnifies as the Seneschal moves not toward his charge, Cavalcanti, but toward the sobbing Rico to console him, "But it is written."[121] He is referring to the words of the poem, but the phrase has a preacher's ring to it that pairs writing with destiny. Pound wants us to hear this line as a very outdated idea. The radiant and cantabile world of Cavalcanti, the opera seems to say, needs no *macchina da scrivere.*

The gaoler is suddenly overcome by the goddess Fortuna, who causes him to sing, "Io son la donna." The radio audience familiar with Italian may catch the bizarre turn of events but will require the announcer's help to know that Fortuna then enters her statue.

Pound referred to the barely sketched character of the seneschal simply as "*deus ex machina,*" but we should not be corralled by the reference to classical models into one area of investigation. The channeling of a voice from the other side into a mortal voice was a device first employed by Pound in *Tristan,* one of the four plays of 1916 based on Noh. Tristan uses the voice of the Sculptor to speak, confusing Yseult so that she does not know whom to address, the apparition or the voice. The play is an early example of Pound's dramatization of the separation of seeing and hearing. The Seneschal is little more than a stereotype of a prison guard, a symbol of time standing still. He enters at the moment Cavalcanti dies, at which instant he undergoes a metamorphosis, not becoming Fortuna, but standing and singing for her until she can appear.

He is a witness to Cavalcanti's death, as the Cobbler was witness to Cavalcanti's youthful follies. Both men are from the lower working class, but the Cobbler is wise; the Seneschal, unconscious of his new knowledge. The characters do not merge, but the marchlike cadences of their songs do (Pound intended they be sung by the same person in production). Their role is to build toward the culminating emotion of the opera, the advance of inexorable fate. The *Oxford English Dictionary* offers a linguistic basis for Pound's construction: "*Cadence* is in form a doublet of *chance,* the direct phonetic descendant of *cadentia.*"

For the audience that followed the subtle meaning of the poetry, the confusion of gender that leads to the doubling of Seneschal with Fortuna (cadence with chance) began with act I's "Era in pensier," in which the two *forosette* tell the poet to consult Love directly if he [Guido] wants to understand his [Love's] modus operandi ("Raccomandati a lui"). Love is male! Act II's "Donna mi prega" explains how Love operates, but the identity and gender of the Donna are wrapped in mystery. Act III's "Io son la donna" commences with a bass or bass baritone, possessed, singing

"I am a woman." Fortuna is revealed as the "donna" operative within the man, and by extension, all men. Love remains perceptually out of reach:

> Guido dies at the end of the poem, Rico sobbing that he has not learned it. Enter *Deus ex machina,* the burly seneschal, sort of prison guard, responsible for Guido's remaining in Sarzana. He is possessed by the spirit of the statue, and losing himself, losing his sense of his own personality, begins the song of Fortune.[122]

> The castelan being energy, and the statue or goddess beyond the need of apparent energy. Or, if you like, so powerful as to be unconscious of opposition. (Destiny, not volition.)[123]

Coming into her own voice with "no need of force, inhuman, impersonal," Fortuna sings over the voice of the Seneschal, of the loan that is life, which all must repay when the loan is called in.[124] Her cadence lacks the corporeality of the seneschal's articulated 4/4 movement (though she stays within the same meter), so that her singing is indicative of a presence outside the constraints of time. When she turns the wheel of fate, time moves again.

Though Fortuna's scene takes place outside of time, as did the final scene of *Villon,* there is no scene change in *Cavalcanti*. This is to be "the 'magic moment' or moment of metamorphosis." It is the Seneschal's "bust thru the quotidien into 'divine or permanent world.' Gods, etc.," Pound's description of the possible momentary glimpse of eternal time.[125] All prior events of the opera must lead the listener to this point, at which time, as in Noh, the import of those events falls away and they are abandoned.

The larger question of legacy is made to pivot on the "loan on life" dispensed by Fortuna to Cavalcanti at her pleasure. Broker for the "universal intellect," the goddess asks us—radio listener, stage or film audience—and the Seneschal to witness the moment of callback when Cavalcanti's "possible intellect" returns to the great bank of shared knowledge upon his death. And our role as witnesses? Are we to assume we are thereby charged with tending Cavalcanti's flame? It is our "destiny not volition." We may have understood little or nothing, but, like Vanna and the soldier, we will sing Cavalcanti's verses, even if blindly.

Pu - pil - let - te, fia m - met - te d'a – mo – re

Figure 7 The musical motif for Pergolesi's *Lo frate 'nnammorato,* Act I, scene 2: Minuetto di Don Pietro.

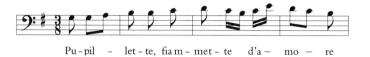

Pound does a bit of hitching to a star to ensure this happens. The music's only repeating motive, barely discernible as it makes sporadic appearances throughout the opera, concludes the work triumphantly, bursting forth as the main melody of "Io son la donna." Have we not heard it before? The ascending line is borrowed from the theme of "Tempo di minué" of the *Pulcinella Ballet* by Igor Stravinsky, who in 1920 borrowed the motive from the opera *Lo frate 'nnammorato* by Giovanni Battista Pergolesi (1710–1736): "Pupillette, fiammette d'amore per voi il core struggendosi" (Little eyes, my heart melts from the little flames of love for you) (figures 7 and 8).[126]

Pound not only extends the noble lineage of Cavalcanti through us, but insinuates an even more illustrious lineage for himself by bridging his setting of "Io son la donna" to eighteenth-century Italian opera, where Fate had already decreed it would be picked up by his favored twentieth-century composer, Stravinsky.

The refrain of "Ailas," posed at the beginning of the act, "What use these eyes that see not my desire?," is answered by Fortuna: these eyes may now see how one's desire is related to the forces of Destiny. (Pound's instruction for vocal delivery by Fortuna strives for an effect similar to that of Verdi's setting of "La Vergine degli angeli" by Leonora in *La forza del destino.*) Pound seems to be saying that the whole of the troubadour tradition as it culminates in Cavalcanti was a love cult whose ruling goddess could only be Fortuna, responsible for love's effects in the second stage of perfection, the lived experience. To see through the unbearable light of the flames of love was to see one's bondage to Time and to Fate.

Fortuna does not appear for Cavalcanti's sake. He dies more or less forsaken. If the goddess wanted to show or tell him something, she, of all the gods and goddesses, could have arrived on time. Pound's solution to the questions posed in "Donna mi prega," Who is Love? and Is Love visible? is to show Fortuna not to Cavalcanti but to us. The scene's isolation

Figure 8 Musical motifs of Pound's second radio opera, *Cavalcanti.*

from the rest of the drama is unsettling until one remembers the Noh, in which the apparent inconclusiveness of everything drops away as the god (goddess) sings and dances.

Pound's poem *Religio* describes how we may know the gods:

Religio
or, The Child's Guide to Knowledge

What is a god?
A god is an eternal state of mind. . . .
. . . When is a god manifest?
When the states of mind take form.
When does a man become a god?
When he enters one of these states of mind. . . .
. . . Are all eternal states of mind gods?
We consider them so to be.
Are all durable states of mind gods?
They are not. . . .
. . . In what manner do gods appear?
Formed and formlessly.
To what do they appear when formed?
To the sense of vision.
And when formless?
To the sense of knowledge.[127]

The Cipher in the Music

Luigi Valli's 1928 publication *Il linguaggio segreto di Dante e dei "fedeli d'amore"* attempted to recover a lexicon of one-for-one word equivalences supposedly used by members of a love cult to communicate clandestinely with one another.[128] As Valli explained it, at the center of the cult and its secret language was "Lady Philosophy" (La Donna Sapienza, Donna, or Madonna) whose wisdom was preferred to the corrupt church (Morte, Gelosia, Pietra). This concept of a true seat of knowledge was personified in terms of a female mystic body (Amore, or Amor Sapientiae), bearing the names of women (Beatrice, Rosa, Giovanna, Primavera, Fiore, Stella, etc.), one for each of the adepts. Pound found the arguments stimulating, but after his own lengthy investigation of the matter he believed Valli lacked substantial proof. Unwilling, however, to dismiss the possibility that a cipher once existed, Pound included Valli's arguments in his own essay "Cavalcanti," counterproposing, "Valli cannot offer us merely two alternatives, he must offer us something like thirty."[129]

Pound again looked into the question of secret writing when drafting the libretto for his second radio work. The attempted transmission of a cipher would introduce suspense and consequences into Guido's imminent, pathetic death, as well as dramatically enrich the role of Rico. On the reverse side of his typed libretto (figure 9), Pound wrote by hand, "Tried to decode the poems thinking the cipher is in the words whereas the cipher was really in the music."[130] The front side of the page also bears marginalia regarding the exact location of the cipher in the music (figure 10).

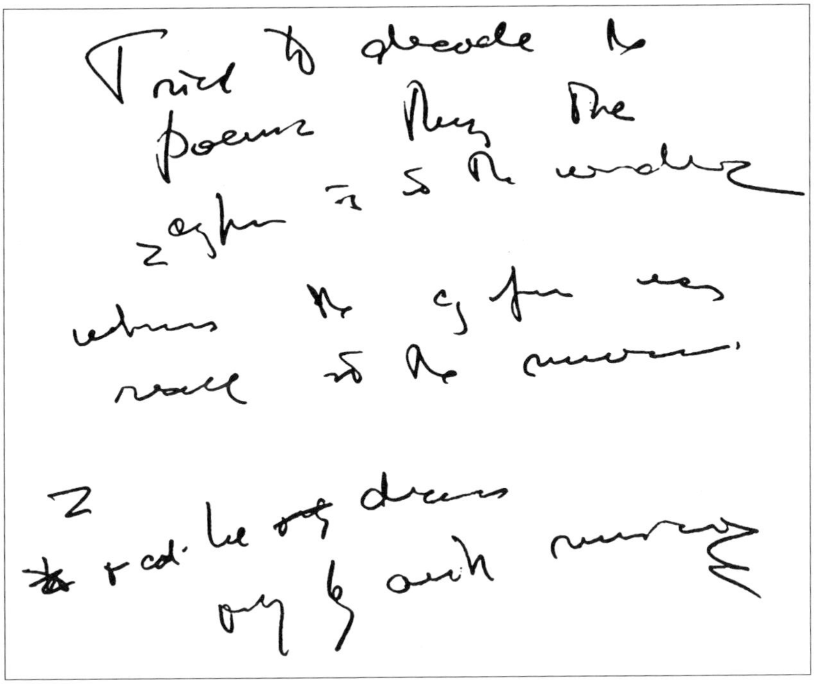

Figure 9 Pound's note on the back of the libretto for act III, *Cavalcanti,* "Tried to decode the poems thinking the cipher is in the words whereas the cipher was really in the music."
© 2002 Mary de Rachewiltz and Omar S. Pound; courtesy Beinecke Library

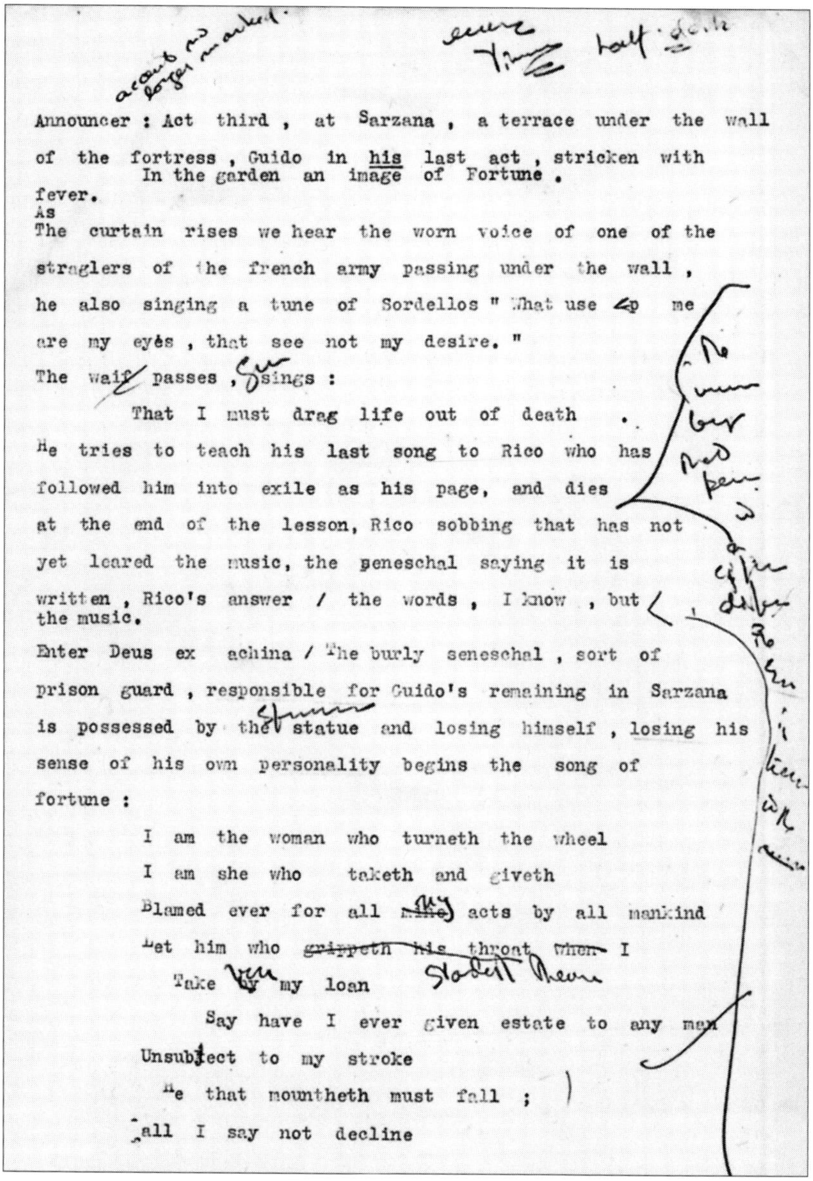

Announcer : Act third , at Sarzana , a terrace under the wall of the fortress , Guido in his last act , stricken with fever.
In the garden an image of Fortune .

As
The curtain rises we hear the worn voice of one of the straglers of the french army passing under the wall , he also singing a tune of Sordellos " What use to me are my eyes , that see not my desire. "

The waif passes , sings :

That I must drag life out of death .

He tries to teach his last song to Rico who has followed him into exile as his page, and dies at the end of the lesson, Rico sobbing that has not yet leared the music, the seneschal saying it is written , Rico's answer / the words , I know , but the music.

Enter Deus ex achina / The burly seneschal , sort of prison guard , responsible for Guido's remaining in Sarzana is possessed by the statue and losing himself , losing his sense of his own personality begins the song of fortune :

I am the woman who turneth the wheel
I am she who taketh and giveth
Blamed ever for all ~~mine~~ acts by all mankind
Let him who ~~grippeth his throat when~~ I
Take ~~by~~ my loan
Say have I ever given estate to any man
Unsubject to my stroke
He that mounteth must fall ;
Fall I say not decline

Figure 10 Pound's notes in the margin of the libretto for act III, *Cavalcanti,* regarding the location of the cipher.

The comments were possibly for the benefit of the copyist, Olga Rudge.[131] Their presence has allowed, possibly ensured, the eventual discovery of Pound's cipher in the music. The cipher is found in the motif at bars 81–83 of "Perch'io non spero" (the fourth strophe that gives the poem its instructions). This musical phrase bears the first instance in which the opera's motif resolves to its tonic note at the cadence. A further indication that the cipher is the motif appears in an early draft of music for "Perch'io non spero," on which Pound wrote at the top, "Fortuna dentro" (Fortuna inside); that is, the theme of Fortuna.[132]

At the top of act III the radio announcer informs the listener that the loyal Rico must learn the cipher to regain entrance into Florence and that the cipher contains a secret message to Guido's political party. The listener is also told that Guido dies before Rico learns the song. Two clues are immediately apparent: the cipher must be heard rather than seen on the page, for Rico does not inscribe the music; he tries to learn it by rote. The musician capable of recognizing the cipher would be someone from the thirteenth century, so that a knowledge of medieval music may be required. Once having heard Rico's attempt to learn the song, the listener might conclude that the cipher must be among the verses Rico did not master, the ones where Guido had to prompt him. By then it is not only too late to remember which verses those were, but so much else happens: Guido dies, Rico breaks into sobs, and the Seneschal sings, I am a woman! The listener is thwarted from returning to the problem.

The cipher will, like all else, be abandoned at the appearance of Fortuna. Pound's notes identifying the cipher's location indicates that he wants to be taken literally—if he says there is a cipher, there is one—but he does not necessarily want to reveal its meaning, at least without sending the quester back to the sources. He also doesn't want to let the cipher disappear entirely despite there being no plot requirement for continued reference to it.

It is possible to follow two lines of questioning regarding the meaning of the cipher. We know that Pound considered two types of listeners—one that must catch the clues as they are sung, and the other already expert and acquainted with the sources. For the former, can we expect to have the information already at hand? What political message would Guido convey to his party? A new leader? Is there a significant sound embedded within the music that authenticates Guido as the sender of the message and Rico as a trusted personage, one whose account of Guido's death will be reliable? A name such as that of Federico III fits the eleven-note motif, indicates a political alliance (or threat), and authenticates Rico's trustworthiness ("fede Rico").[133] But a knowledge of music was not required to reach this conclusion. Lacking a method of decrypting the secret messaged in the motif, the fitting of a name to a cipher is to duplicate Valli's approach. It is stimulating to speculate on the many resonances of a name. The name of Julian in the *Villon* creates an aura or field of associations that enriches by including many otherwise unconnected facts. A political message would be more likely to rely on exclusive information, and for this reason the verification of its source and accuracy is more critical. The difficulty is multiplied when we remember that Pound requires not one or two alternatives, but "something like thirty" reasons to support such a proposition.

Because Cavalcanti at this point in the opera has become Pound's Cavalcanti, a second line of questioning can be directed to Pound. Cavalcanti was sent into exile for perpetuating the violence in Florence. Does Pound want Cavalcanti to encourage an end to the feuding in the city? This was the Cobbler's good advice, but it would fall to Pound, not Guido, to choose whether or not to follow it. Pound's inclusion of a political message within the opera's plot would allow Cavalcanti to demonstrate a desire to overcome his personal fate, and to exert his will on behalf of his party, or perhaps on behalf of all Florence.

Pound as master puppeteer attempts to animate a poet who has been reduced to a temperamental, erudite snob, at times overcome by his own knowledge and sensitivity. Pound's job is to make things right before he buries him. If not for Guido, then for Pound! By this I mean, once we are faced with Pound's Cavalcanti, we are faced with Pound's personal ambition, his elaborate system of knowledge, and the cultivated nuances of difference he inscribes into his poetry and music. We must consider the memory of Cunizza and the ghost of Dante who, to different degrees, infiltrate the opera. Pound's ideas about the relationship that existed between Dante and Cavalcanti cause him to better define within the music his own position relative to both poets (that definition is beyond the scope of this book, though refer to the previous section on "Donna mi prega" for my basic argument that Pound composes a music of representative outline). Referring back to the time frame established for the three acts, the main focus of act III to the moment of Guido's death will be the pursuit of virtue, equated with the activation of the *directio voluntatis* (a direction of the will). Pound has Guido strive again and again to activate his will ("That I must drag life out of death" and "Get it through").[134] What has not been represented by Pound is the psychic or mental change within Guido that would indicate that he has shifted his interest to virtue from his philosophical interest in Love, which is not virtue ("Non è virtute"), the essential determination of the third strophe of "Donna mi prega."

The *Virtù* in the Cipher

Before examining one solution to Pound's cipher in detail, I wish to clarify the terminology pertinent to a cipher constructed with musical elements. A cipher can transmit secret bits of information that correspond one-to-one to bits in a representation of an alphabet. The message to be sent in cipher is called the *plaintext* and its alphabet is called the *plaintext alphabet.* Elements of music used to stand in for or disguise the plaintext are referred to as the *ciphertext alphabet,* and the cipher is of the type called a *substitution* cipher. One-to-one correspondences between the ciphertext and plaintext alphabets, however, are not essential. A single musical note, for example, could represent an entire phrase, and musical elements extraneous to the cipher may be present. The correspondences needed to decipher a secret message are called the *key* (not to be confused with musical key).[135] The Cavalcanti cipher is a dramatic fiction, and we might suspect that Pound is employing it not only to enrich his story but to demonstrate the difficulties in Valli's theories. Pound countered Valli's conclusions with the statement, "There is still perfectly solid ground for arguing that the language of Guido is secret only as the language of any technical science is secret for those who do not have the necessary preparation."[136] Pound's announcer offers all listeners clues to the cipher, warning that only the musician will be prepared to decipher Guido's language. For these reasons, I would argue that the encryption method is not arbitrary and may include compelling reasoning as well as obvious and relevant interpretations and that the criteria for the cipher's method are necessarily related to music, to Guido, and to the Poundian method.

The solmization of the motif offers some interesting possibilities, which do, in fact, combine to impart information that is recognizably relevant to Pound's Cavalcanti as we find him in act III and compellingly Poundian in scope and content. From the outset, I confess that my case is filled with the kinds of holes that would sink a scholarly project. Cavalcanti's work has proven impenetrable; Pound's, intractable. Yet the show must go on. A radio, film, theater, or opera director must have some toehold on the cipher.

Invented by Guido d'Arezzo in the eleventh century, solmization, or sol-fa singing, was a system of Latin syllables to help singers reach their pitches more easily. When sung by solmization, the alphabetic pitch names of the motif are replaced by

ut ut re mi mi fa sol fa mi re ut

("ut" having been the antecedent to our modern syllable "do") (figure 11). There are several very Poundian reasons to hear these syllables as an interleaving of Latin, Italian, and Provençal words, the primary one being Pound's well-established use in *The Cantos* of a sound from one language to partner the meaning in another language. Starting with the central figure of the motif, we find "mi fa sol" (makes me sun, or gives me intense light) at the summit of a phrase that will return to the tonic, a "light motif" for the larger leitmotiv (synonym for the musical motive or motif). A leitmotiv is a representation of recurrent ideas or a representation of individual personalities assigned to a short musical phrase. I believe Pound has composed a light motif/leitmotiv of recurrent ideas; these will be ideas that Cavalcanti, on his death bed, reaches for too late.

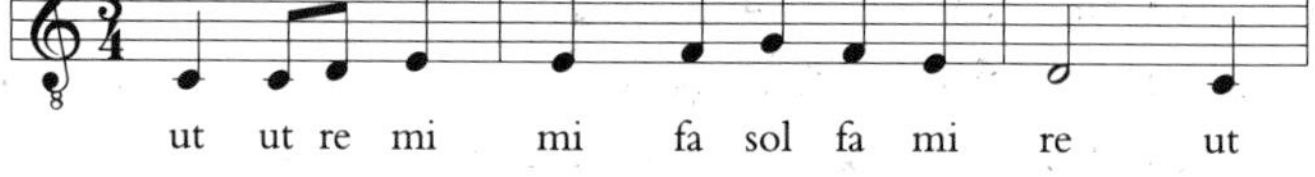

Figure 11 Solmization of the musical motif of *Cavalcanti.*

I have briefly touched on Pound's use of sky and light as mediums through which the gods move (chapter 1), his interest in the light mysticism of the thirteenth-century philosophers (chapter 4, note 37), and the importance of light (versus image) to Cavalcanti in the "Donna mi prega." The light theme recurs throughout *The Cantos;* it parallels the action themes of metamorphosis and visits to the underworld as one of the most important subjects of the poem, spanning the natural and preternatural worlds. The sense of "mi fa sol" is that of mental illumination. Pound wants to link Cavalcanti's thought to the mystical knowledge proposed by the medieval Neoplatonists: "knowledge might be difficult, but when it came it was an 'illumination.'"[137] Pound traces that knowledge to the ninth-century Irish Neoplatonist and theologian Scotus Eriugena (John the Scot), to whom he also attributes the phrase "authority comes from right reason."[138]

One hears the echo of Eriugena's phrase when "mi fa sol" is joined to the motif's descending syllables, "fa mi re" (makes me king, or grants me authority). The Latin "ut" concludes the line.

The eleven-syllable phrase strikes the ear as follows:

ut ut (Latin: so that)
re mi(r) (Provençal: *remir,* to gaze intently; contemplate)
mi fa sol (Italian: gives me light or knowledge)
fa mi re (Italian: it makes me king)
ut (Latin: so)

I do not expect a Latinist or linguist to condone such a reading; however, if my conjecture that Pound has given us a credo of *virtù* in song has merit, we can expect that credo to be something for the ear and the imagination, a musical ideogram that sends us back to original sources.

Assuming then that we have a message with signifiers, I offer these brief notes as to why this particular solmization is compelling, relevant, and obvious:

1. *Ut ut.* My Latin dictionary gives one particularly interesting translation, "so that." The phrase "ut ut" is found after verbs of wishing, commanding, or endeavoring. "So that" is the phrase Pound borrowed from Robert Browning to end Canto I.[139]

2. *remi(r)*. A Provençal word meaning an intense gaze. Pound used the word in Canto XX, borrowing it from the "best poem" of the troubadour poet Arnaut Daniel, "Doutz brais e critz."[140] It is used to imply that new knowledge or heightened sensation rewards such contemplation. Pound's interest in Daniel's music is recounted in Canto XX, a possible anecdotal source for the character of Rico, who must transport the music but cannot sing it. The missing *r* is a problem on the page, but less so for the ear. I leave it to the reader to decide how much of the problem recedes in the wake of Pound's keen interest in having Cavalcanti bring forward the Provençal tradition. Pound's method was to draw a synergetic meaning from the juxtaposition of two cultures. In the opera Guido has already listened intently to two songs of Sordello, and Pound would have him, at the end of his life, reach back to France to Arnaut Daniel, whom Dante praises as "Il miglior fabbro" (*Purg.* XXVI).

3. *mi fa sol*. This overlapping of Latin, Italian, and Provençal, includes the *mi* pronoun we find in Pound's rendering of "Donna mi prega," generally considered incorrect (the correct pronoun being *me*). Pound's use of many languages in *The Cantos* attests to his preference for keeping the sound of different languages simultaneously in the ear, adding to meaning the richness of the experience of sound as movement and texture. "To give me the sun's light" would mean to receive ultimate knowledge or truth. "Mi fa sol" is a joining of reason and nature.

4. *fa mi re*. I translate this as "makes me king." Again, light or wisdom endows one with authority, the implication being that authority acquired in any other manner is spurious. The "re" (king) is apropos to the linked motifs of "Perch'io non spero" and "Io son la donna," the latter concluding with a mention of King Arthur.

5. *ut*. The Latin "ut" generally opens a phrase rather than concludes it. Pound would be using the syllable to signify that this is a beginning.

The historical record of Cavalcanti's elevation of the vernacular to new purpose is another line of support for the solmization interpretation. Pound's idiosyncratic spelling preferences for Cavalcanti's poetry go against the grain of academic consensus and must be seen as an effort to preserve a record of the Provençal influence on Cavalcanti's lyricism. Pound may also be insisting on a curriculum of study that does not segregate Cavalcanti's poetry from that of the Provençal poets. For his printed edition of "Donna mi prega," he selected the "Ld" manuscript of the Laurenziana Library (46–60, folio 32, verso), thereby perpetuating word spellings that draw from Latin, Italian, and Provençal.[141] By and large forced from southern France, the Provençal poets entered Italy at the court of the Holy Roman Emperor Federico II in Sicily, or by way of the northern Italian castles, where they secured the patronage of a lord in exchange for entertaining his court.

The flavor and curriculum of the Sicilian court is not a marginal concern. Federico's new humanism drew upon European, Arabic, and Byzantine cultures and became the seedbed for a specifically Italian culture that saw the flowering of Italian vernacular poetry. Dante called this movement of Italian lyric poetry the *dolce stil novo,* or "the sweet new style" (*Purg.* XXIV). However, it was Dante who chose the Tuscan Italian as the *most worthy* vernacular, and not the Sicilian court or Cavalcanti. Given his decades-long immersion in the field of Cavalcanti studies, Pound's particular choices for print, music, drama, and radio consistently demonstrate the premeditated separation of Cavalcanti's legacy from that of Dante. Pound seems to be insisting that Guido, who stands out from the crowd as an individualist, has much to gain for himself and his city by aligning himself more prominently within his true heritage, Provençal and Provence by way of Sicily. The cipher arranges this alignment and communicates his newly acquired *virtù.*

The Recovery of *Cavalcanti*

The opera has long been the neglected stepsister of the rich *Testament,* a circumstance due not only to its long-term storage but to the primitive appearance of Pound's music notation, the disorganization of the documents in the archive, the intellectual humor, the use of symbols and stereotypes, the repetitive nature of "Donna mi prega," the sparseness of the orchestra, and the assumption that Pound, composing without the assistance of Antheil, turned out an inferior music in this second large work. An analysis of its structure and content, which doubles as criticism, reveals a serious work that exceeds the sophistication of *Testament* in concept if not in actual dramatic results. Perhaps it was a recognition of the high stakes involved (a long-term relationship with the BBC, a salary for musical composition, audition by the prestigious Music Department, and access to a large public) that led Pound to quote Stravinsky and to invest the work with the product of twenty years' research.[142] Crafted independently of Harding, the drama cracks under the burden of Pound's ambition to recreate the radiant medieval world.

The songs are ordered to create a lively contrast that differs from the string of solo arias in *Testament* and demonstrates Pound's increasing skills as a composer. Each opera had its unique "intellectual problem" for radio, and the works, with quite different sound and structure, should be judged according to their dramatic solution to that problem. *Testament* had a greater variety of music theater idioms, building to the large orgiastic chorus and dance. *Cavalcanti* had greater variety in its duets, trios, more challenging vocal parts and ranges, and an interactivity between dialogue and music. Pound avoided placing the poems at the service of a larger musical structure, as was expected of professional composers, because the music was already at least partially made by the poems. The sonic dimension of each of Cavalcanti's poems is heard as a separate expression of the poet.

The fast-paced dialogue between *Cavalcanti*'s songs is on a par with the first radio opera, though *Testament* has the introductory scenes conceived specifically as radio drama, before the music commences. Save for these two radio scenes, both operas present their characters as if center stage, radiating energy outward, making spectacles of themselves, one after another, and never drawing inward. Even Villon in his stillness is cast as the writer who has something to distribute rather than something to keep. Harding's label of "victim" was misconceived. Experiments in *Le Testament* are applied as tried and true formulae in *Cavalcanti:* the crafted distinctions between hearing and seeing, the use of different languages, the interaction of people from different time zones, the warnings, the legal documents, the knocks at the door, the reliance on "voices" and irony for pivotal and concluding scenes, and the baritone register of the protagonists. The different approaches to the final preternatural scenes are unique and cleverly conceived (if difficult for radio), surpassing in their invention historic examples such as the animation of the statue of the Commandatore in Mozart's *Don Giovanni.*

Stage performance that attempts a realism in chronological and historical time and naturalism in stage movement will encounter problems in what Harding perceived as the static nature of *Cavalcanti,* due to the work's commitment to the portrayal of ideas through symbols and code: a "sculptural monymint," the "cantus firmus," Cunizza, the choice of voice register, a nail, a cipher, and so forth. Fortuna represents a multiplex of symbols: desire, destiny, and intervention from the "other side." She makes her presence known first as a disembodied voice, and next as a voice animating a statue. Pound's distinctions between the kind of drama required to depict the complicated rivalries within the Guelph party in one act and the implied importance of the limpid simplicity of a song in another are conveyed by the differing style of each of the narrator's texts, but not by the music or dialogue. Very little in the opera is allowed to be itself, including the simple Cobbler, making realism and naturalism unlikely choices. *Testament*'s characters, except the Gallant, were to be exactly who they were. Even with *Testament,* Pound preferred a stylized approach that resembled puppet theater.

Radiophonic effects could have provided a surrealistic tinge to Pound's *Cavalcanti,* bringing forward some of the intended symbolism through the resonance, echo, and special effects discussed earlier. There is already a suggestion of a surrealist sound design in the penchant toward vocal strain that Pound evinces in his preferences for singers—Gustave Ferrari in the role of Cavalcanti (a man who earlier had done everything wrong in the role of Villon), who was to be given options to go to "head tone" and "falsetto" to meet the range required; the boy soprano; and the ethereal Fortuna.[143]

Comparisons between the two radio dramas bring us to the more significant fact of Pound composing music, writing drama, and scripting for media and stage. This brief analysis of the second opera stops short of bringing Pound's treatment of Cavalcanti in print, in translation, and in *The Cantos* into conversation with the work he prepared for radio, film, and stage. Devoted to the genius in poetry, the opera *Cavalcanti* is a dense work of literary criticism and self-criticism.

The second radio opera is also an important training ground and marker of impulse and technique for Pound's radio broadcasts of the 1940s; it provided Pound with many reasons to continue his association with a broadcasting facility. Radio proved to be a valuable laboratory for his own poetic as well as a forum for his ideas on canon formation, prosody, and criticism. He had been able to dramatize his triangular model of European civilization—the city, the individual ego, and *amor.* Villon and Cavalcanti were brought into conflict with Paris and Florence, respectively, while the passionate experience that was theirs for the asking slipped through their hands. Villon successfully bequeaths the underbelly of Paris to succeeding generations. Cavalcanti, unable to bequeath, receives assistance from the circle of historians and commentators that will include Pound. To his first mass audience, Pound carefully articulated the mystique of these individuals in order to equate their uncounterfeitable sound with an important moment in the history of civilization. By contrast, Ruttmann, Brecht, Sieveking, and Harding used the individual voice on radio to echo the mass voice or be emulated by it.

Postponement

> There is no chance of it [*Cavalcanti*] being done before Christmas, and I think the Spring of next year will be the time to make for, if, indeed, by then it will be possible to persuade anybody to spend money on presenting a work of art, pur et simple. At the rate things are going politically now, it seems to me unlikely. . . . I shall have to go warily about planting the Cavalcanti on the money men. From that angle the Villon met with too mixed a reception for them to welcome your latest with open hands. I shall have to think up a yarn to woo them with, but that should not be hard, and I intend to put it on if I possibly can.[144]

If spending money on art were controversial, Harding pointed out, then spending money on Pound's art was even more so. It appeared from Harding's letter that *Le Testament* had become an *opera non grata* at the BBC. Though it had inspired the composition of *Cavalcanti,* it threatened to lead to its demise as well. Pound had managed to subsume Harding's revolutionary fervor for the future of a "poet's radio" into his own literary aims, and was already at work on his third opera. Harding's radio, on the other hand, was revolutionary in theory but obliged to follow the politics of status quo.

The political activities of Pound and Harding in the winter of 1932–1933 had great consequences for the future of their respective careers and, consequently, for their joint venture, *Cavalcanti*. Harding's New Year's Eve gaffe has already been recounted. Pound's political activities, following a private audition with Mussolini in January 1933, would intensify throughout the duration of the decade, eclipsing his poetry and music. Pound's ever-increasing political presence in the English press may also have contributed to the opera's postponement.

Harding rescheduled again for August, proposing a preproduction meeting in Paris in May: "I'm going to try to get it on in some form at the end of August, but don't know whether I shall be successful."[145] In Paris, Harding confided to Pound a reluctance about Ferrari. An excerpt concert would allay Harding's concerns, as Pound explained to Bedford: "Approves idea of Ferrari doing his numbers of Cavalcanti on BBC as try out for opera."[146] By the end of the month Harding agreed to the excerpt concert and to the full production.[147]

Pound devoted the month of June to readying the music for broadcast and the final scoring of the opera. "THE MAIN THING is to keep complete score there in London, available the minute Harding gets back from Spain. He has the libretto/dramedy etc."[148] By the end of the summer Harding had transferred to Manchester, a dismal outpost of unemployment ripe for his social agenda for radio.[149] The change from the cosmopolitan London days to a new regional activism in Manchester severely compromised the prospects for the *Cavalcanti*. Bedford relayed the information that Harding now thought spring 1934 might be feasible.[150]

News that the finished *Cavalcanti* was being readied for performance appeared in two published sources in 1933—a letter to the editor of *Time* magazine (May 1, 1933), and an account in the *Chicago Tribune* (December 13, 1933).

When eighteen months passed without word from Harding, Pound turned to other projects. Harding left no memoirs or letter explaining the postponement of the opera. His contact with Pound appears to have ended in 1933.

Minister of Kulchur in Utopia

5

The Listener

AT THE END OF JUNE 1936, D. F. Aitken, editor of music articles for *The Listener,* wrote Pound requesting an article on medieval music for a July 14 deadline. Space in the paper usually relegated to "Talks" was freed up owing to the summer reduction in serious programs. Original contributions were solicited to keep the paper intellectually stimulating when in fact variety shows and light music actually dominated the programming.[1] Pound took the initiative to propose further articles: "having done a job in haste as requested.—what about a few at leisure on *Poisibilities* to impediments—or what I wd. do were I minister of Kulchur in Utopia?" (figure 12)[2] He swamped Aitken with possibilities for subjects in both music and art, to which Aitken finally countered, "If you want to be a Minister of Kulchur you will have to broadcast, which is, I regret to say, completely beyond my control."[3]

By October 21, Aitken was compelled to write, "For heaven's sake don't write any more till I say go. I have only four pages a week and the congestion is getting really serious."[4] Softening the rejection of further submissions, Aitken sent Pound a year's subscription to the magazine with an encouragement to send letters to the editor in proper and succinct format. Pound's published output for *The Listener* included: "Mediaeval Music and Yves Tinayre," July 22, 1936; "Mostly Quartets," October 14, 1936; "Music and Brains," December 2, 1936. A fourth piece published at Pound's suggestion was Olga Rudge's article on Vivaldi.

The solicitations by Harding and Aitken of the BBC were the first external influences that eventually led Pound to broadcast on Rome radio

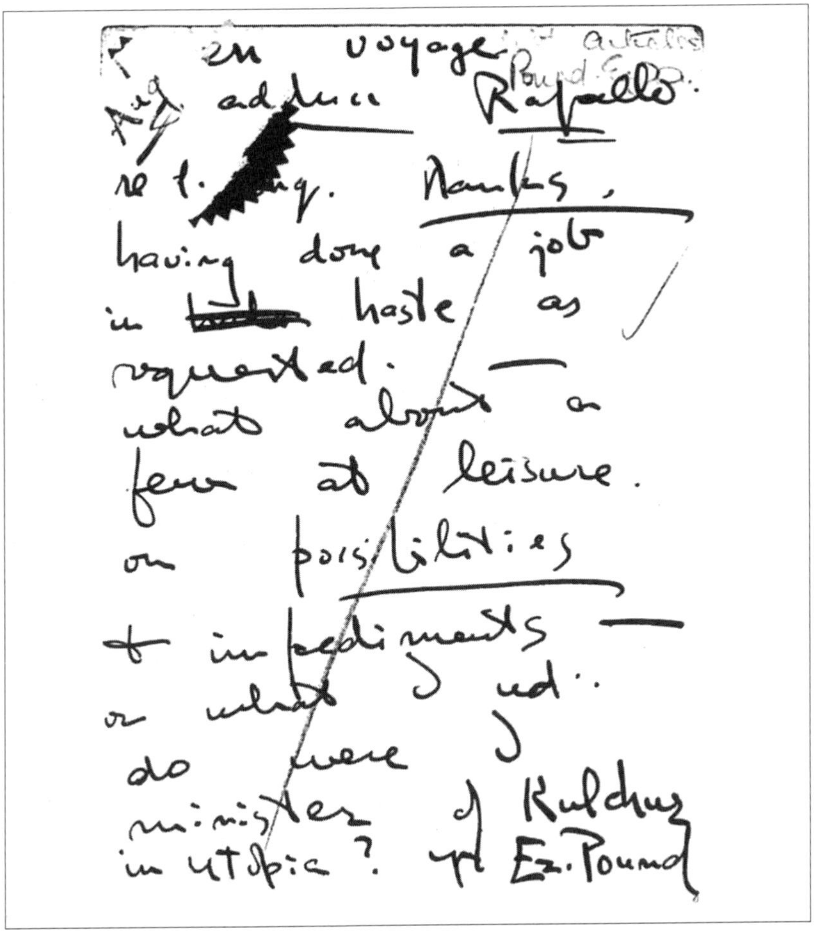

Figure 12 "what I wd. do were I minister of Kulchur in Utopia? yr Ez. Pound." Postcard from Pound to his editor D. F. Aitken at *The Listener,* August 1936.
© 2002 Mary de Rachewiltz and Omar S. Pound, courtesy BBC Written Archives Centre

during the war. Not only had Pound found that radio could pay a regular fee of six guineas for 1200 to 1500 words, but that he could expound as a sort of Minister of Kulchur to millions of Britons on the topics that interested him in the manner in which he thought about them—a cross-fitting of art, music, and literature, though politics and economics would have to wait: "Ez. writin fer three millym Britons in the Listener . . . nacherly on muzik not pulley. ticks . . . wot pop eats IZ details."[5]

The Wartime Broadcasts

When Pound received an invitation from the Italian Foreign Ministry in 1935 to speak on "Italy as I have seen it," for the "American Hour" program from Rome, he delivered instead a talk on Major C. H. Douglas's social credit plan. A listing in the *Radio Corriere,* "Conversazione di Ezra Pound, su 'come il Duce resolve il problema della distribuzione,'" indicates Pound changed his subject several times.[6] Pound brought to radio and to economics some of the assumptions of avant-garde art: the practice of crossing disciplines, the experimental use of a different medium to proselytize (as was seen in the futurist and dadaist use of vaudeville and café theater), and the transnational authority of the artist to converse on any topic.

It would be six years before he would broadcast again. In 1940 Pound began listening to radio more regularly thanks to a gift from Natalie Barney. According to his daughter Mary de Rachewiltz, he felt compelled to respond to what he judged was the "cold, evil voice of mendacity" from England and America.[7] The urge to respond was backed by a self-confidence that he had the technical, political, and artistic experience necessary for radio. Pound's frequent citing of two years' sustained effort to gain access to Rome radio's microphone referred to what he undoubtedly considered a reasonable goal and the unreasonable limits of access.

Pound broadcast over 120 speeches from Rome between January 1941 and July 1943.[8] By prerecording these onto discs he was able to control their content in a way that had been impossible for the preparation of materials for *Testament.* Pound assiduously honed his craft in the intervening years. For example, to avoid the compromised content and quality of *Testament,* he attempted to correct such tendencies in *Cavalcanti* with foolproof notation and notes to the performers (documented in the music and in the correspondence with Bedford). The limitations of radio, now added to the limitations of print and performance, were necessary facts of life to be dealt with.[9] Pound did not turn from a medium once he had engaged it, but sought to bring it under his control. The reason lies in his belief in the autodidact, the depth of interest and intensive self-training he brought to each project. If he seized on something of distinct value made salient by one particular medium to the exclusion of all others, this new element would become essential to his perpetual systematization of knowledge. Once essential, the medium would be subject to Pound's need to improve the existing system. His first radio scripts (end of 1940) were read by regular announcers at Rome radio until Pound was able to gain permission to read his own scripts.[10] He requested that specific selections of music be played on the gramophone at the beginning and end of his talks. Still, there were difficulties to be overcome. The producers at Rome radio mismanaged Pound's instructions, at times confusing the sequential order of the discs. Pound fired off strong letters of censure when radio staff played music other than that specified in his instructions.[11]

We can identify in the Rome broadcasts fragments of a technique developed for the radio operas: the use of radio as a personal bulletin board, the bringing forward from *Cavalcanti* of the theme of the "non-understanders," the use of radio to disseminate what Pound considered privileged information otherwise unavailable, the juxtaposition of music in one language with words in another, and the use of excess and humor as "tricks of the stage" to hold the auditor, including speaking in dialect with a thick drawl. He defended his use of dialect as the only appropriate language with which to address the American listener, who, Pound asserted, was not receptive to "solemn" or "formal" pronouncements.[12] The expectation of an autonomous listener and the complexity of the idea of two audiences underwent a change, though it is difficult to ascertain exactly what audience Pound imagined he was speaking to in Great Britain or the United States. He seems to have been speaking simultaneously to several groups: one audience that, like the various media, needed improvement; another audience comprised of authors of recent radio and newspaper items; another comprised of the institutions of media; another made of the bureaucrats, producers, and performers who stood between him and any of his imagined audiences; and only occasionally to the "expert" audience.

Pound adopted the testiness, word inflection, impatience, and undertone of wry humor he had used to portray his Cavalcanti, a man desperate to bequeath half a lifetime. The substance of accusations made of his listener or reader could be nothing more than an abstracted and displaced censure of himself, when he fell short of his own expectations: "The bastard. the man who hasn't the patience required of his fastidiousness. . . . Appalling crimes I have myself committed."[13] It was not the shined-up language Pound wished to impart in the broadcasts, but the process of mental synapse from one detail to another. Now, however, the details were so crammed one into another and in such accelerated motion, that they cast shadows rather than light and were divorced from their originating sources. Pound cut himself off from his most important font, the spiritual in art, compartmentalizing his ideas rather than integrating them. "Now that the war against Das leihkapital and against the infamy of world usury veers toward a victorious conclusion, one can once again turn to parnassus, to the 'bosco sacro.'"[14]

Postscript Archie Harding, 1936–1953

Archie Harding was called back to London in 1936 first to instruct, then direct the new Staff Training program inaugurated by the BBC.[1] He authored an in-house handbook, *The Past and Future of Staff Training,* and from 1948 worked for Val Gielgud as Assistant Head of Drama, producing Louis MacNeice's translation of *Faust* in the Goethe centenary year, 1949.[2] A hint that Harding was considering a production of Pound's *Cavalcanti* for the year 1950, the centenary year of Cavalcanti's birth, was relayed by Agnes Bedford to Pound in the United States in 1948.[3] A well-accepted practice of the Features producers was to tie a program to a centennial celebration. "Harding said to AB . . . that if only there were some Guido C. 'anniversary'—that he could use as a date to anchor the opera to."[4] But Pound did not know where all the music was located, and Bedford had only drafts in London. Harding's promotion to Acting Head of Drama led to a major falling out with Gielgud over the reorganization of the Department during the latter's transfer to Television Drama (1949–1950) and sabbatical in America. The dispute cast a black cloud over the final years of Harding's career.

That passions at the BBC still ran deep is told by Martin Esslin, who assumed the position of Head of Drama in 1963: "There were still producers in the department almost ten years after these events who strongly supported Archie."[5] Bedford put aside her differences with Harding to become a strong supporter as well. When Harding died in January 1953 at the age of forty-nine, she wrote, "I was going to report that Archie Harding was in hospital, but sad to say he is now dead—he is a real loss to me—we were good friends, & I really valued his opinion on things—Also he was a terrific pro-Villon man, as you know."[6]

Harding had challenged England from within, Pound from without. By war's end each had paid a price for speaking out. When Pound took up the subject of radio in Canto LXXIV, he was a prisoner of the U.S. military in Pisa:[7]

> . . . Oh my England
> that free speech without free radio speech is as zero . . .
> (LXXIV/426)

Appendix BBC Script for *The Testament of François Villon*

A Melodrama by Ezra Pound
Words by François Villon
Music by Ezra Pound
Produced by E. A. F. Harding

Broadcast by the BBC
October 26 and 27, 1931

Advisory

Editor's note: The cover page to Harding's technical script held in the Lilly Library bears a copyright notice, "© This radio script is copyright and may not be printed, performed or reproduced in any form without the written consent of the author or his agents." The transcribed script of this appendix incorporates changes found in Harding's two technical scripts, the second of which is archived in the Beinecke Library. When technical instructions or text other than Pound's have been added by hand, they are shown in italics. Cross-outs are indicated by strike-out lines. —*Margaret Fisher*

"THE TESTAMENT OF FRANÇOIS VILLON"

A Melodrama by Ezra Pound.
Words by François Villon.
Music by Ezra Pound.

~~ANNOUNCER: As a tribute to the memory of François Villon, in the year of the fifth centenary of his birth, we are presenting this evening "THE TESTAMENT OF FRANÇOIS VILLON": a Melodrama by Ezra Pound, with words by Villon, and music by Ezra Pound.~~[1]

"THE TESTAMENT OF FRANÇOIS VILLON"

(Fade in church bell tolling, hold, and stop;
add drum theme, add *full* echo.)

SPEAKER: THE WARRANT

SERGEANT OF POLICE: (pompously) For violence against particular, for violence against the King's officers, for deception of the King's officers that he did in the city of Paris . . .

CAPTAIN OF WATCH: Stt! not so loud, now.

SGT: (softer) . . . that he did speak with foul language . . .

PRIVATE OF THE WATCH: A clerk, sir? Do you think he will plead scortum ante?

CAPT: I don't care if he pleads pickled halibut, your job is to run 'om in. Twenty of you for the six of 'em, easy takin'.

SGT: Easy takin'?

CAPT: A skirt, that'll fetch him.

SGT: A skirt, sir?

(Fade in, to background, drum theme)

CAPT: That window!

SGT: (interrogatively) Aye, eh, sir?

CAPT: What do you think is behind it?

WATCH: Ow! a little bit of awl right, I suppose . . . eh . . . quite handy, booze to the left, sir, and no distance to drag 'em, and that nice little chune from Miss Catherine's.

CAPT: And no place for you, Heiney.

WATCH: They have got a nerve on 'em, buildin' it next to St. Julian's.

2ND WATCH: And next to the jug.

1ST WATCH: (aside) For benefit of the clergy?

CAPT: Not so much lip now; four of you into the church, two of you inside the gaol there, and the rest of you down the five alleys, and be scarce. Git along!

(Off echo, hold little drum theme and slow out. Let clock strike 9.)

~~SPEAKER:~~	~~THE VICTIM~~
BARMAN:	Time o' day, Messir François.
VILLON: (close to microphone: voice utterly weary)	Time, time . . .
(catching himself briskly)	Time o' day, Joe.
BARMAN:	Red, Sir?
VILLON:	Red, no; more like a hangin'. Have you grey for a hangin'?
BARMAN:	Wine, sir? I mean wine, sir.
VILLON:	On credit?
BARMAN:	I might, sir.
VILLON:	For thanks.
BARMAN:	Eh, you'd pay me before you cash in, sir.
VILLON:	How soon would that be?
BARMAN:	Young fellow like you.
VILLON:	Thirty-nine.
BARMAN:	Plenty of time, sir.
VILLON:	The good die . . .
BARMAN:	You're not so good as all that, sir; I'll fetch it.

VILLON:	Dying . . .
(sings)	Et mourut Paris et Helaine,
(*almost sotto voce,*	. . . Qui lors voulsist estre son plege.
close to microphone)	La mort le fait fresir, pallir,
(*Fiddle*)	. . . Ouy, ou tout vif aler es cieulx.
BARMAN:	You've got the 'ump.
VILLON:	Dictes moy où, n'en quel pays,
(sings)	. . . Mais ou sont les neiges d'antan?
(*Fiddle:*)	
	Ou est la tres sage Heloys,
	. . . Mais ou sont les neiges d'antan?
	La royne Blanche comme lis
	. . . Mais ou sont les neiges d'antan?
	Prince, n'enqueroz de sepmaine
	. . . Mais ou sont les neiges d'antan?
BARMAN:	I dunno, I dunno where yer snows are gone,
(puzzled, speaks)	I dunno.

(Fade up, *hold, down a little,* drum theme)

~~SPEAKER:~~	~~HIS WORLD~~
A FRIEND OF VILLON'S:	Say, Frank, yeh gotter clear, AND now!
(approaching, and	Ugh, 'ere comes your boy friend.
breathless)	

(*up echo*)

YTHIER:	Mort, j'appelle de ta rigeur,
(approaching, sings)	

BEAUTY: Mort, j'appelle de ta rigeur,

(echoes, ironically)

YTHIER: Qui m'as ma maistresse ravie,
(Contd.) (*Fiddle only*)

(*add full echo*)

BEAUTY: . . . . vie,
(echoes, ironically)

(*off full echo*)

YTHIER: Et n'es pas encore assouvie
(Contd.)

(*reduce echo*)

. . . Mais que te nuy-soit elle on vie, Mort?
Deux estions et n'avions qu'ung cuer;
S'il est mort, force est que devie,

(*peak echo*)

BEAUTY: S'il est mort,
(echoes, ironically)

(*reduce echo*)

YTHIER: Voire, ou que je vive sans vie
(Contd.) Commes les images, par cueur,
Mort!

VILLON: Not so bad.
(speaks)

YTHIER: What ch'you doin'?

VILLON: Lamentin'. Ever heard of an elegy?

V.'S FRIEND: Wot?

VILLON: Lamentin'.
(sings) Je plains le temps de ma jeunesse,
(*Fiddle only*) . . . Et ne m'a laissé quelque don.

V.'S FRIEND: He ought to be goin'.

VILLON: (Contd.) Ajh!
(sings) Alé s'en est, et je demeure,
. . . Par faulte d'ung peu de chavance.

(*at "Par faulte" fade in drum theme,*
hold a while, down a little, to background)

YTHIER: You DAMN fool, you gotter git out of
(speaks) Paris.

VILLON: Not me.
(replies)

(In Heaulmière's preliminary screech, "Ha!" *with full echo on.*)

(*off echo*)

YTHIER: Wot's 'at?

(*out drum theme*)

V.'S FRIEND: It's the old 'un. They say she used ter work for the blacksmith.

VILLON: (sings) — Advis m'est que j'oy regreter
. . . Et parler on telle maniere.

(*up full echo*)

LA HEAULMIÈRE: Ha! vieillesse felonne et fiere,
. . . Et qu'a ce coup je ne me tue?

Tollu m'as la haulte franchise
. . . Ce que reffusent truandailles.

(~~*Up drum theme and down again*~~)
(*reduce echo notably*)

FRIEND: You fool, don't you know they're a-trailin'
yeh. You hadn't ought to set round.

(*echo on again*)

LA HEAULMIÈRE: A maint homme l'ay reffusé
. . . Et ne m'amoit que pour le mien.

Sy ne me sceut tant detrayner,
. . . Que m'en reste il? Honte et pechié.

Or est il mort, passé trente ans,
. . . Je suis presque toute enragiée.

Qu'est devenu ce front poly,
. . . Et ces belles levres vermeilles?

Le front ridé, les cheveux gris,
. . . Menton froncé, les levres peaussues . . .

(*Villon sings this line without echo.*)

VILLON: C'est d'umaine beaulté l'issue!

(*Heaulmière goes on again with echo.*)

HEAULMIÈRE: Les bras cours et les mains contraites,
Les espaules toute bossues;[2]

(Breaks off and begins on last verse)

Ainsi le bon temps regretons
. . . Ainsi en prent a mains et maintes.

(Pause. Fade *up* drum *theme, hold drum, then* fade slowly in mandolin playing melody of first line of "Faulse Beaulté" *with echo [for music], reduce echo [for words].*)

FRIEND: Look, lummie, what's a-comin' wif his cute little coat and mittens. He couldn't carry his tinkler . . . Yeh! he's a-goin' to sing it hisself, ain't got gloves over his kisser.

(*up echo*)

THE GALLANT: Faulse Beaulté, qui tant me couste chier,
(approaching, sings) . . . Sans empirer, ung povre secourir?
(withdrawing)

(Fade ~~slowly out on last two lines and~~ in sound of drum theme— *hold;* end with sound of door shutting VILLON out significantly; *sharp out as door slams; off echo*)

FRIEND: Did you see how she pulls the shutter?

YTHIER: Wot the hell are you doin', Frankie?
(speaks)

VILLON:	Ajh! Gees! I'm makin' my will.
(answers)	
(sings, ironically)	Item, m'amour, ma chiere rose,
(*unaccompanied*)	
FRIEND:	The little torf is a-goin' after your Rosie.
	Old Bozo looks glad to see him.
VILLON: (Contd.)	Ne luy laisses ne cuer ne foye:
(singing bitterly)	Elle ameroit mieulx autre chose,
(speaks)	Quoy? Une bon bource de soye,
	Bien plein d'escuz.
FRIEND:	AND she's a-gettin' 'em. I can hear ole
(interrupts)	Bozo a-countin' 'em.
GANTHIERE:	Don't mind her, Frankie.
(softly, to VILLON)	
	(*Up echo. Fiddle only*)
LA HEAULMIÈRE:	Or y pensez, belle Gantiere
(interrupts sharply)	. . . Ne que monnoye qu'on descrie.
(*Gantiere*)	Et vous, la gente Saulciciere
	. . . Ne mesprenez vers vostre maistre;
(*Heaul/Gant.*)	Tost vous fauldra clorre fenestre,
	. . . Ne que monnoye qu'on descrie.
(*Heaul.*)	Jehanneton la Chapperonniere,
(*Heaul/Gant.*)	Gardez qu'amy ne vous empestre;
(*Heaul.*)	Et Katherine la Bourciere,
(*Heaul/Gant.*)	N'envoyez plus les hommes piastre:
(*Heaul/Gant./*	Car qui belle n'est no perpetre
Blanche)	. . . Ne que monnoye qu'on descrie.

(*up echo*)

V.'S MOTHER:
(sings)

[*Envoi of above*]
Filles, vueillez vous entremettre
. . . Ne que monnoye qu'on descrie.

(*down echo*)
(~~Cross fade from last line of above into Church Service music, over which she speaks:~~)
(*Gregorian chants*)

V.'S MOTHER:
(speaks)

Yeh ain't got no choice.

(*echo down for this*)

FRIEND:
(ironically, turning to V.)

Mother love! Here's yer old mother,
Frankie.

(*echo*)
(~~Down~~ *In* Church Service music *by Dufay* ~~into Voice of~~:)
(*Fade out on "Amen", in echo*)

V.'S MOTHER:
(begins singing)

Dame du ciel, regente terrienne.

(*echo down for this*)

FRIEND:
(sotto voce)

An' she's a-prayin'.

(*echo*)

V.'S MOTHER:
(Contd. fast)

Emperiere des infernaux palus,
. . . En ceste foy je vueil vivre et mourrir.

(*diminish echo as song proceeds*)

A vostre Filz dictes que je suis sienne;
. . . En ceste foy je vueil vivre et mourrir.

Femme je suis povrette et ancienne,
. . . En ceste foy je vueil vivre et mourrir.

Vous portastes, Viergo, digne princesso,
. . . En ceste foy je vueil vivre et mourrir.

(*A different perspective.*)

(*Add Echo.* Fade in tubular gongs faint from Z,
down 4, *Add echo to 4 & harmonium,* and flick E for:)

VOICE FROM CHURCH: (sings) "Mère au Sauveur."

(~~Cross~~ fade *slowly* to 8, + *echo*, for voice of:)[3]
(*bells stop here*)

PRIEST: (approaching & singing, jeering) Suivez beauté, courez au festes,
Aimez, aimez, tant que vouldrez . . .

(~~As HE sings, following interjections made by voice of~~:)

FRIEND: (ironically) The Reverend Father approaches. And the voice on him.

(In knocking on door)
(*Up echo high*)

BOZO: To hell with you . . . No, you will not go in . . . For a tanner?

PRIEST: What are you to be stoppin' me?

BOZO: I'm the Boss.

PRIEST: (scornfully) Of the establishment.

BOZO: (sings)

Se j'ayme et sers ma dame de bon het,
    . . . En ce bordeau ou tenons nostre estat!
Mais tost apres il y a grant deshet,
    . . . En ce bordeau ou tenons nostre estat.
De paillarder tout elle me destruit,
    . . . En ce bordeau ou tenons nostre estat.

(*take echo out slowly*)

Ventre, gresle, gelle, j'ay mon pain cuit.
Je suis paillart, la paillarde me suit.

(In noise of plop as HE sits down, collapsed)

FRIEND: (to VILLON) The little gentleman is emergin'! and a-wobblin' about on his pins.

(*up echo*)

THE GALLANT: (sings, exhausted) Je regnie Amours, et despite . . .

(*off echo* [*for words*], *then up* [*for song*])

FRIEND: (comments) He denies 'em.

THE GALLANT: (Contd.) Et deffie a feu et a sang . . .

(*off echo for words*)

FRIEND: Looks like he's a-bleedin'.
(comments)

(*up echo*)

THE GALLANT: Mort par elle me precipite,
(Contd.) . . . Se jadis . . .

(*On crowd*)[4]

. . . je fus de leur ranc,
Je desclare que n'en suis mais.

(*Up crowd a shade*)

FRIEND:[5] *Say, Frankie, there's too many folks around here for my likin'.*

(*Diminish echo*)

THE GALLANT: Car j'ay mys le plumail au vent,
(Contd.) . . . "Qui meurt, a ses hoirs doit tout dire".

(*Up full echo*)
(In a crash, *on drums,* as He falls to the ground—which is cue for breaking out into song of voices of:)

THE CROWD: "Père Noé," qui plantastes la vigne,
(*work itself up to dancing pitch*) . . . L'ame du bon feu maistre Jehan Cotart.

(*Orchestral acc. must indicate a dancer & a giggler.*)

~~1ST VOICE:~~[6] It's a nose.
(hoarsely whispers) *2nd* *Yurr a nose.*

2ND VOICE [contd.]: (boozy)	Back alley's half full 'er cops.
THE CROWD:	Jadis extraict il fut de vostre ligne. . . . L'ame du bon feu maistre Johan Cotart!
1ST VOICE: (burly)	~~Les flics!~~ *The cops!*
3RD VOICE:	Ajh. They got nothin' on me.
1ST VOICE:	~~Yurr a noze.~~
VILLON: (close, whispers)	On ne les aime.
THE CROWD:	Comme un veillart qui chancelle et trepugne . . . L'ame du bon fou maistre Jehan Cotart!
VILLON: (close, whispers)	Que pour l'heure.
THE CROWD:	Prince, il n'eust sceu jusqu'a terre crachier; . . . L'ame de bon feu maistre Jehan Cotart.

(Fade slowly out—*then off echo*—~~VOICES replaced with drum theme; down a little for VOICE of~~:)

FRIEND: (*close*)	Gawd, they've pinched him.

(*up lots of echo*)

SERGEANT OF POLICE: (*distant, hearty*)	And you'll come too, me young hearty.

PRIVATE OF WATCH: (*distant, hearty*) And not alone, neither, the two of you.

(*Slow in* drum theme, hold and slow out; pause; In a sighing of wind, *hold, down a little, add creak,* and *no echo for* VOICE of:)

~~SPEAKER:~~ ~~THE GIBBET~~

VOICE: What do you see there?

WOMAN'S VOICE: Six lads of the village,
hung by the neck until dead.

Did you ever hear a man sing on the gallows?

VOICE: Hahj?

WOMAN'S VOICE: I'm a-tellin' you. They're hung. They're
hung by the necks.
Can you HEAR 'em?

(*in echo for song*)

THE CORPSES:[7] (singing) Freres humains qui apres nous vivez,
. . . Mais priez Dieu que tous nous vueille absouldre!
Se vous clamons freres, pas n'en devez
. . . Par justice.

(*fade slow out on this*)[8]

~~Toutes fois, vous açavez~~
. . . ~~Mais priez Dieu que tous nous vueille absouldre~~!

(*in drums to this*)

La pluye nous a buez et lavez, . . .
. . . A son plaisir sans cesser nous charie,[9]

(*fade slow out on this*)

~~Plus Becoquetoz d'oyseaulx que doz a coul-dre.~~
. . . ~~Mais priez Dieu que tous nous vueille absouldre~~!

(*in drums to this*)

Prince Jhesus, qui sur tous seigneurie,
. . . Mais priez Dieu que tous nous vueille absouldre!

(*Up echo.* Sighing wind. *Fade out drums.* Silence)

2 HALBERDIERS: (sing) Icy se clost le testament
Et finist du povre Villon.

(*Off echo*)

SPEAKER: Here ends the will and testament,
It's all up with poor Villon.

Notes

Introduction

1 For his broadcasts from Italy to the United States, for propaganda in favor of the war effort of the Kingdom of Italy and its military allies from December 11, 1941, to May 3, 1945, and for receipt of payment from the Italian government for his broadcast programs, scripts, and consultations, Pound faced two separate indictments for treason (dated July 23, 1943, and November 26, 1945, respectively) against the U.S. government. He was imprisoned in a metal cage in the U.S. Army's maximum security facility at the Disciplinary Training Center north of Pisa, Italy, and later extradited to Washington, D.C., where he was formally charged with treason in October 1945. Early the following year he was determined by a jury to be of "unsound mind" and incarcerated in the district's Saint Elizabeths Hospital for an indeterminate amount of time. After more than twelve years, his indictment was dismissed on April 18, 1958, by Judge Bolitha Laws of the U.S. District Court for the District of Columbia (Cornell, *The Trial of Ezra Pound,* 145–148, 215). Pound's statement to the U.S. Attorney General in defense of his actions is reprinted in *Selected Prose, 1909–1965,* 14–16.

2 Carpenter, *A Serious Character,* 579; E. Fuller Torrey, *The Roots of Treason: Ezra Pound and the Secret of St. Elizabeths* (New York: McGraw-Hill, 1984), 157.

3 Agnes Bedford to EP, n.d., but between September 20 and October 8, 1931 (Beinecke).

4 EP to Dorothy Pound, May 12, 1931 (Lilly). Possum was Pound's nickname for T. S. Eliot. Pound's 1929 essay "How to Read" is reprinted in *Literary Essays of Ezra Pound,* 15–40.

5 A policy of anonymity, as well as the ephemeral nature of radio programs, stripped the British radio producer of an individual voice. Producers and announcers were "symbols of the institution" rather than individual personalities (see Briggs, *History of Broadcasting,* vol. 2, 123, and Scannell and Cardiff, *A Social History of British Broadcasting,* 176). The editor of the BBC's program publication *Radio Times* wrote that yearly revisions to the policy on anonymity at times extended to other members of the BBC staff. "At one time we could not print the name of the producer of a programme, nor of a conductor, nor even a performer, if he was on the staff. An outside performer who joined the BBC vanished completely so far as the public could know" (Gorham, *Sound and Fury,* 58). This situation lasted at the BBC until World War II, when identities were revealed to help the war effort against illicit broadcasting.

6 Olga Rudge (1895–1996) became one of Pound's closest companions and mother of his daughter Mary (now Mary de Rachewiltz). Rudge, an accomplished concert violinist, toured Europe in 1923–1926 with the American composer and pianist George Antheil, premiering two of his violin sonatas as well as several solo works by Pound. She was actively involved as an advisor and performer for the Rapallo concert series that Pound produced from 1933 to 1939. She is known especially for her research on and cataloging of the music of Antonio Vivaldi. Her handwriting is found on many of Pound's music manuscripts. It should be noted that Pound composed the opera *Cavalcanti* without assistance, other than ex post facto advice from Agnes Bedford, his musical advisor in London.

7 Inquiries regarding music materials to augment this handbook, or matters of performance rights, may be addressed to New Directions Publishers, 80 Eighth Avenue, New York, NY 10011. An audio CD containing excerpts from the radio operas, *Ego Scriptor Cantilenae: The Music of Ezra Pound,* is commercially available from Other Minds Music, catalogue number OM #1005-2. Contact them at: <http://www.otherminds.org>.

1

A Dramatic Filter

1 Pound, *The Spirit of Romance,* 180.

2 *Drama* (Chicago, February 1916): 122–132; *Pound/Joyce: The Letters of Ezra Pound to James Joyce,* ed. Forrest Read (New York: New Directions, 1967), 45–46, cited in Longenbach, *Stone Cottage,* 207. I recommend Longenbach's entire chapter, "Theatre Business," 197–221. Pound listed his qualifications for writing about drama as a two-year immersion in reading almost nothing but plays. This period (1906–1907) coincided with his doctoral research for the University of Pennsylvania on the figure of the *Gracioso* in the plays of Lope de Vega.

3 EP to Homer Pound, February 1916 (*Four Plays,* 1). Pound learned about the Noh from the manuscripts of Ernest Fenollosa, which he edited as a posthumous publication, *'Noh'; or Accomplishment, a Study of the Classical Stage of Japan* (London: Macmillan, 1916).

4 Ernest Fenollosa, "Lecture V," *No* (Washington, March 12, 1903), reprinted in *Guide to Pound and Fenollosa,* 325. The analogy originally appeared in Basil Chamberlain's *Things Japanese* (London, 1891).

5 EP to Homer Pound, February 1916 (*Four Plays,* 1). Dulac (died 1953) was a French artist. He designed the sets, costumes, and masks for Yeats as well as composed light music for ethnic instruments. Rummel (1887–1953) was a well-known German concert pianist and composer. He specialized in Debussy's music and in early music. See Adams, "Pound in the Theatre," 154–156.

6 Pound and Fenollosa, *Classic Noh Theatre of Japan,* 11.

7 Yasuo Nakamura, *Noh, the Classical Theater* (New York: Walker Weatherhill, 1971), 17.

8 Pound, *ABC of Reading,* 20.

9 Notes to the opera *Cavalcanti* (Beinecke, Ezra Pound Papers—Addition).

10 On Pound's "homeomorphism of spirits" see Kenner, *The Pound Era,* 33, 170. Pound's own definition was "An epic is a poem containing history" (*Literary Essays of Ezra Pound,* 86). My definition attempts to briefly address the scope of Pound's work, rather than offer an inclusive catalogue. Regarding Pound and the epic tradition, see Bernstein, *Tale of the Tribe.*

11 "I Gather the Limbs of Osiris" (1911), in Pound, *Selected Prose, 1909–1965,* 21, 23; "The Renaissance" (1914), in *Literary Essays of Ezra Pound,* 215.

12 Pound, *The Spirit of Romance,* 92.

13 "The Prose Tradition in Verse" (1914), in *Literary Essays of Ezra Pound,* 373.

14 "Dateline," in *Literary Essays of Ezra Pound,* 74–87.

15 Pound, *The Spirit of Romance,* 92.

16 Pound put aside his song setting of Catullus, unfinished, in either 1932, his last mention of the opera in the correspondence to Agnes Bedford, or in 1933, the year he began a concert series in Rapallo and ceased music composition altogether. I am grateful to Robert Hughes for this information, drawn from his unpublished manuscript, "Ezra Pound's Cavalcanti: A Perspective."

17 Pound and Fenollosa, 12, 37.

18 *Poetry* 10, no. 3 (June 1917): 113–121; 10, no. 4 (July 1917): 180–188; 10, no. 5 (August 1917): 248–254. Regarding Pound's earliest attempts to find a voice for the narrator of the poem and his experiments with dramatic masks, see Bush, *Genesis of Ezra Pound's Cantos,* chapters 4 and 5.

19 Pound, *The Spirit of Romance,* 92.

20 Ur Canto I, Pound, "Three Cantos," 118.

21 Kenner, *The Pound Era,* 284, 579 n. Kenner's explanation of the similarity emphasizes the twin attractions that this particular Noh play and the "Metamorphosis" of Ovid held for Pound. The distance separating the pines, one at Takasago and the other at Sumiyoshi, was easily traversed by the spirits of the pines. It is a play where one finds "people metamorphosing into trees; trees emblematizing the proposition that all things speak, all things are poems, and that the diligent quester may behold a tree become a dancing god" (Kenner, 284). See also *Guide to Pound and Fenollosa,* 10.

22 Pound and Fenollosa, 4.

23 EP to Homer Pound, April 11, 1927 (Beinecke). See also Burton Hatlen, "Pound and Nature," *Paideuma* 25, nos. 1–2 (1996), from which this explanation of Pound's beliefs is drawn: "The omniform intellect as God's fire, shaping itself to all things, infusing them with its own light: here is, I would propose, an explicit statement of

Pound's most fundamental belief—'mystical' perhaps, but by no means transcendental, since 'god' here exists only in the mind and in the things it touches in the act of perception" (171).

24 Terrell, *Companion to the Cantos,* vol. 1, 4.

25 Pound, *ABC of Reading,* 29; *Pound's Cavalcanti,* ix.

26 Pound, *Guide to Kulchur,* 60; preface to *The Spirit of Romance.*

27 The sense of "occult" used here refers to physical qualities that are not obvious. Pound touches upon the subject of knowledge gained through experiment in his essay "Cavalcanti," when discussing Guido's poetic treatise on Love, "Donna mi prega." Pound defines "natural dimostramento" as "proof by experience or (?) experiment," describes it as "dangerous thinking," and translates it first as "nature's source," and a few years later, simply as "natural demonstration." Pound's attraction to Cavalcanti is partly due to a sense of privileged knowledge available only to an elite circle. Regarding Pound's interest in the occult, see Longenbach; Miyake; and Leon Surette and Demetres Tryphonopoulos, eds. *Literary Modernism and the Occult Tradition* (Orono, Maine: National Poetry Foundation, 1996).

28 "Cavalcanti," in *Literary Essays of Ezra Pound,* 154.

29 Ibid., 151.

30 Pound borrows "ply over ply" from Browning's *Sordello* for both the Ur Canto II ("Three Cantos," 182) and Canto IV/15.

31 Harry Partch, *Genesis of a Music* (Madison: University of Wisconsin Press, 1949), 38.

32 EP to Agnes Bedford, n.d., but 1921 (Lilly).

33 Thomson, *Virgil Thomson,* 83.

34 On Pound and Ives, see Michael Ingham, "Pound and Music," in Nadel, ed., *Cambridge Companion to Ezra Pound,* 236–248. Examples from Pound's operas of the different styles mentioned above are, respectively, "Dame du ciel," "Frères humains," "Mère au Saveur" (music of li Viniers); "Tos temps serai," "Sol per pietà" and "Perch'io non spero"; and "Père Noé."

35 Preface to the opera *Cavalcanti.*

36 Pound, *ABC of Reading,* 55, 57.

37 *Literary Essays of Ezra Pound,* 437.

38 Pound, *ABC of Reading,* 198. On Pound's music theory, see Pound, *Antheil and the Treatise on Harmony;* Murray Schafer's "The Develop-

ing Theories of Absolute Rhythm and Great Bass" (*Ezra Pound and Music,* appendix); Adams, "Musical Neofism," 49–69. Antheil countered Pound's idea that something came between music (pure time and sound) and its impact on the human physical organism (George Antheil, "My Ballet Mecanique: What It Means"; Beinecke, Ezra Pound Papers).

39 "Cavalcanti," *Literary Essays of Ezra Pound,* 167.

40 *Ezra Pound and Music,* 12 n. 11.

41 Pound, *The Spirit of Romance,* 222.

42 Pound, *ABC of Reading,* 104.

43 Ibid., 55.

44 I am grateful to Robert Hughes for this information.

45 The reviews, December 1917 to January 1921, are collected by R. Murray Schafer in *Ezra Pound and Music.*

46 EP to Mary Barnard, December 2, 1933 (Barnard, *Assault on Mount Helicon* [Berkeley: University of California Press, 1984], 55, reprinted in *Paideuma* 23, no. 1 (Spring 1994): 161). Barnard (1909–2001) began corresponding with Pound on the subject of sapphic meter in 1933. The above description of Pound's song-setting technique is drawn from the various drafts of his unpublished "Song."

47 Pound, "Introduction," *Sonnets and Ballate* (London: Elkin Matthews, 1912), reprinted in *Pound's Cavalcanti,* 18–19.

48 George Antheil (1900–1959). Antheil's second Paris experiment was also arranged by Pound—the composition of a sound score to *Ballet mécanique* for Fernand Léger's 1924 film of the same name.

The first complete score to *Le Testament* is in the hand of Agnes Bedford. When Pound moved from England to Paris in 1921, and then to Rapallo, she continued to send advice by letter regarding his composition (Hughes). A third complete score in Pound's hand was created in 1934 after the second opera had been finished. Pound took on the work himself, rescoring the music in more practical rhythms and choosing from among the radio broadcast's more successful additions, while discarding others.

49 The latter contains a relatively simple but notorious 7/16 bar of music (part I, scene 1, bar 68) in the midst of flowing 3/4 time, which proved problematic to conductors well into the 1930s. I am grateful to Robert Hughes for guiding me through these metrical comparisons,

for many additional suggestions regarding the technical vocabulary used throughout this book, and for his reflections on Pound's unconventional music terminology.

50 For example, Heaulmière's aria at a tempo of quarter note = M.M. 88 moves from 2/8 to 25/32 to 3/8 to 2/4 meter (bars 25–28). To accommodate the syllables (usually one per note) with the 32d note at such a fast clip, the 25/32 bar needs to be conducted with four beats comprised of 6/32 for the 1st beat, 10/32 for the 2d beat, 6/32 for the 3d beat and 3/32 for the 4th beat.

51 Beinecke, Ezra Pound Papers.

52 Eliot, *On Poetry and Poets,* 21.

53 Ibid., 24.

54 *Radio Times* (October 23, 1931): 276, BBC Written Archives Centre. Other headers for prebroadcast publicity included "A Melodrama by Ezra Pound, with words by François Villon and music by Ezra Pound" (*Radio Times,* October 23, 1931: 287), and a prebroadcast column announcing "A STRANGE play is that entitled *Villon,* to be broadcast on October 26 (National) and 27 (Regional)" ("BSOM," *Radio Times,* October 16, 1931: 175).

55 Booth, *English Melodrama,* 35–36, 52–53, 91–92, 145–146, 163. Realistic melodramas in the neighborhood minor theaters offered social portraits of urban squalor, alcoholism, and labor issues in "temperance" and "factory" dramas (136). Another trend in the second half of the nineteenth century was the "sensation" drama, a specialty of the Drury Lane Theatre. These melodramas used increasingly spectacular sets and scenic effects (145). See also note 58 below.

56 Ezra Pound, "The Drama," *Outlook* 44, no. 1132 (October 11, 1919): 363. Pound reviewed melodramas at the "patent" theaters and not at the theaters where biting social commentary was a staple. Even if he did not attend the London neighborhood theaters, he would have known about the Abbey Theatre's presentations of Irish patriotic historical dramas (characterized as "political melodramas" by Cheryl Herr in *For the Land They Loved: Irish Political Melodramas, 1890–1925* [Syracuse: Syracuse University Press, 1991], 59). This particular review may reflect his interest in Yeats's involvement in the Irish national theater movement, though I have chosen to analyze Pound's statements in terms of his own agenda for art.

57 Aldous Huxley, "The Three Sisters," *Athenaeum* 94, no. 4690 (March 19, 1920): 378.

58 Ezra Pound, "In Their Degree" and "Vaudeville," *Athenaeum* 94, no. 4689 (March 12, 1920): 348, and no. 4692 (April 2, 1920): 457–458. Pound's reference to "Semitic luxuries" may be interpreted as a reference to Eastern or Oriental opulence in general, which, since the time of the Crusades, was considered one of the main influences leading to cultural decadence in the West. The comment anticipates Pound's later, sustained expression of anti-Semitism in connection with the subject of usury. These early drama reviews return repeatedly to the relationship between production cost and the quality of the art. Pound particularly objected to the industrial scale of American designers David Belasco and Steele MacKaye ("The Rivals," *Athenaeum* 94, no. 4689 [March 12, 1920]: 348). In this context, Pound's complaint echoes that of many theater professionals, who, since the end of the nineteenth century, rebelled against the grandiose sensationalism of melodrama and Wagnerian opera. An alternative theater movement was launched with the members-only Théâtre Libre (Free Theater) in Paris, followed by the democratic Freie Bühne (Free Stage) in Berlin, the professionally oriented Moscow Art Theater, and two subscription-based theaters, the Independent in London and the Abbey in Dublin, among others.

59 Pound, "The Drama," 363.

60 Ezra Pound, "Society, Ltd.," *Athenaeum* 94, no. 4692 (April 2, 1920): 456.

61 Ezra Pound, "Dramedy," *Athenaeum* 94, no. 4688 (March 5, 1920): 315.

62 "The versification of musical comedy is presumably the only active stage versification in England, unless we, with considerable tolerance, include the occasional translation of a more 'serious' opera libretto" (Pound, "Society, Ltd.," 456).

63 Pound, *Guide to Kulchur,* 367. Henry Lawes (1596–1662) was an English composer who set the poetry of Milton and Herrick, but not of Shakespeare. Upon learning that Pound composed music, people often assume that he set his own words to music.

64 Pound, "Society, Ltd.," 456. The unfolding structure of "the journey" proved to be a theme well suited to radio plays. I will touch on

this subject again in the second part of this book, where I compare experimental radio dramas of the 1920s and 1930s. Many of these works used the episodic journey as an excuse to stimulate the visual imagination of the listener.

65 Ibid.

66 Ibid. We should not limit our understanding of this passage to the stage, as Pound may be citing principles formulated during his 1916 collaboration with the photographer Alvin Langdon Coburn (on which occasion Pound designed a simple technical device from a shaving mirror that could produce a vorticist perspective in photography; see the cover image of the dust jacket to this book). See Standish Lawder, *The Cubist Cinema* (New York: New York University Press, 1975), 256. The passage is also interesting in light of Pound's direct influence on Fernand Léger and Dudley Murphy's 1923–1924 film project *Ballet mécanique* (see Lawder, 117–168, and Moritz, "Americans in Paris," 118–136). Pound and Murphy first met in Venice in 1908 (EP to Homer Pound, August 30, 1923; Beinecke). When Murphy came to Paris in 1923, Pound made arrangements for him to join Man Ray in shooting *Ballet mécanique* for Fernand Léger. Moritz reports that Pound then worked with Murphy and Léger in the film editing room (Moritz, 129). Pound worried about the project after he left Paris for Rapallo: "Also work on vorticist film-experiment interesting, but probably Murphy hasn't brains enough to finish the job in my absence or without pushing" (EP to Homer Pound, January 29, 1924; Beinecke). Pound's handwriting appears on the working diagrams for the film, reprinted in Lawder (132). His work with Murphy overlapped his work with Antheil on the orchestration of *Le Testament*.

67 Galway Kinnell, ed., *The Poems of François Villon* (New York: New American Library of World Literature, 1965), 10.

68 EP to Agnes Bedford, December 18, 1919 (Beinecke). Bedford (1892–1969), an English pianist and vocal coach, would be Pound's musical advisor and a lifelong friend. Pound reviewed her performance for *The New Age* in 1919. He provided English lyrics by Chaucer to fit Provençal texts for five songs that she arranged and published (*Five Troubadour Songs* [London: Boosey & Co., 1920]).

69 See Canto XLV: "They have brought whores for Eleusis," regarding the spoiling of the sexual mysteries of Eleusis. Villon's own words, "painted paradise on his church wall/*harpes et luz*" appear in the canto and were set to music in *Le Testament*'s "Dame du ciel."

70 See Surette, *Light from Eleusis,* and Carl Kérenyi, *Eleusis, Archetypal Image of Mother and Daughter,* trans. Ralph Manheim (Princeton: Princeton University Press, 1967).

71 "Staging of the Villon" (Beinecke, Ezra Pound Papers—Addition).

72 The role of the priest has been misunderstood in productions of the opera since 1962. This is clarified in the analysis of the radio opera below. An unpublished page of Pound's notes, which begins with the words "Coition the Sacrament," reads, "Xtianity profaned all the sacrapents [sic] in substituting permanent and legal bond for act of enlightenment. Ceremony only to impress the value of the act" (Beinecke, Ezra Pound Papers—Addition).

73 Author's translation. Sexual entendres, such as the shared linguistic root of the words *testament* and *testicles,* permeate Villon's work. Many of these disguised meanings have been recovered. See Jean Toscan, *Le carnaval du langage,* Ph.D. dissertation, Université de Paris III, 1978 (published by Université de Lille III).

74 Hughes, "Ezra Pound's Opera," 14.

75 EP to W. B. Yeats, June 1924, reprinted in Stock, *The Life of Ezra Pound,* 255.

76 Noh drama does not have scene changes. Pound could simply have been avoiding the appearance of competition with Yeats's own dance dramas based on Noh, or attempting to promote his work along the lines of contemporary experiments with music in Greek drama.

77 *Guide to Pound and Fenollosa,* xx.

78 If Pound intended the final act to be modeled on the Greek drama itself, one would expect his opera to be episodic, complete with a moral ending. If so, Villon would surely be among the hanged. If the ending were modeled on the Noh, the interest would lie in the ghost psychology of the hanged men, with Villon responsible for the vision of the scene.

79 Unpublished stage instructions (Beinecke, Ezra Pound Papers).

80 On the two-language passion plays of Benediktbeuren (c. 1231) and Montecassino (c. 1130), see Peter Dronke, ed. and trans., *Nine*

Medieval Latin Plays (Cambridge: Cambridge University Press, 1994), 185–235; and Sandro Sticca, "The Literary Genesis of the Latin Passion Play and the Planctus Mariae: A New Christocentric and Marian Theology," in Sandro Sticca, ed., *The Medieval Drama: Papers of the Third Annual Conference of the Center for Medieval and Early Renaissance Studies* (Albany: State University of New York Press, 1972), 39–68. Regarding individual playwrights, see Pound's review of a 1920 London production of the 1836 play by Nikolai Gogol (1809–1852), "'The Government Inspector' by Gogol at the Duke of York's Theatre," *Athenaeum* 94, no. 4695 (April 23, 1920): 553. Regarding Pound and Dante, see Wilhelm, *Dante and the Epic of Judgment*.

81 Kenner, *The Pound Era,* 33, 170.

82 Robert West, *The Rape of Radio,* 74.

83 EP to Mary Barnard, December 2, 1933 (Barnard, *Assault on Mount Helicon,* 55, reprinted in *Paideuma* 23, no. 1 [Spring 1994]: 161).

2
Radio

1 Wells, ed., *World Broadcasting,* 80–81.

2 EP to Homer Pound (Wyncote, PA), November 29, 1924 (Beinecke). Homer Pound would have been familiar with radio as nearby Philadelphia had ten commercial stations by June 30, 1924 (though some broadcast only a few hours a day). The first American station, KDKA in East Pittsburgh, Pennsylvania, began public broadcasts at the end of 1920 (whereas the BBC did not offer programs until 1922). The numerous independent American stations were commercial enterprises. Geared to entertainment and advertisement, they did not eschew colloquial speech as did the BBC. Even though he did not own a radio until 1940, Pound managed to hear programs that interested him (*Pound and Laughlin: Selected Letters,* January 6, 1936, 53). I am grateful to Mary de Rachewiltz for supplying me with a photocopy of the EP-Homer Pound letter.

3 EP to Homer Pound, November 29, 1924 (Beinecke).

4 EP to Sarah Perkins Cope, January 15, 1934, in *Letters of Ezra Pound,* 250.

5 EP to Ronald Duncan, March 31, 1940; in ibid., 342–343.

6 The comment is dated June 10, 1950. See Dudek, ed., *DK/Some Letters of Ezra Pound,* 32.

7 Hugh G. J. Aitken, *The Continuous Wave: Technology and American Radio,* 1900–1932 (Princeton: Princeton University Press, 1985), 69, 74; Briggs, *The BBC,* 6.

8 The legend opens Francis Chase's *Sound and Fury,* 1.

9 EP to Ronald Duncan, March 31, 1940, in *Letters of Ezra Pound,* 342–343.

10 See chapter 5, "The Poetics of Copying: The Scribe as Artist in the Chansonniers and Dante's Vita Nuova," in Elizabeth Poe's *From Poetry to Prose in Old Provençal.*

11 Excellent surveys of the performance activities by artists of the movements in western and eastern Europe have been published and should augment this reading by anyone unfamiliar with the European art movements of the early century: Berghaus, *Italian Futurist Theatre 1909–1944;* Gordon, *Dada Performance;* Kirby and Kirby, *Futurist Performance;* Goldberg, *Performance Art, from Futurism to the Present;* Annabelle Henkin Melzer, *Dada and Surrealist Performance.*

12 For an account of the corner the dadaists had painted themselves into, and their reliance upon a limited bourgeois audience to achieve their goals, see Christopher Schiff's "Banging on the Windowpane," in Kahn and Whitehead, *Wireless Imagination,* 150–153. By the time of Antonin Artaud's dada-surrealist, drug-induced iconoclastic performance "To have done with the judgment of God," recorded for radio in 1947, dada was considered the somewhat respectable antecedent to modern and postmodern art, as Artaud himself would be to postmodern theater. The tape of Artaud's performance was not broadcast for thirty years. The text is reprinted in Kahn and Whitehead, 309–329. The tape has since been commercially released on audiocassette by Editions Le Manufacture, Lyon, 1986.

13 "Gadji Beri Bimba" is printed in Gordon, 41. Hugo Ball (1886–1927), a German philosophy student turned theater experimentalist, teamed up in Berlin with the singer and dancer Emmy Hennings (1885–1948). Arriving in Zurich in 1915, they performed their cabaret-style shows on the road until they were able to open the

Cabaret Voltaire in February 1916, site of the first dada performances (Gordon, 11–12).

14 This does not preclude, however, the appearance of names such as Pound's (and Stravinsky's and Picasso's) on dadaist tracts and posters (Y. Poupard-Lieussou and M. Sanouillet, eds., *Documents Dada* [Geneva: Librairie Weber et Jacques Lecat, 1974]). On the fluidity of the dadaist movement and its application to any area of human concern, see Huelsenbeck's *Memoirs of a Dada Drummer.*

15 An exception was the dadaist artist Kurt Schwitters, who recorded his works *Ursonate* and *Anna Blume* in the spring of 1932, at the Süddeutsche Rundfunk (Webster, *Kurt Merz Schwitters,* 241). In this case, the matter of a foreign accent was not an issue. The BBC considered a broadcast of the *Ursonate* in 1947, but balked upon hearing the work. Schwitters intoned his works in performance, which bordered on song. I am grateful to Gwendolen Webster for this information.

16 Marinetti, *Taccuini 1915–1921,* 616 n. 4 (1926, appendix). Regarding Marinetti's knack for publicity, see Claudia Salaris, "Marketing Modernism," 109–127. Also see Lawrence Rainey's account of Marinetti's publicity machine at full throttle in London between 1912 and 1914, and Marinetti's tactical errors in 1914, which Rainey ascribes to the chosen venue of a music hall—the Coliseum ("Creation of the Avant-Garde," 195–219).

17 Marinetti, *Taccuini 1915–1921,* 520–521. The radio station in Rio was first operated as a private club, with listeners paying membership fees. Marinetti's reference to an elite may indicate that the broadcast went out on two bandwidths simultaneously. His notes indicate the May 21 broadcast from the "Radio Club" was addressed to all of Brazil and the May 22 broadcast from Radio Rio to all of Brazil and to an elite of Rio. See also Wells, 190, 196.

18 Wells, 196. Bernardes pushed toward the gradual encroachment of the federal government on states' rights. He would be succeeded that same year by the paulist Washington Luis Pereira de Sousa. By 1930, the Fascist dictator Getúlio Vargas strictly controlled the medium of radio, a control he maintained through the end of the war.

19 Marinetti, *Taccuini 1915–1921,* 532. For various accounts of Marinetti's voice and delivery, see Kahn, 60–61.

20 Marinetti, *Taccuini 1915–1921,* 522–523.

21 See his remarks, however, on police activity against the crowd of students outside the theater, which led to a riot (Marinetti, *Taccuini 1915–1921,* 524–525).

22 The manifesto for a futurist Radiophonic Theatre, written by Marinetti and Pino Masnata, is also called *La Radia.* The most extensive analyses in English on the institutional difficulties related to the broadcast of foreign points of view on a state-controlled broadcasting system regard British radio. See particularly, Scanell and Cardiff, chapter 3, "The Management of News and Political Debate," and chapter 8, "Forms of Talk."

23 These notes on futurism and Fascism are drawn from Berghaus, 329–345; supplemented by Mack Smith, *Mussolini;* and Hettinger, *Radio.*

24 For that occasion the Fascist government officially welcomed the futurists back into the fold, with a showcase of painting and sculpture in the national pavilion of the Venice Biennale. Denis Mack Smith reasons that Marinetti's 1929 promotion to the Academy, first as "poeta in feluca" and then as secretary of the Writers and Journalists' Union, may have also helped the cause of the futurists. In earlier years Marinetti did not hesitate to ridicule the director of the Biennale publicly, but after induction to the Academy he softened his tone, and the futurists were accommodated to some extent in the Fascist cultural circles. Futurist art was not well received at the Biennale; a preference for Soviet social realism began to take hold in Fascist official circles, and reflected Mussolini's personal preference as well. It should be noted that Mack Smith gives the founding date of the Academy as 1926. A different point of view is taken by Berghaus, who cites many examples of Marinetti's attempts to "exploit" his ties to Mussolini to intercede on behalf of futurist artists and projects, such as a futurist theater in Milan, but Berghaus concludes that Marinetti's requests were consistently turned down, even after considerable review (Berghaus, 335–345).

25 See the 1915 manifesto "Il teatro sintetico futurista," by F. T. Marinetti, Emilio Settimelli, and Bruno Corra, reprinted in Marinetti, *Selected Writings,* 123–129. These notes on futurist drama are drawn from Berghaus, 156–186.

26 Shock value gave way to pleasing the public. In 1924, lacking the financial backing of Marinetti, the Nuovo Teatro Futurista, directed by Rodolfo De Angelis, was forced to charge admission. They offered a light musical program to attract ticket sales (Salaris, *F. T. Marinetti,* 191).

27 Berghaus, 409–410.

28 Berghaus, 484.

29 *Il teatro aeroradiotelevisivo* was published in April 1931 in the *Gazetta del Popolo* (Berghaus, 489). It is reprinted in *Teatro F. T. Marinetti,* vol. 1, 207–211.

30 Berghaus, 526–527.

31 Berghaus, 487–490.

32 *Il teatro aeroradiotelevisivo,* reprinted in *Teatro F. T. Marinetti,* vol. 1, 211.

33 The next incidence of broadcast given in Berghaus's exhaustive study is that of Fortunato Depero, who read from his published work on Radio EIAR, September 23, 1933 (Berghaus, 480). Because few broadcasts are included in the available published histories, it is unclear to me if this reflects the infrequency of futurist broadcasts or a lack of data. It should be noted that Pound traveled to Rome in the fall of 1932 for a break from the composition of his radio opera. There he had "amiable jaw" with Marinetti (Norman, *Ezra Pound,* 309–310). By then, both had experienced their first taste of the artistic potential of radio.

34 Marinetti, "The Founding and Manifesto of Futurism," is reprinted in his *Selected Writings,* 41.

35 The didactic thrust of the drama, its focus on children, and dramatization of futurist values have precedence in Bertolt Brecht's 1929 learning play for children based on Charles Lindbergh's transatlantic flight. Walter Benjamin also wrote a series of moral tales for children from 1929 to 1933 for Frankfurt and Berlin Radio; see Jeffrey Mehlman, *Walter Benjamin for Children: An Essay on His Radio Years* (Chicago: University of Chicago Press, 1993).

36 Luigi Russolo, "The Art of Noise" (Milan; March 11, 1913), reprinted in Kirby and Kirby, 166–174. Italian futurist experiments with sound began with Russolo's manifesto, which proclaimed the necessity of a new "art of noises" to take futurist music to its logical

extension: "THIS EVOLUTION OF MUSIC IS PARALLELED BY THE MULTIPLICATION OF THE MACHINE" (Kirby and Kirby, 167). Russolo built an orchestra of noise machines, called *intonarumori*. The premiere performance in Milan in 1914 caused a riot. The Parisian dadaists signaled the demise of futurist noise concerts as early as 1921 at a concert at Jacques Hébertot's Salon Dada at the Théâtre des Champs-Elysées (Christopher Schiff, "Banging on the Windowpane," in Kahn and Whitehead, 152–153).

37 Arnheim, *Radio,* 67–68. For example, Arnheim's chapter "Direction and Distance" begins with an explanation of the ears' ability to distinguish sounds from right and left, front and behind, taking into account the physiology of the ears and the body's impulse to respond to sound by moving toward it. He transposes the same situation to the ears in relation to a loudspeaker and finds different results, concluding that sound from a microphone or loudspeaker has qualities only of distance but not of direction (Arnheim, 55). Arnheim goes on to say that all kinds of artistic effects can be created by distance, and that this potential has barely been explored in actual practice.

38 The invocation at the play's end of the mystical elements of light and paradise, which have no particular sound associated with them and therefore must be conjured by the visual imagination, bears a similarity to the endings of Pound's two operas discussed earlier. And we will see that the originating concept (more so than the design itself) of Pound's second opera also reflexively referred back to the radio process itself.

39 Claudio Segrè, *Italo Balbo: A Fascist Life* (Berkeley: University of California Press, 1987), 255–257. While commander of the militia, Balbo had been implicated in a spate of violent crimes in the Veneto region at the end of 1922, a period during which Mussolini's government came close to dissolution. Perceiving Balbo as his most likely political rival, Mussolini at the time praised Balbo publicly, giving him the "velvet glove" (Mack Smith, 83–84). Such public adulation on the occasion of the *crociera del Decennale* may have provided Mussolini with the means to show the world that Balbo and Marinetti, both considerable opponents at one time, were now to be considered at the behest of the Fascist party.

40 Edward Tannenbaum, *The Fascist Experience* (New York, 1972), 227, reprinted in Segrè, 255.

41 F. T. Marinetti and Pino Masnata, "La Radia," *Gazzetta del Popolo* (October 1933), reprinted in Kahn and Whitehead, 265–268 (trans. S. Sartarelli). See also "Il teatro radiofonico, manifesto dell'ottobre 1933," in *Teatro F. T. Marinetti,* vol. 1, 212–220.

42 German broadcasting had just been centralized by Joseph Goebbels, minister of the Reich Ministry for Public Enlightenment and Propaganda (RMVP) in March 1933 (Ernest Hakanen, "Germany," in Wells, 65). The new policy was to be enforced by Costanzo Ciano. By 1937, Ciano's post expanded into the new Ministry of Popular Culture, future sponsor of Ezra Pound's wartime broadcasts from Rome radio.

43 Kahn and Whitehead, 265–266.

44 The manifesto astutely recognizes that the influence of technology upon human perception is politicized by the very nature of who owns, has access to, and is affected by technology. It reaches beyond drama, poetry, and other manifestations of the aural avant-garde to political, spiritual, and conceptual realms not limited to art, so that its fields of reference need not be limited to the avant-garde. By 1937, Marinetti sustained an attack against anti-Semitism, as well as a denouncement of censorship and the campaigns against modern art stimulated by Mussolini's pact with Hitler. Marinetti would broadcast on Rome radio in support of modern art and devote the final futurist cultural evening in December 1938 to its defense (Berghaus, 529). Berghaus cites Yvon de Begnac, *Taccuini mussoliniani,* ed. F. Perfetti (Bologna, 1990), as a source of new information regarding Marinetti's personal appeal to Mussolini to stem anti-Semitism.

45 Brecht's article in English appears in Kaes, Jay, and Dimendberg, eds., *The Weimar Republic Sourcebook,* 615–616.

46 Jeanpaul Goergen, "Il montaggio sonoro come 'ars acustica'," in Quaresima, ed., *Walter Ruttmann,* 190.

47 One of the works *La Radia* criticized was F. W. Bischoff's 1928 "Hörsymphonie," *Hallo! Hier Welle Erdball!* According to Goergen, Bischoff, who was director of the Schlesische Funkstunde in Bratislava, made a concerted attempt in this work to sever *Hörspiel* from theater. His impetus was a literary one, and he employed actors and arranged

the spoken text in scenes. Other German producers singled out by *La Radia* were Viktor Heinz Fuchs, Bischoff's coauthor and director, and Friedrich Wolf, who produced the well-known *Hörspiel* simulation of a rescue attempt at the North Pole *SOS—rao, rao—Foyn, Krassin rettet Italia*. *SOS* was broadcast on Berlin Radio in November 1929 and on Radio-Paris in 1931, and has been preserved in its entirety. Goergen mentions a different Mendelssohn, an M. Felix (as opposed to *La Radia*'s Friedrich), who wrote the 1931 *Malpopita* with music by Walter Goehr, although there is no mention of a broadcast date (Quaresima, 187, 191 n. 38).

48 The five *Sintesi radiofoniche* received their first broadcast in 1980, produced by Juan Allende-Blin for the WDR (Westdeutsche Rundfunk), which promoted them as "short noise-Hörspiele" (Schöning, "The Contours of Acoustic Art," 313).

49 Arnheim, 72.

50 Glenn Frank, "Radio as an Educational Force," in Hettinger, 120.

51 Arnheim, 276, 286. The unsubtle radio had proved itself popular, effective, and, by Arnheim's date of publication, a powerful weapon. In the 1935 plebiscite in the Saar, mandated by the League of Nations, the Germans were victorious over the French largely because of their more effective radio propaganda (W. J. West, *Truth Betrayed,* 67ff.). In 1935 the German government had millions of cheap receiving sets built. These "People's Receivers" were installed in every factory, public square, and school, and issued to businesses to prepare citizens for decrees of mandatory community reception (R. West, *The Rape of Radio,* 290). Radio reportage of the 1936 Olympic games proved that, even at a remove, crowd euphoria was infectious and could be employed to marshal large groups of people. On this basis Hitler decided to occupy the Rhineland with a minimum of military preparation by broadcasting throughout Germany a radio commentator's "actuality" report of troop movements toward the Rhineland, to which was mixed the sound of cheering crowds. The troops, however, were ordered not to actually enter the Rhineland if any resistance were shown. The French troops, positioned at the edge of the demilitarized zone, made no protest and the occupation was a success (W. J. West, 67ff.). In 1940 Pound expressed his impatience with the potential for deception in radio script and style, deploring "the

histrionic developments in announcing. And the million to one chance that audition will develop: at least to a faculty for picking the fake in the voices" (*The Letters of Ezra Pound,* 342–343). Pound's concern here was not over the communications' being sent out, but rather that they were acted or theatrically inflected. He feared that listeners lacked the skills to interpret what was heard.

52 The recommendation may not seem unreasonable if one considers the irony behind the fact that Rudolf Arnheim's 1936 perceptual studies put forward in *Radio* are directed toward successfully feigning the human condition in radio plays with a new microphone technique, while imagination, in *La Radia,* is the tool proposed to improve the human "ear," or powers of perception, directing it toward a new truth.

53 The examples do not aspire to be a comprehensive study of the early stages of a new audio art, but rather to contextualize Pound and Marinetti, and I apologize to readers who note omissions important to their field and interest.

54 Throughout this section, I refer to the English translation of *La Radia* (Kahn and Whitehead, 265–268), and the Italian printing in *Teatro F. T. Marinetti,* 215–220). Sartarelli's translation employs the closest English word equivalents when possible, which obfuscates to some degree the technical implications of the Italian word choices. When La Radia is presented both as a subject and as a title, the type font indicates which use is intended.

55 In radio technology, the variable electrical current from the microphone, a high-fidelity "image" of the aural information, is sent from the broadcasting station to a transmitter that generates carrier waves. The transmitter uses the incoming electric audio signal to modulate the carrier wave. The modulated wave is then amplified to a specific high-frequency wavelength. Once radiated from the transmitting antenna, this wave, now called the "program signal," travels at the speed of light as radiant energy. The specific frequency of the wave can be detected by a receiver, which eliminates the carrier wave from the signal. The modulation information is reconverted into an electric current that is a copy of the variable current originally sent from the broadcasting station.

56 The fifth of Marinetti's radio *sintesi* from 1933, "La costruzione di un silenzio" (The Construction of a Silence), proposes to shape silence from four "walls" of sound. A brief "left wall" of drums, a "right wall" of strident horns, a "floor" of noisy water pipes, and an even briefer "ceiling" of chirping sparrows prepare the ears to discern silence after one minute and fifty seconds (*Teatro F. T. Marinetti,* 225).

57 Arnheim, 103 (see the entire chapter "Spatial Resonance," 95–104); Pawley, *BBC Engineering,* 119–120. The 1931–1932 letters from BBC producer E. A. Harding to the Pounds affirm that the creative manipulation of resonance was of primary concern in radio art. "Mr. Pound probably missed a good deal of the finer points of production, like resonance differentiation. . . . I should like to have . . . a final talk over the thing, especially on the points which are almost impossible to discuss in a letter" (E. A. F. Harding to Dorothy Pound, November 3, 1931; Beinecke).

58 Arnheim, 97. This "trick" points up the difference between John Cage's formal presentation of a given silence that already and always exists, and Marinetti and Masnata's proposal to shape many new and different kinds of silence with technology. See n. 56 above.

59 Arnheim, 99.

60 Arnold Schoenberg, "'Space-Sound', Vibrato, Radio, ETC., 1931," in Schoenberg, *Style and Idea,* ed. Leonard Stein (New York: St. Martin's Press, 1975), 150.

61 Scannell and Cardiff, 137.

62 James C. McNary, "New Technical Horizons for Broadcasting and Their Significance," in Hettinger, 208–213.

63 Anthony Burgess, a critic and author of fiction and nonfiction (*A Clockwork Orange* and *Re Joyce*), also remembered the BBC producers Bridson and Sieveking as some of the great artists of early radio ("European Culture," *Theatre Journal* 43 [1991]: 302).

64 Parker, *Radio,* 63. The king died on January 20, 1936.

65 The distinction also extends to an actor's voice, which passes for a fictional character but is recognized as the true sound of the actor.

66 Hettinger, 4. The United States, with its commercial network of broadcasters, achieved high marks in cultural education without any

government directive other than the "development of an operating system which will render program service most in keeping with the desires and the needs of the listeners" (4).

67 Matheson, *Broadcasting,* 48. Matheson's book contains a valuable informal comparative analysis of broadcasting in Britain and Germany with additional commentary on Italy, France, Denmark, Japan, America, and the Soviet Union.

68 Matheson, 116–117, 153.

69 Mark Cory, "Soundplay: The Polyphonous Tradition of German Radio Art," in Kahn and Whitehead, 334.

70 Ibid., 337. For an overview of German radio, see the entire chapter (331–371). Cory's survey of German radio plays and the *Hörspiel* movement from the 1920s to the present traces the trend toward verisimilitude, its countertrend by Brecht, and the political bind of the avant-garde artist working for state-controlled radio. Also see Klaus Schöning's article "The Contours of Acoustic Art," in which he states that *Hörspiel* is not confined to radio (309–310). Germany continued experimentation as a state-supported endeavor after the war under the name *das neue Hörspiele,* a movement that continued to grow throughout the 1960s not only in Germany but in Switzerland and Austria as well.

71 Quaresima, 261.

72 Leonhard Adelt, "The Filmed Symphony," *Berliner Tageblatt* (April 21, 1921), reprinted in Robert Russett and Cecile Starr, *Experimental Animation* (New York: Van Nostrand Reinhold, 1976), 42.

73 The five-act division of the film is traditionally compared to a symphony's five movements. Edmund Meisel's orchestral score for *Berlin* aspired to render the noises of the city as a soundscape, while adhering closely to Ruttmann's pictorial rhythms. A seventy-piece orchestra was dispersed throughout the auditorium for the film showing (Quaresima, 120). Pound admired Ruttmann's filmic ability to rhythmically organize visual pattern in the service of larger ideals ("Data," *Exile* 4 [Autumn 1928]: 104–117, reprinted in *Ezra Pound's Poetry and Prose,* 59–62). Ruttmann would later work with the German filmmaker Leni Riefenstahl during the shooting of the 1935 film *Triumph des Willens* (Triumph of the Will) (Quaresima, 77, 332, 398–406).

74 Gielgud, *British Radio Drama,* 90.

75 Cavalcanti moved to England in 1934 to direct and sound-edit documentaries for the Government Post Office Film Unit.

76 Walter Ruttmann, *Kopfnotiz über den Funk-Tonfilm* (reprinted in Quaresima, 67). The statement implies a departure from the approach used for the music of *Berlin.*

77 "Der Film hat seine Grenzen gesprengt" (Quaresima, 67). The following July, Ruttmann presented his second sound film, *Melodie der Welt* (Melody of the World), at the same Baden-Baden festival for which Brecht would create *Der Lindberghflug.*

78 A showing of *Weekend* took place in London, but no details are available (Goergen, 177). Ruttmann's work was also known in Italy. He shot his film *Acciaiao* (Steel) in Rome and environs from September to December 1932.

79 Quaresima, 351.

80 Ibid.

81 Goergen, 181–182. The technique of sonic film dissolve was employed for the first time in Bischoff's 1928 *Hallo! Hier Welle Erdball!*

82 Schöning, 307–324.

83 The first printing of the libretto in the April 1929 issue of the Berlin magazine *Uhu* gave the title as *Lindbergh,* with the subhead, "Ein Radio Hörspiel" (reproduced in Schebera, *Kurt Weill,* 137). The title was changed several times, to *Der Lindberghflug, Der Flug der Lindberghs* (note the plural name), and *Der Ozeanflug.* For an analysis of Brecht's influences, objectives, and achievements in the area of the *Lehrstück,* see Mueller, "Learning for a New Society," in Thomson and Sacks, eds., *The Cambridge Companion to Brecht,* 72–95. She writes, "The learning plays belong to the nexus of Brecht's most innovative writing" (72). *Der Lindberghflug* was commissioned for the 1929 Baden-Baden music festival devoted to music and radio. Music was by Kurt Weill and Paul Hindemith, though Weill later substituted his own songs for those of Hindemith. Produced by Ernst Hardt for Cologne Radio, and performed by members of the orchestra of the Südwestdeutscher Rundfunk (Frankfurt), the work was performed live July 27, and then broadcast to other German receiving stations (except Munich) on July 28 and 29. The work has been called a "cantata

for radio" (Everett Frost and Margaret Herzfeld-Sander, eds., *German Radio Plays* [New York: Continuum, 1991], x), a "didactic ballad for chorus and individual voices," and a "school oratorio for radio" (Cory, "Sound play," 344).

84 From the libretto by Bertolt Brecht, *Der Lindberghflug,* trans. Lys Symonette, audio CD booklet (Königsdorf: Capriccio 60012–1, 1990), 27. The quotation is from the revised libretto of *Der Ozeanflug.* Remarks regarding *De Lindberghflug* are culled from Schebera and the audio CD booklet with libretto and notes by Josef Heinzelmann, unless otherwise noted. Schebera, an authority on the culture of Weimar Germany and coeditor of Weill's collected writings, concludes that "the project . . . remained in the realm of utopia" (135), and that "there is no evidence that the work was ever performed by amateur ensembles" (137).

85 Schebera, 137.

86 Willett, *The Theatre of Bertolt Brecht,* 31–32.

87 Brecht speaking on Berlin Radio, "Vorrede zu Mann ist Mann" (March 27, 1927), reprinted in Willett, *Brecht on Theatre,* 19.

88 The earlier cited article, "Radio as an Apparatus of Communication," originally delivered as a speech, ended on the note that innovation was intended for the "existing social order" but directed against that order to "force them to surrender that basis" (Willett, *Brecht on Theatre,* 53). For a dadaist's perspective on Brecht, see Huelsenbeck, 73.

89 Horst Dressler-Andress, "German Broadcasting," in Hettinger, 62.

90 Ibid., 61.

91 Willett, *Brecht on Theatre,* 53.

92 Ibid., 31–32.

93 Arnheim, 27–28.

94 Matheson, 120.

95 Comments on the structure and operation of the BBC are culled from Briggs's *History of Broadcasting,* vol. 2, unless otherwise indicated. The organization began as a consortium of six manufacturers chartered by the Post Office in October 1922 as the British Broadcasting Company. It became an independent public corporation under royal charter on January 1, 1927, with Reith continuing as its director-general. The corporation broadcast two programs on different bandwidths, a national and regional program. Eckersley built the transmitter

that carried the first broadcast in 1922, and would later build the powerful long-wave Daventry transmitter in 1925. He also entertained the public with his singing, acting, and talks in the earliest programs. Director-General John Reith, later Lord Reith, firmly ruled the organization as a benevolent dictatorship (1923–1938). He was charged with developing guidelines for the new media of public broadcast as well as keeping pace with the rapidly developing technology of transmitters and the expansion into airwaves beyond the British Isles.

96 Eckersley, *The Power Behind the Microphone,* 21. His memoirs are filled with proposals for radio as well as criticisms of the BBC. He anticipated cable television with the shocking proposal that wired radio would be better than wireless, because it would permit more stations and therefore encourage theme programming, such as we have today on HBO or the Education Channel. On the other hand, he forecast a doubtful future for television because of the technical limitations of wireless.

97 Boyle, *Only the Wind Will Listen,* 238.

98 Gielgud, 27. Briggs refers to the research unit as the Production Research Section and the Research Department (Briggs, *History of Broadcasting,* vol. 2, 89).

99 Scannell and Cardiff, 135.

100 Eckersley was forced by Reith to resign in 1929 for personal reasons related to his pending divorce (Eckersley, 152). A glance at Andrew Boyle's index under "Reith/idealism" previews Reith's brand of Calvinism: idealism, identity, image, imagination, immaturity, impatience, impulsiveness, inadequacy, independence, indifference, inefficiency (attitude to), infallibility, inflexibility, ingenuity, initiative, innocence, inscrutability, interest, intolerance, inventiveness. See Boyle, 366.

101 Boyle, 187.

102 Agnes Bedford to EP, n.d., but November 1931 (Beinecke). Also see Briggs, *History of Broadcasting,* vol. 2, 167.

103 A climate of rudeness developed in the drive for prestige; senior employees bullied juniors; and sex played a large part in interoffice communications as well as artistic decision making. See Gorham, 17, 30.

104 Raymonde Collignon to EP, March 3, 1933 (Beinecke).

105 Gielgud (1900–1981) was head of Drama from 1933 to 1963. He also served a brief term as head of Television Drama. He was the brother of British actor Sir John Gielgud.

106 Whitehead, *The Third Programme,* 111–112.

107 Gielgud, 24–29. No recordings of Sieveking's work survive at the BBC. The production was broadcast on September 4, 1928. Sieveking offers a description of it in the opening of his book *The Stuff of Radio,* 18–24.

108 Gielgud, 24. Peter Eckersley credited A. G. D. West, a senior member of his staff, as the BBC engineer who finalized the design of the DCP (Eckersley, 111–112). A schematic diagram of the chain of connections from the studio to transmission lines and the control rooms is found in Sieveking, appendix B, 400–401.

109 Paulu, *British Broadcasting,* 137; Sieveking, 17–23.

110 E. A. F. Harding to EP, April 15, 1931 (Beinecke).

111 Briggs, *History of Broadcasting,* vol. 2, 96.

112 Gielgud, 50; Val Gielgud, "Mr. E. A. F. Harding," obit., *The Times,* London, January 27, 1953.

113 Bertolt Brecht, "Can Radio Programmes Become More Artistic and More Concerned with Actuality?," *Börsen-Courier* (Berlin, 1927); trans. Stuart Hood, "Brecht on Radio," *Screen* 20, nos. 3, 4 (Winter 1979–1980): 18. See also Otto Alfred Palitzsch, "Gefunkte Literatur," in Kaes, Jay, and Dimendberg, 600–603.

114 The idea of actuality programs was perhaps first recorded by the Russian cinematographer Dziga Vertov in 1925. He theorized about a Radio-Eye, partner to his idea of cinema or Kino-Eye, which could be everywhere at once reporting to the people. This required an athletic responsiveness to meet situations with energy, equipment, and ideas. See his essay "Kinopravda and Radiopravda," in *Kino-Eye: The Writings of Dziga Vertov,* ed. Annette Michelson (Berkeley: University of California Press, 1984).

When the American broadcaster César Saerchinger joined with the British to broadcast the progress of the 1935 plebiscite in the Saar, their accomplishment redefined for world radio the meaning of "actuality" programming. They had no time for dramatic interpolations or recourse to effects. Their historic broadcast included an interview with an American expert on plebiscites, the British and American points of view, and patriotic sounds from the crowds in the street conveying the newly sanctioned allegiance to Hitler. It was also the first broadcast ever from the Saar and involved great technical resourcefulness and international cooperation to capture the story (W. J. West, 70).

115 *Radio Times* (November 15, 1929): 493, reprinted in Scannell and Cardiff, 139.

116 *Crisis in Spain,* radio feature, "composed" by E. A. Harding, prod. Lance Sieveking (BBC Written Archives Centre, Scripts, 1931), 11, reprinted in Scannell and Cardiff, 139. Harding later had his Staff Training School record the program as an exercise. Housed in the BBC Sound Archive Library, T28022, it recreates the original but with a slower pacing (Scannell and Cardiff, 396). *Dramma di distanze* was the second of five works for radio under the collective title *Sintesi radiofoniche.*

117 Scannell and Cardiff, 154.

118 Scannell and Cardiff, 139. The foreign news compiled in the listener's home was understood, even if emotionally or subliminally, from the larger vantage point of international affairs. A listener many miles away in another country had the sense of being included in these affairs as one more international overseer. This contrasted with the sense of removal or distance characteristic of news conveyed in print. The sounds of radio, when they overlapped and juxtaposed regional borders, intercut by new rhythms, led to creative interpretation. Harding was thus able to turn a passive listener into an active one. His method echoed Pound's own ideogrammic method of joining together essential ideas to create a synergetic effect. The denotative meaning of the words became supercharged with the nonverbal emotive sonic information.

119 Scannell and Cardiff, 139–140. *Testament* would receive a similar treatment. Harding appears to have sent Pound a script for this work: "I am sorry I haven't done anything about 'Villon' before now, but I have been 'sunk' in a Spanish programme, of which I will send you a script . . ." (E. A. F. Harding to EP, June 23, 1931; Beinecke). If Pound received this script, his education in radio production was at a level offered novice producers a decade later when the script became part

of the curriculum of the Staff Training School. His education also preceded the first published book on radio theory, Arnheim's *Radio* (1936).

120 Bridson, *Prospero and Ariel,* 53.

121 "One has to remember that during the thirties—indeed, until after the war—nearly all speech on radio was live, and had to be pre-scripted. The microphone was regarded as such a potentially dangerous weapon that nobody was allowed to approach it until it was fully known what he intended to do with it. . . . A case can be made out for checked and censored scripts in wartime on the grounds of national security. But that spontaneous speech should have been banned by the BBC for the first odd twenty years of broadcasting is almost unbelievable. The fact remains that it was" (Bridson, *Prospero and Ariel,* 52–53).

122 Marinetti, "Destruction of Syntax," 48.

123 Kahn, 52–53.

124 Scannell and Cardiff, 130.

125 Scannell and Cardiff, 139.

126 Bridson, *Prospero and Ariel,* 20–21. The Empire Service, launched December 19, 1932, broadcast on shortwave to five zones: Australia, India, South Africa, West Africa, and Canada (Briggs, *History of Broadcasting,* vol. 2, 381–386).

127 Bridson, *Prospero and Ariel,* 28–29. In the 1930s the BBC presented a leftist bias for which it was often criticized; the presence of self-avowed Marxists on staff was not uncommon. For a discussion of Marxist influence at the BBC, see W. J. West, *Truth Betrayed,* chapter 3.

128 Bridson, *Prospero and Ariel,* 28–31. Midcareer, Harding found he could pinpoint regional issues such as the poverty of the working classes in the north of England and filter these through radio to close the gap between rich and poor on a most fundamental level—alteration of spatial perspective. The voice of the northern coal miner was no longer a distant world—it merged with other sounds in the now less-privatized (thanks to radio) world of the middle and upper classes.

129 Bridson, *Prospero and Ariel,* 22.

130 Scannell and Cardiff, 140.

131 W. J. West, 24.

132 Scannell and Cardiff, 140. Harding's script is available in the BBC Archives: *New Year Over Europe,* radio feature prod. by E. A. F. Harding, 1932 (BBC Written Archives Centre, R 19/825/1).

3

Broadcast of a Melodrama

1 Scannell 150, 397f. G. A. Wyndham Lewis read from his prose work for the BBC as early as January 1928 (Omar Pound and Philip Grover, *Wyndham Lewis: A Descriptive Bibliography* [Kent: William Dawson & Sons, 1978], 165–167). He was represented as an artist and a philosopher, rather than as a poet. By the late 1930s the situation changed: Dylan Thomas made his first broadcast for the Welsh Region of the BBC in 1937 and W. H. Auden wrote *Hadrian's Wall* for the BBC in the same year (Parker, 145).

2 E. A. F. Harding to EP, December 15, 1930 (Beinecke).

3 E. A. F. Harding to EP, January 9, 1931 (Beinecke).

4 EP to Agnes Bedford, February 10, 1931 (Lilly).

5 E. A. F. Harding to EP, March 6, 1931 (Beinecke).

6 Ibid.

7 Ibid. The Arts Theatre Club, located between Charing Cross Road and St. Martin's Lane, was London's smallest stage—a basement theater, with an audience capacity of 324 persons. It had been the site of successful "outside" or on-site broadcasts of new music from 1928 to1930, featuring works by the composers Milhaud, Hindemith, Webern, and Berg. In 1931 the Music Department was restructured, and broadcasts of new music London concerts sponsored by the BBC were either live from the BBC's No. 10 studio situated near Waterloo Bridge or broadcast from Queen's Hall. Stravinsky, Schoenberg, Berg, and Webern personally visited London in 1931 for BBC concerts of their music. See Wendy Trewin and J. C. Trewin, *The Arts Theatre, London, 1927–1981* (London: Society for Theatre Research, 1986), 2, 76–81, and Doctor, *The BBC and Ultra-Modern Music,* 166, 198–199, 220, 350–353, 375, 392, 409.

8 Antheil remembered that the stakes of a salon concert were very high: "In 1923 musical opinion and prestige in Paris was formulated only

in its salons. If one wanted to be recognized in musical Paris, one had first to be properly introduced to the various all-powerful musical salons, and for this one had to have a sponsor whose opinion was worth something in them" (Antheil, *Bad Boy of Music,* 119). The Salle Pleyel was founded in 1830 by Camille Pleyel, manufacturer of pianos and piano rolls. At the time of the 1926 performance of *Testament,* the salon was located at 22 rue de Rochechouart in Paris. Stravinsky maintained a studio on an upper floor of the building in the 1920s (Nigel Simeone, *Paris—A Musical Gazetteer* [New Haven: Yale University Press, 2000], 195).

9 "Leslie Woodgate," BBC Gallery, no. 3, *Era* (December 29, 1933), BBC Written Archives Centre.

10 Music Department, internal documents regarding a commission to Constance Lambert (BBC Written Archives Centre, R27/55/1, November 11, 1930), reprinted in Doctor, 161. The BBC poorly administrated its first commissions and produced no results. Music was not organized to produce its own in-house opera performances until 1938. Broadcasts of standard opera repertory in 1931 were still made on location from concert halls such as Queen's Hall, Covent Garden, and Sadlers Wells (Scannell and Cardiff, 193–243).

11 His reputation would peak at the BBC with his appointment as Chorus Master in 1934. "Though on Music Staff as conductor and programme arranger, [Woodgate] is often 'loaned' to compose and conduct incidental music for radio plays and light dramatic shows. In this he is an outstanding success" ("Leslie Woodgate," BBC Gallery, no. 3, *Era* [December 29, 1933], BBC Written Archives Centre).

12 Scannell and Cardiff, 241; E. A. F. Harding to EP, June 26, 1931 (Beinecke).

13 Doctor, 220–221. Roger Eckersley was the brother of Peter Eckersley.

14 EP to Dorothy Pound, October 10, 1931 (Lilly). The fee was actually paid to Dorothy Pound to avoid taxation.

15 William Walton, an English composer, was commissioned in 1930 to compose specifically for the microphone. The BBC niggled back and forth over Walton's fee, stating that it was unwilling to pay more, as he had requested, because the piece, *Belshazzar's Feast,* in the end was

considered too long and serious for the commissioning programs' goal (Doctor, 156–162).

16 The Labour Party was split over Labour leader Ramsay Macdonald's acceptance of a proposal to form an all-party coalition government to institute economic measures to stem the depression in England. The majority of the Labour party opposed the coalition while the minority, under the name National Labour Party, favored it and accepted Conservative backing. The BBC Talks Department appropriated every available time slot for election discussions. Many listeners, expecting election news, must have been surprised to hear Pound's opera.

17 "The Testament of François Villon," *Radio Times* (October 23, 1931): 287.

18 "Ezra Pound's Opera 'Heaulmière,' with Villon's Words, to Be Broadcast," July 2, 1931, reprinted as "Ezra Pound et il film sonoro," *Il Mare* (Rapallo), August 29, 1931.

19 E. A. F. Harding to EP, n.d., but after October 10, 1931 (Beinecke). The suitability of the experimental Alberto Cavalcanti to direct a *Testament* film project is confirmed by Paul Rotha's description of Cavalcanti as a filmmaker "not interested in the usual devices favoured by the *avant-garde,* being generally concerned with the slow unfolding of a human being's life" (Rotha, *The Film till Now,* 310).

20 Dorothy Pound to EP, October 8, 1931 (Lilly).

21 Pound, *Guide to Kulchur,* 366–368.

22 Pound used the concept of graph, for example, to explain the differences in notation between the 1923 Antheil and the 1926 Paris versions of the counterrhythm in the "Père Noé" song: "The music [is] not supposed to be changed. . . . The difference in the graph is due merely to question *which* graph was most likely to convey the idea of the music" (foreword to *Le Testament*). Pound added the comment to the 1923 holograph score sometime in 1931 for the BBC production. This becomes clear in viewing the score (sometimes referred to as the "gold" score for the color of its cover) in the Beinecke Library. It should be noted that the microfilm of the score made by the Library of Congress (and used for the Bridson/Schafer and Hughes productions) reproduces the color markings in black and white where they

can (and have been) easily mistaken as part of the original 1923 Antheil edition. Pages 62 and 63, missing from the LOC microfilm, are now in the Beinecke archive.

23 E. A. F. Harding to EP, January 9, 1931 (Beinecke). That Pound absorbed Harding's radio "primer" is shown by his restatement of this particular lesson for his friend Ronald Duncan, a writer: "Anyhow what drammer or teeyater *wuz,* radio is. Possibly the loathing of it [radio] may stop diffuse writing. No sense in print *until* it [i.e., the radio script] gets to finality" (*The Letters of Ezra Pound,* 342–343).

24 The word *dialogue* is used here as a technical term, and signifies that the script contained spoken lines for more than one character. It is not meant to convey discourse between characters, which was kept to a minimum. Speech was often no more than a rhetorical remark related to the music text, a comment to help the listener, or a sonic impulse used to further the plastic qualities of the montage.

25 E. A. F. Harding to EP, April 15, 1931 (Beinecke).

26 EP to Dorothy Pound, May 10, 1931 (Lilly).

27 E. A. F. Harding to EP, October 10, 1931 (Beinecke).

28 E. A. F. Harding to EP, April 15, 1931 (Beinecke). Without knowledge of Harding's letter, Robert Hughes's 1971 stage production in Berkeley essentially followed Harding's original tack. Verse from Villon's *Testament* was selected by Hughes and translated by Peter Dale Scott, poet and Poundian at the University of California, Berkeley. Those translations may be heard on Fantasy recording #12001.

29 E. A. F. Harding to EP, April 15, 1931(Beinecke).

30 E. A. F. Harding to EP, October 10, 1931 (Beinecke).

31 EP to Dorothy Pound, May 12, 1931 (Lilly). A sheet of undated stage instructions, "Staging of the Villon" by Pound are in Beinecke, Ezra Pound Papers—Addition. The comments on the difficulty of the work with Harding are an interesting gauge given Pound's capacity for and eagerness to acquire difficult new skills such as music notation and composition.

32 "Continuity" (no. 52 [July 6, 1942], in "*Ezra Pound Speaking,*" 192).

33 *Le Testament,* music score, 1923 Antheil edition, 16.

34 Domenico de Paoli of the Italian RAI wrote to Geoffrey Bridson at the BBC about his interest in broadcasting *Le Testament,* but insisted

the songs would need to be translated into Italian for Italian broadcast (unpublished letter, February 14, 1960, BBC Written Archives Centre). Dorothy Pound insisted on Pound's behalf that the songs should not be performed in any language but French (unpublished letter, Dorothy Pound to Robert Hughes, November 15, 1960, courtesy of Robert Hughes).

35 E. A. F. Harding to EP, April 15, 1931 (Beinecke).

36 E. A. F. Harding to EP, July 11, 1931 (Beinecke).

37 Sieveking, 48. The proposal for a "vast auditory palette" was by T. H. Pear, *Voice and Personality* (London: Chapman and Hall, 1931). The debate may have been sparked by the proximity of the *Testament* program to James Weldon Johnson's American drama *God's Trombones*, performed by Paul Robeson (*Radio Times* [November 13, 1931]: 506). Johnson's sermons on Biblical texts represented the African-American with "straight speech" and eschewed dialect and rhyming patterns.

38 The BBC maintained a Spoken English Advisory Committee, with Robert Bridges as chair. G. B. Shaw joined the Committee in 1926. Other members included L. Pearsall-Smith (of the Society for Pure English), and L. James (Lecturer in Phonetics, School of Oriental Studies) ("Wireless Accent—Bernard Shaw to Help," *Manchester Guardian*, July 16, 1926). Asa Briggs attributes the development of an impersonal and upper-class BBC speaking style to the attitudes and posturing of the personnel, who wore dinner jackets to broadcast. "The language of discourse—accent, vocabulary, style—was so separate that it was always a matter of 'them' and 'us'" (Briggs, *History of Broadcasting*, vol. 2, 40). A complaint lodged in 1929 claimed that education by radio disseminated "unintelligible words and unfamiliar metaphors" (Briggs, *History of Broadcasting*, vol. 2, 195). While Talks sought to introduce the concerns of the working classes into their programs, we have Sieveking's comments to suggest Drama did not share this view. On BBC "standard English," see Matheson, 59–83.

39 E. A. F. Harding to EP, July 11, 1931 (Beinecke).

40 Alternation of speech and song, both in French, recalls the troubadour tradition in which the performer entertained the audience with *vidas* (biographies) and *razos* (paraphrase of the song, or anecdote) before singing. The hint of a connection would have been misleading.

Pound's dialogue avoided such content. The sense of time between speech and song was to be immediate, not a commentary on something that happened or was composed in the past. Theoretically, troubadour performance of speech alternating with song moved between the temporal space of the past (the *vida* and *razo*) to that of the present/eternal (the *canso*), as Elizabeth Poe describes it in *From Poetry to Prose,* 48–55).

41 E. A. F. Harding to EP, September 15, 1931 (Beinecke).

42 Arnheim, 49.

43 EP to Homer Pound, April 11, 1927 (Beinecke).

44 Arnheim, 48.

45 Arnheim, 51 (interior quotation marks added; when referring to Arnheim's work in the text below, I have freely interchanged the terms "interest" and "conceit" for "intellectual problem"). The year 1936 was a pivotal year for formalized instruction in the field of radio in England. Not only was Arnheim's *Radio* published in English translation by Faber & Faber, but the BBC initiated Staff Training with Archie Harding as its first director.

46 *Pound's Cavalcanti,* 18.

47 Beinecke, Ezra Pound Papers.

48 Another experiment in language across centuries is Luigi Pirandello's 1922 play *Enrico IV.* A confrontation of illusion and reality, it juxtaposes the eleventh and twentieth centuries, contrasting archaic and modern Italian speech (Luigi Pirandello, *Naked Masks,* ed. Eric Bentley [New York: E. P. Dutton, 1952]).

49 D. G. Bridson to Matyas Seiber, March 8, 1960 (Ezra Pound S/W File 1953–1962, BBC Written Archives Centre). Seiber was a composer asked to advise BBC on the feasibility of a new broadcast of *Testament.*

50 Matheson, 63. Matheson specifically listed Cockney vowels as one of the forms of speech capable of arousing "violent criticism from different quarters." She also recommended Cockney be avoided for practical considerations, when broadcasting verse (66–68). Regarding the vernacular language, she wrote, "Broadcasting is clearly rediscovering the spoken language, the impermanent but living tongue, as distinct from the permanent but silent print" (74). Much of the remainder of her chapter "Living Speech" will be of interest to readers analyzing Pound's radio speeches from Rome during World War II.

51 EP to Homer Pound, November 29, 1924 (Beinecke).

52 As I write this, the Gate Theatre of Dublin is presenting its production of Samuel Beckett's *Waiting for Godot* in nearby Berkeley. Finely honed cadences of Irish brogue contrast with Pozzo's Queen's English to create an exquisite and dramatic music of speech. As with *Testament,* debate focuses on the use of dialect, with critics deeming it an injection of colonialism into the author's text (Karen Fricker, "Waiting for Beckett," *Stagebill* [October 2000]: 12). Also along these lines, an unpublished letter from Julian Beck to Pound dated January 25, 1961 (Beinecke, Ezra Pound Papers), reported on the Living Theater's production of Pound's *Women of Trachis.* Beck said the critics could not interest themselves seriously in the translation, choruses, or monologues and were shocked by the slang.

53 Ezra Pound, "The Drama," *Outlook* 44, no. 1132 (October 11, 1919): 363.

54 Pound and Fenollosa, 69.

55 Arnheim, 194–195.

56 Ibid.

57 Pound and Fenollosa, 27 (Fenollosa's notes on *Suma Genji*).

58 Drakakis, ed., *British Radio Drama,* 20–21. The play was broadcast January 15, 1924. See also Crook, *Radio Drama* (5), who gives a brief account of the first American dramas written for the microphone by the New York station WGY. A more detailed description by Elizabeth McLeod, "The WGY Players and the Birth of Radio Drama," is found at <http://www.midcoast.com/~lizmcl/wgy.html>. All the early dramas sought to create stunning sound effects. Hans Flesch's *Zauberei auf dem Sender* (Magic at the Radio Station), one of the first *Hörspiel* dramas broadcast (October 24, 1924), was about a magician who, anxious to demonstrate his powers, creates pandemonium in a broadcast studio. The play has been the focus of studies on the use of acoustic transmission to extend the concept of realism (*Encyclopedia of Contemporary German Culture,* ed. John Sandford [New York: Routledge, 1999], 299–300). Karl Valentin, Germany's famous misanthropic clown, created a parody on this theme in 1926 for the cabaret theater, *Im Senderraum* (At the Radio Station). This text is reprinted in Laurence Senelick, ed. and trans., *Cabaret Performance,* vol. 2: *Europe 1920–1940* (Baltimore: Johns Hopkins University Press, 1993), 40–50.

59 *Squirrel's Cage* was broadcast on March 6, 1929, in London. Guthrie later staged this play under the title *The Top of the Ladder.* He is quoted from the foreword to a printed edition of his play (reprinted in Val Gielgud, 44–45). Gielgud's figure for the number of pieces produced by Drama in 1930 was close to two hundred plays a year (Gielgud, 42).

60 McWhinnie, *The Art of Radio,* 27.

61 Eliot, "Matthew Arnold," 111. The McWhinnie and Eliot quotes are reprinted in Crook, 66–67.

62 Louise Cleveland, "Trials in the Soundscape: The Radio Plays of Samuel Beckett," *Modern Drama* 11, no. 3 (1968): 269.

63 Guralnick, *Sight Unseen,* 98. With psychology as a focal point, Tim Crook, having conducted his own research into the theory of the "blindness" of radio, contends that "the degree of signification in radio or sound goes beyond the superficial and subtextural layers of the sound itself and must encompass the interaction with memory, other media and contextualisation." Concluding that the listener may be brought into a state of imagination that evokes the full sensory spectrum, Crook divides the listener's experience not into seeing and hearing, but the physical and the psychological: "The space for radio/audio drama lies in the physicality of aural experience and the psychological space of the mind's imagination which is, of course, visual and aural" (Crook, 60, 36). He bases this idea partly on the research of T. H. Pear, professor of psychology. Pear believed that radio listening involved a process of thinking that was a response to radio drama's unique rhetorical structure (Crook 60).

64 Pound, *Guide to Kulchur,* 59.

65 Pound, *The Spirit of Romance,* 88–89.

66 All dialogue is derived from the BBC script printed at the back of this book.

67 Cantril and Allport, *Psychology of Radio,* 121.

68 E. A. F. Harding to EP, April 15, 1931 (Beinecke).

69 Villon's words would later be harnessed to the famous line of Canto LXXIV/464, "Time is the evil."

70 E. A. F. Harding to EP, April 15, 1931 (Beinecke).

71 As Pound would counsel readers of *The Cantos* (January 15, 1934; *The Letters of Ezra Pound,* 250).

72 EP to E. A. F. Harding, October 27, 1931 (Beinecke). This was Pound's sole commentary to Harding regarding the extramusical matters of *Testament*. Another indication of the intent to point to a merger of past and present was the occasional substitution of the name "Jean Cocteau" for Villon's "Jean Cotart" in the "Père Noé." Jean Cotart was the magistrate and drunkard who earlier had obtained a favorable court opinion for Villon. Cotart died in 1461, the year preceding Villon's writing of *Le grand testament*. Cocteau's name was first substituted in the 1926 Salle Pleyel performance of "Père Noé." "Cocteau" was written into the lyrics of the 1923 Antheil edition once, the final time Cotart's name was to be sung, obviously for a surprise effect. At a later date, either for the 1926 or the 1931 performance, the above substitution of lyrics was indicated for several additional bars of music.

73 Noah's cultivation of the vine led to his drunkenness which in turn led to a curse upon the Canaanites—the descendants of his son Ham who had shamed him. Lot's drunkenness caused him to lie with his three daughters. Archetriclin, governor at the wedding at Cana, recognized the first miracle wrought by Jesus, the conversion of water into wine. On Cotart, see n. 72 above.

74 Originally Pound called Bozo the brothel keeper the "Pornoboskos," one who has a nose for whores (Beinecke, Ezra Pound Papers—Addition). Pound may have intended "It's a nose" as a double entendre, referring both to police informant and to Bozo's nose. I believe that Pound discarded the name "Pornoboskos" for the radio script in order to avoid a confusion of noses.

75 Slang for cops. The word was undoubtedly also intended as a double entendre for film.

76 Crossouts in the BBC script have been retained. Italics indicate last-minute script changes. Pound wrote his father that he should distinguish between voices in Cantos XVIII and XIX by the printed punctuation (EP to Homer Pound, November 29, 1924; Beinecke). I have considered this statement in forming my remarks above.

77 This can be heard in the 1962 Schafer/Bridson production for the BBC. I am grateful to R. Murray Schafer and Robert Hughes, through whose auspices I was able to hear a tape of the production.

78 Emendations to Libretto of Villon (Beinecke, Ezra Pound Papers—Addition). The BBC script chose to replace Heaulmière with "Woman's Voice":

VOICE:	What do you see there?
WOMAN'S VOICE:	Six lads of the village, hung by the neck until dead.

The image has the potential to draw its power from Heaulmière's earlier boast of the many young men drawn to her. I have paused to remark on Pound's specific reference to Heaulmière simply to note that there is a textual reason for selecting her, though Pound may have wanted to offer a practical alternative.

79 D. B. Wyndham Lewis notes that it was fashionable on summer nights for the gallants of Paris to take their girlfriends out to the gibbet of Montfaucon. One such adventure was the subject of verse (*Repues franches*) written to glorify Villon after his disappearance (Lewis, *François Villon,* 49).

80 Perhaps worried about the ability of the radio audience to sustain that image, compounded by difficulties with the music itself, Harding marked two cuts in the song. He devised a clever method to cross-fade the music without having it rewritten. "This trick gives effect of them going on singing though one can't hear them. It enables one to make a cut sound natural" (marginalia, *The Testatment of François Villon;* Beinecke). Dorothy Pound, however, was displeased with the results and asked if the song were not "hopeless" (Dorothy Pound to EP, October 28, 1931; Lilly). Woodgate, a seasoned choral conductor, rewrote the aria for monophonic voices and put the polyphonic dissonance into the instruments.

81 "Radiario I believe is O.K. you can get Har / to let you see it" (EP to Agnes Bedford, August 28, 1932; Lilly). A similar term, "radario," was used by *Radio Digest* (October 1923), reprinted in Crook, 5.

82 The four scene titles may have been Harding's contribution. The word "Victim" does not fit the character Villon, as the following synopsis will make clear. The *Radio Times* program announcement of

October 23, 1931, combined scenes two and three into "The Victim's World." A late correction to the final script canceled a plan to announce the name of each scene. For ease in discussing the melodrama, I have maintained the four scene divisions throughout.

83 Reprinted in Stock, 297.

84 Pound and Fenollosa, 4.

85 *Radio Times,* October 23, 1931: 262.

86 Mgr. Joseph Nasrallah, *The Church Saint-Julien-le-Pauvre* (Paris: St.-Armand [Cher], Impr. CLERC, no. 817, 1961): 1. The Paris dadaists, searching for new forums in which to stage their public events, chose the grounds of St.-Julien-le-Pauvre as the first (and it turned out, the last) in a series of tours to city sites. See Melzer, *Dada and Surrealist Performance,* 149, 153.

87 *The Testament of François Villon* (Beinecke).

88 EP to Dorothy Pound, October 29, 1931 (Lilly).

89 Pound and Fenollosa, 36.

90 E. A. F. Harding to EP, April 15, 1931 (Beinecke).

91 His biographer Guillaume Colletet (1650) conjectures that he died about 1482 (Lewis, *François Villon,* 220–221).

92 By which he explained the "outline of [the] main scheme" of *The Cantos* to his father (EP to Homer Pound, April 11, 1927; Beinecke). The Bridson adaptation established through a narrator that the year was 1462.

93 Pound may have also been pointing to his own rewriting of *Testament.* His 1923 *Testament* opera, previewed twice in various concert excerpt formats, was now being adapted for radio and film.

94 E. A. F. Harding to EP, April 15, 1931 (Beinecke).

95 The narrator of the 1962 Bridson script placed Villon's appearance at "late afternoon," his mother's prayer at "evening," the priest's attempt to enter the brothel at "dusk." The gibbet scene was accounted for with the words "It is dusk again." Bridson's narrator also supplied vivid visual detail for each scene. The image of one character watching another dominates the *mise-en-scène* with an attempt to create imaginary freeze frames or visual backgrounds to the singing. This experiment of having the characters "see" each other while the listener can see no one was one of many of Bridson's changes to the

script. With no intention of producing a film of the script, Bridson turns the script's sole focus on radio. His alterations to the 1931 script should be viewed as an adaptation rather than as a recension.

96 Pound, *Selected Prose, 1909–1965,* 168.

97 Bridson rewrote the script according to chronological time. By doing so he missed the drama's two allusions to voices outside of time. He gave the "voice from church" to the priest, then reordered the sequence of arias so the priest would not sing his two songs consecutively. The complex role of Villon's mother was diminished by these choices. Pound told Bridson the production had been a "mess." The blame eventually landed (unfairly) on the shoulders of R. Murray Schafer, who arranged some of the music (Carpenter, 885).

98 Although "ostinato" is more accurate, the phrase "drum theme" has been used in the text above to conform with the radio script. In the Pound/Antheil edition the drum theme was associated with the brothel. For the radio script it has the much broader application of indicating time movement.

99 The use of a clock to mark the passage of time in film was already a well-used formula. Two examples show this device was used by filmmakers who interested Pound. To follow the movements of two figures in *Rien que les heures,* Alberto Cavalcanti worked with a "pattern of shots of Paris, interspaced at regular intervals by close-ups of a clock marking the hours" (Rotha, 310). The earlier film *Danse Macabre* (1922) by Pound's friend, the American filmmaker Dudley Murphy, opens with an animation of the striking of the hour by the church tower clock. The action then moves indoors to a castle where pleasure seekers dance and pantomime to synchronized music. Death, stalking the lovers through the castle, was portrayed both in animation and by an actor, using special film effects to give an otherworldly sense. The similarities found in Pound's Villon are notable—the church tower, the heavy reliance on the stage arts of music and mime to tell the story, the stalking of the main character(s), the attempt to create a semblance of the other world. The description of Murphy's film is from Moritz, 118–136).

100 These are Psalm 50, the Prayer of Repentance ("Have mercy on me, O God"), Psalm 69, a Prayer for Remembrance ("O God, come to

my assistance!"), and Psalm 142, a Prayer of Confidence in the Lord ("O Lord . . . enter not into judgment with your servant since of all the living none is just before You").

101 *Radio Times,* October 23, 1931: 262.

102 Pound delivers the ballad to Catherine in the person of the Gallant (scene 3), who serenades her from the square. Her enduring hostility to Villon is registered as she receives the Gallant: "End with sound of door shutting VILLON out significantly."

103 Pound and Fenollosa, 4.

104 The Angelus prayers, not technically part of the canonical hours, were so popular that they were integrated into the morning, noon, and evening service according to local custom. Church bells rang three times for each of the versicles and nine times for the concluding prayer. The evening Angelus recalled the Annunciation by the Angel to Mary and the Incarnation (John Harthan, *The Book of Hours* [New York: Thomas Crowell, 1977], 13).

105 François Villon, *The Complete Works of François Villon,* trans. Anthony Bonner (New York: Bantam Books, 1960), 16.

106 Lewis, 3.

107 Beinecke, Ezra Pound Papers—Addition.

108 Beinecke, Olga Rudge Papers.

109 "Ezra Pound's Opera 'Heaulmière,' with Villon's Words, to Be Broadcast." Interview, *Herald Tribune,* reprinted from *Il Mare* (Rapallo), July 2, 1931. Yvette Guilbert (1865–1944) performed in cafés and vaudeville houses. Her accompanist, Gustave Ferrari, also arranged her songs (*Ezra Pound and Music,* 493–494). After she refused to perform the work, Pound wrote, "It will take the nasal tone of tough, open-air singing. [If only Ethel Merman or Pinza would!]" (*Guide to Kulchur,* 366–368).

110 Yvette Guilbert, *L'art de chanter une chanson* (Paris: Bernard Grasset, 1928). The book surveys a great variety of motifs, each accompanied by a photographic still of Guilbert demonstrating the corresponding facial technique.

111 Beinecke, Olga Rudge Papers.

112 The word *rose* is not a woman's name, but an epithet directed to Catherine (Villon, *Complete Works,* 199, n. 77). Versions of the opera since 1971 have portrayed "Catherine" as the character "Rose."

113 The music by Dufay (1400?–1474) would have been one of three short selections of his sacred music available on 78 rpm record at that time: "Christe Redemptor," "Conditor alme siderum," or "Gloria 'ad modum tubae'" This information was kindly provided by Richard Koprowski at the Stanford Archive of Recorded Sound, Stanford University.

114 The words of "Dame du ciel" are a variation of the traditional "Prayer for the Intercession of our Lady Theotokos" recited at compline, the last service of the day ("O Lady, Bride of God . . . despise me not a wretched sinner, who have defiled myself with unclean thoughts . . .").

115 Medieval liturgical and passion plays sometimes employed two languages, Latin with German, Italian, French, Hebrew, or Greek, to indicate characters as well as a hierarchy within the church, chronology of time, or psychology of the secular juxtaposed to the sacred. For a selection of such plays, see David Bevington, *Medieval Drama* (Boston: Houghton Mifflin, 1975).

116 Agnes Bedford to D. G. Bridson, September 21, 1959 (BBC Written Archives Centre); *The Testament of François Villon* (Beinecke); *The Testament of François Villon* (Lilly). "Mère au Saveur" was one of two songs in *Testament* that were not Pound's melodies; "Suivez beauté," the priest's song, was the other. The authentic melody and text of "Mère au Saveur" were by the thirteenth-century troubadour Williaume li Viniers. Collignon first sang the song in London, April, 1918, from the published arrangement of li Viniers's tune by Walter Morse Rummel for voice and piano (*Ezra Pound and Music,* 97). The song was part of Rummel's 1912 collection *Hesternae Rosae: Nine Troubadour Songs from the XIIth and XIIIth Centuries.* Pound knew the songs well as he had assisted Rummel with their modern rhythmic notation and supplied English translations for the publication (Peter Whigham, ed., *The Music of the Troubadours,* vol. 1 [Santa Barbara, CA: Ross-Erikson, 1979], 74).

The Bedford, Pound/Antheil scores and the Pound/Harding radio script all place "Dame du ciel" before "Mère au Saveur." Confusion was caused by the removal of pages 62 and 63 from the 1923 score, probably during the broadcast rehearsals. When the score was microfilmed by the Library of Congress, these pages were missing and therefore lacking in the microfilm supplied to conductors of future productions. The Schafer and all subsequent music editions place "Mère au Saveur" before "Dame du ciel." (The order of the music should be corrected for future performances.) For the 1962 broadcast, Schafer composed a simple accompaniment of tubular chimes and assigned the "Mère au Saveur" to a lower register for the priest. The idea was probably to give the priest a larger role, one that included his priestly occupation (an interpretation that has been challenged in this book) and to separate his two songs with the mother's song. Bridson, working from the 1931 BBC script, did broadcast the songs in their original order (*Le Testament,* audiotape, London: BBC Sound Archive Library, 1962).

117 See the section titled "Radiophonic Effects" below. Bedford remembered the performance as having been unaccompanied, but her inability to recall instrumental accompaniment may indicate only that the chimes and harmonium were prerecorded. If so, the producer at the control panel and the engineer would have heard them in their headphones as they were transmitted, but no one else in the studio would have heard them.

118 Pound's specific use of the word *voice* to indicate a preternatural sound can be traced to his explication of Cavalcanti's Ballata V, "Vedrai la sua virtù nel ciel salita." Pound commented on the poem's final line, "Guido speaks of seeing issue from his lady's lips a subtle body, from that a subtler body, from that a star, from that a voice, proclaiming the ascent of the virtu" (Pound, *The Spirit of Romance,* 90, n.).

119 Beinecke, Ezra Pound Papers—Addition. Page 63 of the score was lost until recently. The priest is accompanied by cello and contrabass. The drum theme and nose flute were to enter before the priest's song and be audible during "Suivez beauté," but Harding's radio script makes no indication for this.

120 See Carl Kerényi, *Eleusis* (Princeton: Princeton University Press, 1967).

121 *The Testament of François Villon* (Lilly).

122 For this source I am grateful to Charles Mundye, who, on the occasion of his 1992 production of *Le Testament* at York, England, was in communication with Robert Hughes and supplied information

regarding the "Gaite de la tor" from Andrew Minor, ed., *Music in Medieval and Renaissance Life* (Columbia: University of Missouri Press, 1964), 10–15.

123 Beinecke, Ezra Pound Papers—Addition.

124 Beinecke, Olga Rudge Papers. Pound's stage instructions were made from the audience's perspective. This would translate to "extreme upstage right."

125 Beinecke, Olga Rudge Papers.

126 Lambert, *Ariel and All His Quality,* 41; Gorham, 35–36. The incidents may explain Pound's epithet for the BBC—"that b/(loody) B(ooby) C(urrumpusCo)" (EP to Agnes Bedford, March 6, 1935; Lilly). See also Bridson's account of the BBC's censorship of his 1937 broadcast of *The Wasteland* by T. S. Eliot (Bridson, *Prospero and Ariel,* 63–67).

127 *Manchester Guardian,* October 28, 1931 (BBC Written Archives Centre).

128 *Star,* October 27, 1931 (BBC Written Archives Centre). It appears odd, given that the anniversary celebration was the fifth centenary year of Villon's birth, that *The Star* referred to the opera's "13th century atmosphere." The first third of the broadcast opera evinced a late medieval quality due to the restricted gamut of the voice range and the purity of the solo violin accompaniment. Starting with medieval monophony, Pound added new harmonic ingredients to each aria as the opera progressed, culminating in the second third of the opera with the dissonance of "Dame du ciel" and climaxing in the final third with the polyrhythms of "Père Noé." The final number abruptly changes character with its slow-moving monorhythmic dissonances gradually resolving to a final unison. Thus, musically, "13th century atmosphere" is an apt description, even if "Mère au Saveur" is the only authentic thirteenth-century melody in the production. *Radio Times* referred to the play as being set in the fourteenth century. See review cited below.

129 Beinecke, Ezra Pound Papers.

130 *Radio Times,* November 13, 1931: 506.

131 *Radio Times,* November 13, 1931: 506. The *Testament* broadcast has since been singled out by BBC historians Asa Briggs, Paddy Scannell, and David Cardiff as one of radio's most extraordinary features pro-

grams. The work was still considered extremely experimental in the 1960s by Third Programme producer D. G. Bridson, who called it "an almost unique example of composition by a major poet with ideas about the setting of words and vowel tones" (unpublished letter from D. G. Bridson to the Controller of Third Programme, October 28, 1959, Ezra Pound S/W File 1953–1962, BBC Written Archives Centre).

132 EP to E. A. F. Harding, October 27, 1931 (Beinecke).

133 Agnes Bedford to EP, n.d., but November 1931 (Beinecke). One should read her comments in the context of her sense of responsibility to Pound as music advisor, her limited influence, and her disappointment at the level of performance of the production. Harding's focus had been on the electronics and the overall organization rather than on the music. He also evidenced signs of buckling under the weight of trying to produce simultaneously a second script on Germany titled *L'Unity* (E. A. F. Harding to EP, n.d., but after October 10, 1931; Beinecke).

134 EP to Dorothy Pound, October 29, 1931 (Lilly).

135 Dorothy Pound to EP, November 2, 1931 (Lilly); EP to Olga Rudge, July 21, 1931, and Olga Rudge to EP, November 24, 1931 (Beinecke).

136 Dorothy Pound to EP, November 2, 1931 (Lilly). Run by the actor and clown Peter Godfrey, the Gate Theatre in 1931 was a private club that specialized in expressionist plays and a genre called the "intimate revue," a spin-off of the popular revue (Oscar Brockett, *History of the Theatre* [Boston: Allyn and Bacon, 1999], 488).

137 *Il Mare* (Rapallo), July 2, 1931. Pound proposed an article for *Radio Times,* "What it feels like to be broadcast" (E. A. F. Harding to EP, November 27, 1931; Beinecke). The article never materialized. He also finished a work for solo violin, the *Sonate 'Ghuidonis' pour violon seul,* premiered by Olga Rudge on December 5, 1931, in Paris (Gallup, 437). The music would provide the protomelodic material for the second opera *Cavalcanti.*

138 Notes to *Cavalcanti* (Beinecke, Ezra Pound Papers—Addition). Pound's remarks indicate that he was aware of the early Baird system of mechanical television (1928), which had regular experimental

broadcasts on the BBC in 1931. The previous year Harding's colleague Sieveking produced the first televised drama, Luigi Pirandello's *The Man with the Flower in His Mouth* (Briggs, *History of Broadcasting,* vol. 2, 550).

139 Lambert, 168.

140 Gregory Whitehead, "Out of the Dark: Notes on the Nobodies of Radio Art," in Kahn and Whitehead, 253–264.

141 E. A. F. Harding to EP, September 25, 1931 (Beinecke).

142 *Ezra Pound and Music,* 67–70.

143 She performed chamber music for the BBC and followed the *Testament* broadcast with an appearance in a BBC vaudeville program on November 24, 1931 ("BSOM," *Radio Times,* November 13, 1931: 504).

144 *Ezra Pound and Music,* 194–197.

145 Arthur Jacobs, *A New Dictionary of Music* (Middlesex: Penguin Reference Books, 1958), 37; and *Ezra Pound and Music,* 499.

146 E. A. F. Harding to EP, September 15, 1931 (Beinecke). Marquesita, née Violetta Hume, a descendant of the philosopher David Hume, continued to perform acting roles as well as singing roles, appearing after the *Testament* broadcast in at least two BBC productions in 1932 by Lance Sieveking (Sieveking, 167). I am grateful to Omar Pound for information about Violetta Marquesita.

147 E. A. F. Harding to EP, September 25, 1931 (Beinecke). Ferrari, who was Swiss, frequently broadcast with the BBC (*Ezra Pound and Music,* 491). Pound and Bedford assumed he would bring to the production some of the qualities they initially had expected from Guilbert (Agnes Bedford to EP, n.d., but September 20 to October 8, 1931; Beinecke).

148 Handwritten by Ezra Pound onto the title page of 1923 Pound / Antheil edition of *Le Testament.* The musicians had access through Bedford to the many extant versions of the orchestration. Two of the arias—"Je renye amours" and "Mort j'appelle"—had been privately published by Pound in February 1926. The numerous versions of the music made it easy for the musicians to turn away from the unusual meters of the Antheil edition, but also caused considerable confusion.

149 E. A. F. Harding to EP, June 26, 1931 (Beinecke).

150 E. A. F. Harding to EP, September 15, 1931 (Beinecke).

151 EP to E. A. F. Harding, October 27, 1931 (Beinecke). The most complete documentation referring to the various editions used is a list compiled by the BBC Music Library in 1959 (Ezra Pound, S/W file 1953–1962, file 1, BBC Written Archive Centre).

152 "Word from Madge—who heard in Winchester—& seems to have noted some orchestra. I thought the orchestra really almost non-existent—This was internal BBC politics—not to be struggled with by me" (Dorothy Pound to EP, October 28, 1931; Lilly). Edith Madge was a family friend who taught music for many years in Kashmir. "Internal BBC politics" referred to frequent disagreements between engineers and producers on balance control. I am grateful to Omar Pound for information about Edith Madge.

153 Quotations are from EP to Agnes Bedford, October 29, 1931 (Lilly); EP to E. A. F. Harding, October 27, 1931 (Beinecke). Pound's remark about a frieze was probably not based on a visualization he made during the broadcast (or a memory of what he had heard), but rather an image invoked to describe a proportion between the basses and the voice. Transmission of bass frequencies varied from station to station in Europe. Arnold Schoenberg stated that he thought Britain and Italy were satisfactory in their bass tones, but otherwise condemned radio in general for presenting only the upper half of the spectrum of sound, like "a lady sawn in half" (Arnold Schoenberg, "Modern Music on the Radio" (1933), in Schoenberg, *Style and Idea,* ed. Leonard Stein [New York: St. Martin's Press, 1975], 151).

154 EP to Dorothy Pound, October 28, 1931 (Lilly). The comment contains the underlying assumption that once the piece was notated, performers would adhere to his notation, granting him the same authority granted to opera composers. For many reasons pertaining to the music's appearance and content, Pound was not accorded this authority, and his music was rewritten, rearranged, and "corrected" in the productions that followed, until the 1971 Hughes performance.

155 Notes on act III, *Cavalcanti.* The aria was "Quando di morte." For his Rome radio broadcasts, Pound is reported to have told the engineers to "turn on more current" if his delivery was too soft. The retelling of the account by Humphrey Carpenter builds the impression that

Pound was at such a fevered pitch to gain access to the microphone that he could not be bothered with its technique (Carpenter, 584). But Pound's experience with the *Testament* broadcast suggests that he knew better than to let the engineers cow his performance at the microphone. A technical adjustment such as boosting the signal would not compromise his delivery as much as the unnatural modulation of his own voice, "the fake in the voices" (*The Letters of Ezra Pound,* 342–343). Pound had earlier investigated ways that a producer, working directly with the musicians, could regulate the signal sent to the engineer. Referring to the overly loud mandolins in the *Testament* broadcast, Pound asked Bedford, "What about adjusting the 'mike' [?] me friend Cauda has several ideas of that subjek" (EP to Agnes Bedford, August 28, 1932; Lilly). Adjustments might have included the type and number of microphone(s), the individual level settings (controlled at the DCP), and microphone placement. Pound knew Ernesto Cauda as a sound engineer who wrote technical articles for trade publications in the film industry (Letter, EP to Langston Hughes, July 8, 1932, reprinted in David Roessel, "The Letters of Langston Hughes and Ezra Pound," *Paideuma* 29, nos. 1 and 2 [Spring and Fall 2000]: 221). Cauda authored *Cinematografia sonora: elementi teoricopratici* (Milan, 1930) and wrote on all aspects of cinema in the 1930s.

156 Sieveking, 73.

157 Sieveking, 61, 87–89.

158 Pawley, *BBC Engineering 1922–1972,* 45.

159 Raymonde Collignon to EP, n.d., but after October 27, 1931 (Beinecke). The tin bath was most famous for its imitation of locomotive sounds made by the drag of roller skates against the metal, the operator being connected to the control booth by headphones (Sieveking, 72).

160 Agnes Bedford to EP, November 1931 (Beinecke). Pound, of course, did hear the two broadcasts in Rapallo. Another example of Pound's intervention was his request to the Italian radio service to install a radio receiver in Rapallo. "The Turin people (either in response to yr/ letter or mine or both) have been very amiable , telegraphed their bo' here to put an apparatus . 5 other apparati apparently got nothing. the doc's down stairs got some" (EP to E. A. F. Harding, October 27, 1931; Beinecke).

161 E. A. F. Harding to EP, July 11, 1931 (Beinecke).

162 Pound's subsequent recording projects provided an opportunity for him to realize some of the solutions developed in response to the compromised *Testament* broadcast and destined for the abandoned *Cavalcanti* opera. On May 17, 1939, he accompanied himself on drums for a recording of his reading of *Seafarer, Sestina Altaforte,* and Canto XVII for the Harvard Department of Speech (Norman, *Ezra Pound,* 365–366). By November 1940 when Pound arranged to register his talks on discs for Rome radio, he had the experience of both the *Testament* drum and "Harvard Vocarium" recordings behind him.

163 The steel tape was "6mm wide and 0.08 mm thick, spooled in lengths of a little over a mile, which at a speed of 5 ft/s gave a playing time of 20 minutes. A full spool weighed 21 lb. The drive was from a dc motor, the speed of which had to be regulated by watching a stroboscope and manipulating a sliding rheostat" (Pawley, 179). The machine was installed in Room 66 of Savoy Hill.

164 E. A. F. Harding to EP, January 9, 1931 (Beinecke).

165 EP to Dorothy Pound, May 12, 1931 (Lilly). Pound remained interested in access to recording technology. Regarding a future possibility of recording on the Blattnerphone he wrote Olga Rudge, "he cd he believes get her recorded" (EP to Olga Rudge, April 26, 1932; Beinecke).

166 E. A. F. Harding to EP, January 27, 1932 (Beinecke). The penultimate rehearsal was 10:30 A.M., Saturday, October 24 (E. A. F. Harding to Dorothy Pound, October 23, 1931; Beinecke). The recording has not been located.

167 Sound waves impacted the diaphragm sufficiently enough to "mechanically compress carbon discs and granules in accordance with the intensity and frequency of the sound." This caused variations in air pressure, reflected in the electric current flowing through the transmitter (Cowan, ed., *Recording Sound for Motion Pictures,* 35). Other isolated microphones at Savoy Hill were the Western Electric condenser microphone, the RCA condenser microphone, and Bell Recording Company's "slack-diaphragm" microphone. The RCA ribbon microphone, available in 1931 and used immediately for film, was not installed at the BBC until a BBC-engineered clone of it was approved for use in 1935. The ribbon mike had a double-sided response,

reducing the effect of reverberant sound. It allowed artists to face each other rather than standing side-by-side. The delay in the BBC's acquiring the better-quality microphone was due to funding. They required far more microphones, for example, for a symphony orchestra than were required on a film set (Pawley, 119–120).

168 Cowan, 35.

169 Pawley, 119–120.

4

Dramedy

1 Hugh Witemeyer, "Early Poetry 1908–1920," in Nadel, 48.

2 Ezra Pound, "Vortex Pound," *Blast,* June 20, 1914, reprinted in *Ezra Pound and the Visual Arts,* 151.

3 Ezra Pound, "A Few Don'ts," *Poetry* 1, no. 6 (March 1913), in *Literary Essays of Ezra Pound,* 4.

4 Ezra Pound, "Vorticism," *Fortnightly Review,* September 1, 1914, reprinted in *Ezra Pound and the Visual Arts,* 205–206.

5 Ibid.

6 *Blast,* June 20, 1914, reprinted in *Ezra Pound and the Visual Arts,* 151–152. Marjorie Perloff has written that the vorticist emphasis on energy and motion, coming after the string of 1910–1914 futurist presentations in London, appeared indebted to the machinelike, industrial character of futurism. Despite Pound's repeated rejection of the futurist aesthetic, she demonstrates the importance of futurism to vorticism through a comparison of statements from artists in both movements, a chronology of futurist and vorticist events in London, and a review of shared concepts between the movements. "Energy, force, dynamism—these were to be key terms in Poundian poetic. Another was simultaneity . . ." (Perloff, *The Futurist Moment,* 174, but see 163–193).

7 See Marinetti, "Destruction of Syntax," 45–53. Harding's 1931 invitation to Pound to entirely "free poetry from the limitations of print" becomes multivalent in the climate of indebtedness of vorticism to futurism, when we follow Perloff's account (E. A. F. Harding to EP, January 9, 1931; Beinecke).

8 An excerpt is translated in Kirby and Kirby, 169–170. Benedikt Livshits's explanation of the Russian futurists' critical reception of Marinetti is reprinted in Perloff, 64.
9 EP to Agnes Bedford, April 15, 1933, in *The Letters of Ezra Pound,* 245.
10 Pound, *Guide to Kulchur,* 87–88.
11 Ezra Pound, "Epstein, Belgion and Meaning," *Criterion* (April 1930): 470–475, reprinted in *Ezra Pound and the Visual Arts,* 166.
12 *Ezra Pound and the Visual Arts,* 165.
13 Ezra Pound, "Mediaevalism and Mediaevalism," *Dial* 84, no. 3 (March and April 1928): 231–237, reprinted in *Literary Essays of Ezra Pound,* 154–155.
14 Ibid.
15 The extent of Pound's belief in intangible structural form is captured by the statement, "The mind making forms can verbally transmit them when the mental voltage is high enough. It is not absolutely necessary that the imagination be registered either by sound or on painted canvas" (*Guide to Kulchur,* 77).
16 Schiff, 139. The surrealists insisted that art was political in all of its manifestations (166).
17 Pound, *Guide to Kulchur,* 189–190.
18 Regarding Pound's aversion to psychoanalysis, see Terrell, *Companion to the Cantos,* vol. 2, 551. Pound's exploration of the psyche came under the more general auspices of a "psychology" that takes account of comparative, behavioral, environmental, and cultural phenomenon.
19 Misch Orend, "Der magische Realismus" (January 1928), reprinted in Kaes, Jay, and Dimendberg, 495.
20 Pound, Guide to Kulchur, 189–190.
21 D. G. Bridson, "An Interview with Ezra Pound," *New Directions 17* (New York: New Directions, 1961), 170.
22 Pound, "Epstein, Belgion and Meaning," 470–475.
23 Ezra Pound, "Dramedy," *Athenaeum* 94, no. 4688 (March 5, 1920): 315.
24 E. A. F. Harding to EP, November 23, 1931 (Beinecke).
25 EP to Dorothy Pound, October 19, 1932 (Lilly).
26 E. A. F. Harding to EP, August 25, 1932 (Beinecke).

27 I am grateful to Robert Hughes for this brief description, drawn from his unpublished manuscript, "Ezra Pound's Cavalcanti: A Perspective."

28 *Paideuma* 12, nos. 2 and 3 (Fall/ Winter 1983): 502. Pound used two spellings, *Rico* and *Ricco.* With the exception of direct quotations, I have chosen the first spelling for this text to conform with the reproduced page from his libretto.

29 Though Cavalcanti's authorship of the poem has since been refuted, Pound believed that the first strophe could be attributed to him, and that the poem was later finished by Niccolò Machiavelli (1469–1527). For Pound's notes from the 1927–1931 manuscript of *Rime,* see *Pound's Cavalcanti,* 195. Pound's musical setting reinforces this idea. See the discussion of the opera's main motive, below.

30 Announcer's text, act I, *Cavalcanti* (Beinecke, Olga Rudge Papers). Pound reviews the brief known details of Cavalcanti's life in his essay "Cavalcanti," reprinted in *Literary Essays of Ezra Pound.* I recommend the account in Nelson, ed., *The Poetry of Guido Cavalcanti.*

31 *Sonnets and Ballate of Guido Cavalcanti,* trans. and with an introduction by Ezra Pound (Boston: Small, Maynard and Co., 1912); and Pound, *The Spirit of Romance,* 110.

32 Ezra Pound, "Guido Cavalcanti," unpublished essay in Italian, c. 1940s (Beinecke, Ezra Pound Papers), translated by the author.

33 *Pound's Cavalcanti,* 19.

34 Jacqueline Kaye, "Pound and Heresy," *Paideuma* 28, no. 1 (Spring 1999): 90.

35 Averroës was the Latin name given to the Arabic scholar Ibn Rushd. Confirmation of Cavalcanti's link to Averroism was made by Paul Oskar Kristeller in his discovery of "A Philosophical Treatise from Bologna dedicated to Guido Cavalcanti: Magister Jacobus de Pistorio and his 'Questio de felicitate,'" *Medioevo e Rinascimento,* vol. 1 (Firenze: Sansoni, 1955): 425–463. Kristeller concludes that the *Questio,* indubitably Averroistic, establishes a link between the philosophers on the faculty at the University of Bologna and the poets of Tuscany named by Dante as belonging to the "dolce stil novo." J. E. Shaw's *Guido Cavalcanti's Theory of Love* offers the most extensive analysis of "Donna mi prega" in English, though he discounts the validity of Guido's Averroism. On Cavalcanti's Averroism, see Corti, *La*

felicità mentale, 3–37; on Cavalcanti's Avverroism and Pound, see Jacqueline Kaye's article, "Pound and Heresy," 89–111. On the steps taken by the Church to ban the writings of Averroës, see Edward Grant, ed., *A Source Book in Medieval Science* (Cambridge: Harvard University Press, 1974), 45–46.

A review of the dates of Corti's bibliographical listings augments George Dekker's conclusion that Pound's contribution to twentieth-century studies of Cavalcanti, despite his "lack of scholarly underpinnings," lay in his recognition and efforts on behalf of a poet deserving a major modern treatment and reevaluation (Dekker, *Sailing after Knowledge,* 119). The last English translation of Cavalcanti had been published in England by Rossetti, *The Early Italian Poets from Ciullo d'Alcamo to Dante Alighieri;* the complete works in Italian had been last issued by Ercole Rivalta, ed., *Le rime di Guido Cavalcanti* (Bologna: Nicola Zanichelli, 1902). Since Pound's work, the field of Cavalcanti studies has been very active.

36 Gilson, *Dante the Philosopher,* 169.

37 Pound recognized the Averroistic strain of Cavalcanti's thought but was reluctant to relinquish the belief that Cavalcanti incorporated aspects of a Neoplatonic light mysticism within his views. He believed Cavalcanti's ideas could also be traced to Avicenna (Ibn Sina, 980–1037), but definitely not to Aquinas (1225–1274) (*Literary Essays of Ezra Pound,* 149, 158). Regarding other trends in Cavalcanti's "Donna mi prega," Pound wrote, "It would seem that Guido had derived certain notions from the Aristotelian commentators, the 'filosofica famiglia,' Ibn Sina [Avicenna], for the *spiriti, spiriti* of the eyes, of the senses; Ibn Rachd [Averroës], *che il gran comento feo,* for the demand for intelligence on the part of the recipient; Albertus Magnus, for the proof by experience; and possibly Grosseteste, *De Luce et de Incohatione Formarum,* although this will need proving" (ibid., 158). Avicenna was the more influential interpreter of Aristotle for Western philosophy; he promoted a theory of God's creation through emanation. Albertus Magnus (Albert the Great, 1193?–1280), a Dominican based in Cologne, was the leading interpreter of Aristotle in his time. Though he concurred with Averroës's interpretation of the immortality of the possible intellect, he (and his student Thomas Aquinas) attempted to

reconcile Aristotle with the teaching of the Church. Robert Grosseteste (d. 1253), Bishop of Lincoln, wrote a philosophy of light in the 1230s and agreed with Averroës on principles of the separation of the soul and the possible intellect.

38 Dante Alighieri, *De vulgari eloquentia,* II.12.

39 Bird, ed., "The Canzone d'Amore of Cavalcanti according to the Commentary of Dino del Garbo," 150–203, 117–160.

40 Alison Cornish, declaring Cavalcanti's philosophy "secondhand," correctly represents the scholarship on the subject, which attempts to locate the sources of Cavalcanti's language within the medieval tradition of commentary and interpretation of Aristotle (Cornish, "A Lady Asks," 170). Pound suggests the possibility that Cavalcanti's philosophy, if not germinal, is an original negotiation of Neoplatonic, Avicennist, and Averroist ideas; that is, Cavalcanti's originality was as a philosopher-poet whose science lay between word and meaning.

41 The telling passage according to Maria Corti are lines 21–24 of the second stanza:

> Vien da veduta forma che s'intende,
> Che prende—nel possibile intelletto,
> Come in subietto,—loco e dimoranza.
> In quella parte mai non ha possanza.

I refer the reader who is interested to her chapter "Guido Cavalcanti e una diagnosi dell'amore," in Corti, *La felicità mentale,* especially pp. 23–24, in which she explains that "subietto" (subject) is associated with the possible intellect of the previous line and must be a separate substance from the individual person. This is explained by Cavalcanti's use of the vernacular—*come in subietto*—to represent the philosophers' technical language, which, in Latin would be *sicut subiecto* ("as subject"). Corti describes this as "a very dense allusion of philosophical significance in that it is the negation of the individual intellectual soul" (Corti 24, my trans.). I am grateful to Amir Baghdadchi for his assistance with the translation of Corti's sources. Pound, too, isolated this passage of the poem for commentary. Corti and Pound, however, differ in their use of the technical term *subject.* Corti writes that Averroist thought held the possible intellect to be the subject, and that it serves the individual human soul, the *object*; that is, the idea of Love derives from the possible intellect and is on loan to the individual. Pound identified the individual as the *subject* penetrated by Love. Interrupting the "Donna mi prega" aria of the radio opera, he has Guido's friend Orlando attempt an analogy of this difficult philosophical distinction: "as a nail enters a wall" (act II, *Cavalcanti* opera).

42 Cavalcanti's repeated theme of the death of the will led Dino del Garbo to write a commentary on the canzone as a medical account of a pathological condition rather than an account of *fin'amors* (Shaw, 159).

43 Andrew Barker, ed., *Greek Musical Writings,* vol. 2, *Harmonic and Acoustic Theory,* trans. Oxford Classical Texts (Cambridge University Press, 1989), 77.

44 See Pound, "Epstein, Belgion and Meaning."

45 Canto XX/92–93. Pound's notes reference the "nel fuoco" to the Canticle of St. Francis (Miyake, *Ezra Pound and the Mysteries of Love,* 11, 229 n.). Individual flames of course are not V-shaped, but upside-down V's. The V shape, the negative space between the flames, could imply the space of the gaze that goes through the flames. Canto XX contains the anecdote of Pound's trip to Freiburg, Germany, to deliver his discovery of the music of Arnaut Daniel from the Ambrosiana Library to Professor Emil Lévy, authority on the Provençal language. The poet-narrator comments, "Not that I could sing him the music" (XX/89). Having in the meantime learned to compose music, Pound passes down the courier role that he has outgrown to the *Cavalcanti* character Rico, who, charged with delivering a song to Guido's allies in Florence, cannot learn it.

46 Poe, *From Poetry to Prose in Old Provençal,* 7.

47 The comment on the return to the same note is from a letter by EP to Agnes Bedford, August 20, 1932 (Lilly); Gallo, *Music in the Castle,* 33–34. Gallo presents a number of possible aims of the rhetorical device of repetition: highlighting of the "verbal sonorities," a correspondence to the "positive-negative verbal juxtapositions" commonly used, or to create a retrograde pattern of syllables within the verse (32–34).

A convincing interpretation of the aria can turn the repetition to mesmerizing effect, as sung by baritone Marco Camastra at the

Nuovo Teatro di Bolzano, Italy, where Pound's *Cavalcanti* was performed on July 13 and 14, 2000, by the Conductus Ensemble, with Marcello Fera conducting.

48 Pound, "Vorticism."

49 "Coition, the sacrament," unpublished draft (Beinecke, Ezra Pound Papers—Addition).

50 However, Pound structures commentary within his music for act III's "Perch'io non spero" to readjust that alignment. See liner notes, *Ego scriptor cantilenae* (OM 1005-2).

51 Pound and Fenollosa, 4.

52 See Shaw, 87.

53 *Accident* is a technical term of Aristotelian philosophy, one of several terms used to explain how sense and intellect "are affected, moved, or changed by perception and learning" (Jack Greenspan, "On Alberti's 'Sign': Vision and Composition in Quattrocento Painting," *Art Bulletin* 79, no. 4 [December 1997]: 676). Greenspan's article contains an excellent and concise primer on Aristotle's technical language and divisions of the soul.

54 Judging from twelve pages of music sketches in the Beinecke marked "Collis" and "Poi etc." (Ezra Pound Papers—Addition), the work appears to follow the formula of two languages: a song in Greek, "Poikilothron" by Sappho (sketches with abbreviated title and symbols, no lyrics), and the Latin, Carmen LXI, the greater wedding song of Catullus (sketches titled "Collis" include the first seventy lines of the poem, with placement of a few selected lyrics to music). Reference to the music appears in three letters: a sketch of the musical setting that invokes the name of the goddess "Aphrodite" (EP to Agnes Bedford, June 7, 1933; Lilly); and references by Pound to his composing, "Think I have found someone who wants to do the Latin song 25 minutes long. which you once considered pleasantly impractical. Got that to write now" (EP to Agnes Bedford, August 3, 1932; Lilly); "Have been fool enough to restart the Catullus" (EP to Agnes Bedford, September 9, 1932; Lilly).

55 "Cavalcanti," *Literary Essays of Ezra Pound,* 168. Pound based the text for his edition on the manuscript "Ld" from the Laurenziana Library in Florence. The design was prepared for the 1929 Aquila Press in

London. When it went bankrupt, Pound rescued these pages and inserted them into the 1932 Marsano edition printed in Genoa.

56 "Song," second draft. For the terms *logopoeia, phanopoeia,* and *melopoeia,* also see "How to Read," *Literary Essays of Ezra Pound,* 25. I have chosen to quote from the unpublished essay because it introduces the terms in relation to music.

57 "Song," first draft. Pound's divisions of poetry are threefold: *logopoeia,* poems in which the interest is "in words and their usage as words" or the meaning of words; *phanopoeia,* poems in which the "author is trying to do with words (for the imagination) very much what the painter or sculptor do for the senses"; and *melopoeia,* defined above in the text.

58 "Song," second draft.

59 "Song," second draft.

60 EP to E. A. F. Harding, August 25, 1932 (Beinecke).

61 E. A. F. Harding to EP, September 13, 1932 (Beinecke).

62 Act II, *Cavalcanti* (Beinecke, Olga Rudge Papers). Translated by Pound as "Not necessary that every animal should understand."

63 Ibid. I am grateful to Dr. Ruggero Stefanini, emeritus professor of Italian Studies, University of California at Berkeley, for assistance with the dialect and translation.

64 E. A. F. Harding to EP, September 13, 1932 (Beinecke).

65 Announcer's text, act I, *Cavalcanti* (Beinecke, Olga Rudge Papers).

66 Ibid. On Cunizza and Sordello, see Makin, *Provence and Pound,* 80, 186–214.

67 Announcer's text, act III, *Cavalcanti* (Beinecke, Olga Rudge Papers).

68 Ibid., act I.

69 Ibid., act II.

70 Pound's handwritten note to typescript of announcer's text, act III, *Cavalcanti* (Beinecke, Olga Rudge Papers).

71 Ibid.

72 Act III, *Cavalcanti* (Beinecke, Ezra Pound Papers). Guido would harp on the question "Why don't you pronounce the words?" even on his deathbed. This is an example of Pound's identification with his character—he has Guido repeat the same ideas and demands about language from youth to his grave, as Pound intended to do.

73 Pound, *The Spirit of Romance,* 88–89.

74 Act II, *Cavalcanti* (Beinecke, Ezra Pound Papers). The Bianchi are members of Cavalcanti's White faction of the Guelph party, as well as personal friends. The dialogue echoes scene two of the *Testament* production, in which the confused barman confesses he does not know where Villon's snows have gone.

75 Act II, no. 3, *Cavalcanti* (Beinecke, Ezra Pound Papers).

76 Ibid., Act II, no. 4. Pound's Italian text reads, "Quel scrofanino!!" The word *scrofa* (in both English and Italian) refers to a breeding sow, *scrofanino* being Pound's neologism, the *ino* adding a hint of endearment. Pound appears to have made an effort to avoid the obvious expression, *porca misera.* Though commonly occurring in Italian speech, the phrase is considered uncouth. Pound's Italian libretto is a combination of dialect and neologisms. For example, the banter that interrupts Cavalcanti's "Donna mi prega" reads, "Basta, basta, non ze scuola di filosofia/ ze per cantar. bprco [sic] d'un porco acidempopumpili. corpo dun can" (Beinecke, Ezra Pound Papers). *Acidempopumpili* is a play on the expression, *Accidente!* (Good Heavens!) Dr. Stefanini provided invaluable assistance in translating Pound's lines.

77 Act I, *Cavalcanti* (Beinecke, Ezra Pound Papers).

78 Ibid., Act III.

79 Ibid., Act II. Pound's Italian text deviates slightly, the dialogue between Guido and Vanna culminating in her attempt to remember and sing "Ailas" (Beinecke, Olga Rudge Papers). In the surviving music drafts and final copy, "Ailas" opens the third act and is sung by a soldier. This version of the script suggests that Pound wrote the libretto first in Italian, then in English:

GUIDO:	Cosa che canta.
VANNA:	Una canzonina, cantava sempre Madonna Cunizza e nella lingua veja.
GUIDO:	Ah! sai di chi è.

VANNA: Di che? una cosetta cantava sempre la Cunizza. cosa di Cunizza.

GUIDO: Non, ma no? sarebbe di Sordello.

VANNA: Non so. . . . Il resto. Non mi ricordo

GUIDO: E cantava altro; che tu ricordi?

VANNA: Si, si zera un altra. ma non so cantarla.

GUIDO: Prova.

hesita

GUIDO: Prova, prova; come cominciava?

VANNA: Si, si,
Ailas e que fau.

[GUIDO: What are you singing?

VANNA: A small song, always sung by Madonna Cunizza in the old language.

GUIDO: Ah! You know whose it is?

VANNA: Whose? Something always sung by la Cunizza. It's one of Cunizza's.

GUIDO: No, well why not? It would be by Sordello.

VANNA: I don't know. As for the rest, I don't remember.

GUIDO:	She sang other [songs] that you remember?
VANNA:	Yes, yes, there was another. But I don't know how to sing it.
GUIDO:	Try.
	She hesitates
GUIDO:	Try, try. How does it begin?
VANNA:	All right, Ailas e que fau.]

80 I have supplied Pound's edition of the poem (*Pound's Cavalcanti,* 42), with my translation. On Cavalcanti's sonnet, and its sister sonnet by Dante, "Tanto gentile" (*La vita nuova,* XXVI), in which the men stammer and go mute at the approach of a beatific lady, see Harrison's chapter 4, "The Ghost of Guido Cavalcanti," in *The Body of Beatrice,* 69–90. Having introduced the conundrum of Vanna's role and silently invoked "Chi è questa," Pound turns his interest to Dante's admission in *La vita nuova* of a fluctuating affection for his "first friend." When Dante's regard for Guido lessened, he transferred the authority of influence he attributed to the older Cavalcanti to another poet named Guido, generally believed to be the Bolognese lyric poet Guido Guinizzelli (born c. 1240s) (Harrison, 84). Pound intercepts Dante's game of "who's in and who's out" by demonstrating through music that Cavalcanti's poetry is more profitably studied in connection with that of Sordello.

We will come closer to Pound's conception of Vanna for radio if we use for a guide the several precedents within *The Cantos* of cameo appearances of beautiful, intelligent, and influential women who enter the poem just at the moment the poet, or his warring personae, need mental and spiritual rejuvenation: Eleanor of Aquitaine (1122–1204), Galla Placidia (fifth century A.D.), and Cunizza da Romano

(1198–1279). Each made a name in history by her independent social or political action. The women have in common the fact that they nurtured, inspired, and protected the legacy of a king, an emperor, or a master poet. Pound associates Eleanor with sound, and uses her name to initiate some word play on her alter ego Helen of Troy: *Elena, helenaus* (destroyer of men) and *heleptolis* (destroyer of men) (Canto VII/24). Placidia always evokes a special light in the poem (Canto XI/51). Early in *The Cantos* Cunizza is associated with neither light nor sound, but the meaning of words. She is represented by the legal document that granted freedom to her brothers' slaves (Canto VI/22).

81 For an overview of interpretations of line 21 of the canzone, "veduta forma che s'intende," I refer the interested reader to Shaw, 38–40; Guido Favati, *Inchiesta sul dolce stil nuovo* (Firenze: Felice Le Monnier, 1975), 198–199; and Corti, 24–27.

82 Announcer's text, act II, *Cavalcanti* (Beinecke, Ezra Pound Papers).

83 Ibid., act III.

84 The octave represents the first overtone in the harmonic series. Pound's first published notice of his interest in overtones appears in the introduction to *Sonnets and Ballate* (1912, reprinted in *Pound's Cavalcanti,* 11–20). His *Treatise on Harmony* (Paris: Three Mountains Press, 1924) further explores overtones and the importance of the bass frequencies in harmony. See also the exegesis of "great bass" in Schafer, 467–480.

85 Barker, 81. Aristotle's science of anatomy locates the testes within a network leading to the heart and the voice. The network commences at the "seed-bearing tubes," which are attached to a vessel originating at the heart and adjacent to the physical organs that produce the voice (*De generatione animalium,* sections 787a and b; Barker, 83). When measured by Aristotle's science, Rico's failure would be a matter of vocal weakness caused by sinews not yet stretched to their full tautness, rather than by intellectual or psychological inadequacy: "Most creatures when they are young, and most females, are high-voiced, because they move little air, on account of their lack of power. A little air travels swiftly, and in sound what is swift is high-pitched" (Barker, 82). When the sinews are stretched to their maximum, they are

capable of moving a great amount of air. At bar 109 of "Perch'io non spero," Guido has to conclude the line for Rico because Rico is unable to descend to the middle C required. Moerbeke's translations of Aristotle are listed in Grant, 40.

86 EP to E. A. F. Harding, August 25, 1932 (Beinecke); EP to Agnes Bedford, June 9, 1933 (Lilly).

87 Act III, *Cavalcanti* (Beinecke, Ezra Pound Papers). *Filly* not only connotes a female foal; it is also a verb meaning to give birth to a filly. Earlier the opera made reference to Dante as a breeding sow.

88 Giovanni Villani, *Cronica,* 47; Filippo Villani, *Le vite d'uomini illustri fiorentini,* 142 (excerpts reprinted in Nelson, xviii); Compagni, *Cronaca,* book One, chapter 20 (excerpts reprinted in Nelson, xvi).

89 See chapter 4 in Harrison, 69–90.

90 Though the literary circle to which Pound appends himself is not as illustrious as the circle of poets in Dante's *Inferno* IV, a parallel may be made to Dante's insinuation of himself as sixth member into a group of epic poets that consisted of Homer, Ovid, Horace, Lucan, and Virgil, and would later include Statius.

91 Announcer's text, act I, (Beinecke, Ezra Pound Papers—Addition).

92 *The Testament of François Villon* (Lilly).

93 "We do NOT know the past in chronological sequence" (Pound, *Guide to Kulchur,* 60).

94 "Era in pensier" refers to the *spiriti* of the eyes. Attribution to Cavalcanti of several of the poems has since been proven incorrect. These are "Guarda ben dico," "Sol per pietà," and "Io son la donna." Pound, aware of their questionable attribution, employs them for dramatic contrast, and, as we have seen, puts them in the mouths of either Guido's enemies or of persons of a different class or from a different century.

95 Pound, *ABC of Reading,* 55.

96 EP to E. A. F. Harding, August 25, 1932 (Beinecke).

97 "Ballate & Canzoni mainly for music. Sonnets ceased, I think, to be for music; hence . . . defective in certain sensibility" (EP to Laurence Binyon, August 30, 1934, *The Letters of Ezra Pound,* 261).

98 Dante Alighieri, *De vulgari eloquentia,* II. 6.

99 Pound omits the fourth line "dirò com'ho perduto ogni valore" (I will tell how I have lost all worth), as it would give the poet no room to grow.

100 EP to E. A. F. Harding, August 25, 1932 (Beinecke).

101 EP to Agnes Bedford, August 6, 1932 (Lilly).

102 EP to E. A. F. Harding, August 25, 1932 (Beinecke).

103 *Monymint* becomes *munyment* in Canto XXXIV/171.

104 This is Pound's translation of the third line of "Guarda ben dico," just before the cobbler sings it. David Anderson notes that Pound excluded the poem from Cavalcanti's canon and did not print it in the 1932 *Rime,* but translated it, "probably while writing the libretto for his opera 'Cavalcanti'" (*Pound's Cavalcanti,* 275). The translation, catalogued in Gallup under the reference number C1986, was published posthumously in *Antaeus* 44 (Winter [1981/1982]): 16–33, and dated by the editor Charlotte Ward as c. 1920. Pound's setting of the poem in marching cadences marked "moto perpetuo: marcato robusta" conforms to the sixteenth-century square-cut, forward-driving rhythms of the song form known as the Italian frottola. With a keen ear for cadence, and a point-for-point composition style (one syllable to each pitch), the rhythm of the tune matching the rhythm of the verse, Pound used music composition to question the attribution of "Guarda ben dico" to Cavalcanti.

105 I am indebted to Dr. Stefanini for guiding me to the author of "Guarda ben dico," Antonio di Matteo di Meglio (1384–1448), as presented in *Lirici toscani del '400,* vol. 2, ed. Antonio Lanza (Rome: Bulzoni, 1975), 57–58, 90–94. "It's an interesting rule, that in the presence of a textual crux Ezra Pound is apt to be utterly literal" (Kenner, "Ezra Pound and Homer," 18).

106 The poem that Pound worked from and his translation, reprinted in the 1983 program of the *Cavalcanti* concert premiere, were kindly provided by David Anderson to Robert Hughes on that occasion.

107 EP to E. A. F. Harding, August 25, 1932 (Beinecke).

108 Ibid.

109 The subject of the rains of love was taken up by Cavalcanti again in "Se m'hai del tutto" (which opens the opera's second act). It has

precedence in the Provençal poem of Arnaut Daniel, "Lo soleills plovil." *Forosette* are country women.

110 On extramission, see David Lindberg, *Theories of Vision from Al-Kindi to Kepler* (Chicago: University of Chicago Press, 1976).

111 Pound follows Francesco Zanzotto's ordering of strophes published in the mid-nineteenth-century Venetian anthology *Parnaso italiano.* In this arrangement, the most dramatic moment, the felling memory of Mandetta that slays the poet anew, occurs just before the envoy.

112 "Guarda ben dico," trans. Ezra Pound (unpublished manuscript, courtesy of David Anderson).

113 Act I, *Cavalcanti* (Beinecke, Olga Rudge Papers).

114 Dialogue sketched in at the bottom of music draft of "Guarda ben dico," Act I, *Cavalcanti* (Beinecke, Ezra Pound Papers).

115 EP to E. A. F. Harding, August 25, 1932 (Beinecke).

116 "Se m'hai del tutto," act II, *Cavalcanti.*

117 EP to E. A. F. Harding, August 25, 1932 (Beinecke).

118 Nelson, xviii; Pound, *Guide to Kulchur,* 153. Pound's examples of "music of representative outline" are Janequin, Vivaldi, and Couperin. In contrast are the composers of music of structure—Bach and Hindemith.

119 EP to E. A. F. Harding, August 25, 1932 (Beinecke).

120 Act III, *Cavalcanti* (Beinecke, Olga Rudge Papers).

121 Ibid.

122 "Synopsis, act III," *Cavalcanti,* reprinted from the program notes, *Ezra Pound: Composer.* Concert premiere, San Francisco: The Arch Ensemble, March 28, 1983.

123 Announcer's text, act III, *Cavalcanti* (Beinecke, Ezra Pound Papers—Addition.

124 Notes on act III, *Cavalcanti* (Beinecke, Ezra Pound Papers). Harding would probably have added plenty of echo, as with the "Mère au Saveur" of the *Testament.*

125 EP to Homer Pound, April 11, 1927, in *The Letters of Ezra Pound,* 210. "For Pound metamorphosis is a revelation of the godhead, but it is not something that exists apart from the natural world" (George Dekker, "Myth and Metamorphosis," in *New Approaches to Ezra Pound,* ed. Eva Hesse [Berkeley: University of California Press, 1969], 302).

126 The "Tempo di minué" is the seventeenth number of the *Pulcinella Ballet,* taken from act I of Pergolesi's opera ("Minuetto," sung by Don Pietro). The lines repeat the theme, the eyes as witness to the passion of the heart, from "Era in pensier." Stravinsky made very few alterations to Pergolesi's music. See White, *Stravinsky,* 244–251. Pound believed Stravinsky's genius surpassed all other living composers, including Antheil (*Ezra Pound and Music,* 372). "After Strawinsky's Pulcinella, there wd. be 'no sense' in continuing certain forms of mediocrity and wateriness in our handling of early Italian masters" (Pound, *Guide to Kulchur,* 251).

Pound wrote his wife he had seen the sound film *Pergolesi* and, while not impressed with the film, found it helpful in formulating his ideas about how sound for radio differed in its requirements from sound for film (EP to Dorothy Pound, October 21, 1932; Lilly).

127 Ezra Pound, *Pavannes & Divisions* (1918), reprinted in *Selected Prose, 1909–1965,* 47.

128 Valli, *Il linguaggio segreto di Dante e dei "fedeli d'amore."* A second volume, *Discussione e note aggiunte,* was issued in 1930.

129 *Literary Essays of Ezra Pound,* 181.

130 Act III, *Cavalcanti* (Beinecke, Ezra Pound Papers).

131 Rudge twice copied out a new score for the "Perch'io non spero" from Pound's original manuscript.

132 Act III, *Cavalcanti* (Beinecke, Ezra Pound Papers).

133 Federico III (1272–1337), ruler of Sicily from 1296 to 1337, was actually Federico II of Aragon but referred to himself as III to distinguish his name from that of his grandfather, Federico II of Sicily (1212–1250, *stupor mundi,* of the Hohenstaufen dynasty of Swabia). There is no historical basis that I can locate to place Federico III's name in relation to that of Cavalcanti. Federico III received harsh words from Dante (*Convivio* IV.12; *Paradiso* XIX.133–135), though the *Enciclopedia dantesca* notes a brief friendship between the two men. Pound considered him a just ruler (Terrell, vol. 1, 583). The name has much to recommend it in the context of Pound's drama: it bears the lineage of Federico II, under whose patronage the Sicilian court became a seedbed for the flowering of Italian lyric vernacular poetry.

134 Act III, *Cavalcanti* (Beinecke, Ezra Pound Papers). Pound later wrote the direction of the will into Canto LXXVII/487: ". . . directio voluntatis, as lord over the heart . . .".

135 I am grateful to Dr. Doug Tygar, expert in the field of cryptology, University of California at Berkeley, for fielding questions about the cipher, suggesting several strategies for finding a key, and checking my phrases for technical accuracy. Terminology and definitions are from David Kahn, *The Codebreakers* (New York: Scribner, 1996), xv.

136 *Literary Essays of Ezra Pound,* 182.

Those who have "the necessary preparation" for Pound's dramatic treatment of Cavalcanti will also be familiar to some degree with Dante studies, enough so, perhaps, to remember the prophetic cipher in *Purgatorio* 33 that foretells the corrective influence of Enrico VII, known as the "Eagle," on the corrupt "material" Church. Dante refers to an object or person "messo di Dio" (sent by God), named only by number, "un cinquecento diece e cinque" (five hundred, ten, and five). To insure that his meaning is understood, Dante describes a mysterious descent of eagle feathers onto the chariot. Subject of debate since Dante's time, the reference is commonly read as DVX (a rearrangement of the Roman numerals DXV), or DUX (the U is written as a V in the Latin alphabet), a reference to Enrico VII's rule as emperor commencing in 1308. (Specific words quoted above and these notes on Dante's symbolism are from Charles S. Singleton's comments in *Dante Alighieri, The Divine Comedy: Purgatorio, Text and Commentary* [Princeton, N.J.: Princeton University Press, 1973], 813-815.)

Because Pound studied and wrote about Dante (*Spirit of Romance*), considered him one of the world's five most important writers (*Guide to Kulchur*), referenced Dante in his strategies and objectives for *The Cantos,* and, as we've seen above, structured the three acts of his second opera according to Dante's humanism (as written in *De vulgari eloquentia*), and because Pound may have chosen Cavalcanti as the subject of his opera to correct Dante's notable omission of Cavalcanti from the personages encountered in *The Divine Comedy,* it was necessary to investigate the possibility of a connection between Dante's cipher and the Cavalcanti opera cipher. Pound undoubtedly was familiar with the variety of theories about Dante's cipher (now collected in the *Enciclopedia dantesca,* vol. II [Rome, 1970], 10-14). Before describing my effort to construct a cipher from Pound's music that is related to Dante's DUX cipher, I want to mention the obvious fact of the word's potent political implications in the fall of 1932 (the tenth anniversary of Mussolini's march on Rome and rule as prime minister), and the more obscure fact that Pound had already identified his own "Dux" in the music archives at Perugia—Dux Burgensis, or Duc de Bourgogne, listed as a fifteenth-century composer in the July 7, 1924, Salle Pleyel program that included Pound's and Antheil's music (Mary de Rachewiltz, *Discretions* [Boston: Little Brown, 1971], plate 1). In lieu of a title, Pound wrote "Dux" as his header on the working and final manuscripts of his violin transcription of the manuscript attributed to Bourgogne. (I am grateful to Robert Hughes for this information. *The New Grove Dictionary of Music* doesn't list Pound's composer, but does identify a François Bourguignon, a French or Franco-Netherlandish composer of four songs and a Latin motet, who flourished in the years 1533-1540.) Had Pound borrowed his cipher from Dante in the spirit of piquing the interest of an informed audience with "the necessary preparation," his radio-opera cipher might have had extremely serious consequences on the subsequent indictments against him for treason; that is, had the cipher been known.

Friedman and Friedman calculate that a message in cipher must contain approximately twenty-five letters for a solution to a single-alphabet substitution cipher to be considered conclusive (William Friedman and Elizebeth Friedman, *The Shakespearean Ciphers Examined* [Cambridge: Cambridge University Press, 1957], 18-23). Accepting their determination, it follows that there may be multiple approaches to finding a *Dux* cipher within Pound's music given our lack of his original key, and if *Dux* is indeed a message in cipher. No single solution can be verified as the sole solution, while only solutions involving music can be verified. Attempts to retrieve the message in cipher will necessarily involve working backward from predetermined solutions, as Valli had done. With these limitations noted, it remains to say that a procedure that produces intelligible and reproducible results may be considered a reasonable conjecture.

I employed a double-alphabet substitution cipher. My ciphertext alphabet is drawn from the musical notation of the Cavalcanti opera's principal motif (see figure 11 in this book). I created a system of equivalences for the motif's note durations (half note = 2; quarter note =4; eighth note = 8) to correspond to the numeric positions of the letters in my plaintext Italian alphabet. I added the letter X to the modern 21-letter Italian alphabet, its inclusion justified by the use of X in the dialects of Italy's Veneto region (for example, the antique spelling of *Venezia* as *Venexia,* still used today; see also the conjugation of the verb *essere* in Eugenio Vittoria's *Detti veneziani* [Venice: Editrice E V I, 1977], 112). We know that Pound liked the Venetian dialect (Anderson, 286) and made reference to it in his opera: the young page Rico is scolded by Cavalcanti for slipping into Venetian dialect, and the character Vanna in act II, as the announcer explains, is affiliated with Cunizza of the Eccelino da Romano family that ruled over many areas of the Veneto. Pound spelled the family name E-x-x-z-i-l-i-n-o (announcer's text, Olga Rudge Papers). Pound also used the letter J in his opera, as in *viejo.* I paired the J to the I, as they are interchangeable in Italian.

I ordered the letters of this plaintext alphabet so that the first four rows of letters contain four letters each (see the diagram below). The last two rows contain three letters each. After pairing the rows into three groups, I shuffled the sequence of letters in a systematic way: the first eleven letters are checkered sequentially and diagonally across two rows at a time, top, bottom, top, bottom. I then reversed the procedure from bottom to top, checkering the last eleven letters sequentially into the remaining available positions. Each letter was assigned a numbered position. The first row reads A, X, C, U in positions 1, 2, 3, 4; the second row reads Z, B, V, D in positions 5, 6, 7, 8, and so forth.

I next employed a simple set of numeric substitutions. The six eighth notes correspond to position 8, which contains the letter D. The four quarter notes correspond to position 4, which contains the letter U. The single half note corresponds to position 2, or the letter X. (I am grateful to Professor Tygar for suggesting that numeric values of the note durations might be associated with letters of the alphabet.)

position	1	2	3	4
Row 1	A	X	C	U
Row 2	Z	B	V	D
position	5	6	7	8
position	9	10	11	12
Row 3	E	S	G	Q
Row 4	T	F	R	H
position	13	14	15	16
position	17	18	19	
Row 5	I/J	O	M	
Row 6	P	L	N	
position	20	21	22	

At first appearance this cipher looks quite arbitrary. In fact, it is closely related to and represents a simple variant of a rather famous system called the Playfair cipher, arguably the best-known cipher at the turn of the last century. The Playfair cipher was invented in 1854 by Sir Charles Wheatstone (1802–1875), who published on acoustics, phonetics, and electromagnetic telegraphy. He is also credited with the invention of the concertina. The cipher was mistakenly attributed to his friend, Baron Lyon Playfair (Kahn, 196–198).

I suspect that Pound looked at one or more books on cryptography when he devised his cipher. By doing the same, the reader will discover entries that are provocative because of their origin, if not their means. Thomas Jefferson's "wheel cypher," invented at the beginning of the nineteenth century, was forgotten until 1922, when an explanation of it was found in his correspondence to Robert Patterson, a University of Pennsylvania mathematician (Kahn, 193). Pound referred to Jefferson's use of cipher in Canto XXXI (line 154). The research and writing of this canto overlapped the time period in which the opera was composed. Canto XLI concludes this new section of *The Cantos* with an anecdote about Mussolini (il Duce) and the date 1933. In act III of the opera, Rico's attempt to learn the cipher is followed immediately by the song, "Io son la donna che volgo la ruota" (I am the woman who turneth the wheel [Pound's translation, act III, Ezra Pound papers]). Scored for the prison guard's bass voice, Pound's song about the turning of the wheel makes use of a substitution (a man singing for a woman) and strongly suggests a hidden significance. I found nothing further that associates a cipher in the music with Jefferson's wheel.

Despite the difficulty of recovering the precise meaning or method Pound intended, it appears that he used the character of Rico to point to the meaning of the cipher. Rico is a means of verification, a tangible symbol comparable to Dante's use of eagle feathers in *Purgatorio* 33 to insure that his message would be deciphered. When Pound spells the page's name R-i-c-c-o he may do so to obtain a spoken emphasis, as the double *c* requires a stronger glottal action, produces a slight pause, and lends emphasis to the second syllable, which otherwise drops off. A man of Cavalcanti's stature would have retired to Sarzana with a retinue of servants. We may surmise that Pound's selection of Rico from among Cavalcanti's loyal circle was a symbolic gesture, given the boy's inabilities (discussed above in chapter four), a gesture that points to the meaning of the cipher.

137 Makin, *Pound's Cantos,* 188.

138 Terrell, vol. 1, 143; Pound, *Selected Prose, 1909–1965,* 61. See also Dermot Moran, *The Philosophy of John Scottus Eriugena* (Cambridge: Cambridge University Press, 1989), 84–85. Following his musical setting of "Donna mi prega," Pound made a second translation of the canzone, placing it in its entirety within Canto XXXVI. The remainder of the canto is devoted to the medieval philosopher Scotus Eriugina (c. 815–877, Pound's spelling), including the quote above, "authority comes from right reason," and its qualifier, "never the other way on." Pound then turns Thomas Aquinas upside down (presumably for reason serving authority), after which the sacred mystery of love is inscribed: "Sacrum, sacrum, inluminatio coitu" (Sacred rite, sacred mystery, illumination in coition). Concluding with Sordello, the canto reworks the themes Pound believes are implicit to Cavalcanti's poem, ones that have been made explicit by his musical setting of

the poem (Canto XXXVI/179–180; Terrell, vol. 1, 143). Sordello of Mantua (c. 1180–1255) was a troubadour who lived in Italy. His fame is preserved in Dante's *Commedia, Purg.* VI and VII. Regarding Pound's Canto XXXVI sources, see Makin, *Pound's Cantos,* 186–214.

139 Book I, lines 565–567 of Browning's *Sordello:* "—to display completely here/The mastery another life should learn,/Thrusting in time eternity's concern,—/So that Sordello . . ." (Robert Browning, *Strafford–Sordello,* ed. Charlotte Porter and Helen Clarke [New York: Thomas Crowell, 1898], 110–111).

140 Canto XX/90. Ezra Pound, "Il Miglior Fabbro" (1909), in *The Spirit of Romance,* 22–38; "Arnaut Daniel" (1920), in *Literary Essays of Ezra Pound,* 109. Pound admires the mixture of languages, including Latin, that Daniel brings into his poetry (109). See particularly the fourth strophe, line 32 of "Doutz brais e critz": "e qe'l remir contra'l lum de la lampa" (and I contemplate the light from the lamp). See Arnaut Daniel, *Canzoni,* ed. and trans. Gianluigi Toja (Florence: Sansoni, 1960), 300. See also James Wilhelm, *Il Miglior Fabbro: The Cult of the Difficult in Daniel, Dante, and Pound* (Orono: National Poetry Foundation, 1982), 9–35. Daniel's dates are uncertain, though his presence in southern France from 1180 to 1200 is generally agreed upon (Wilhelm, 9).

141 *Pound's Cavalcanti,* 170.

142 The *Cavalcanti* contains 1230 bars of music. A fledgling composer might spend half an hour to two hours finishing a single bar of vertically scored music for a small ensemble. Pound orchestrated the work himself, writing two to three different drafts to finalize each number. Each revision required recopying the entire aria. He also composed additional movements for the *Ghuidonis Sonate,* from which the overture was selected. Based on a very conservative estimate, Pound's time investment in the *Cavalcanti* was at least six hundred to one thousand hours. Compare Robert Fitzgerald's 1932 comments about Pound's "visionary music" as poetry in the imagination still awaiting words (reported in Norman, 310) to Domenico de Paoli's comments to D. G. Bridson: de Paoli of the RAI was interested in producing *Testament.* With Pound's permission he entered the house in Rapallo to look for music and described to Bridson a trunk filled to the brim with sketches, outlines, and fragments of different versions of the music for an opera (February 14, 1960; BBC Written Archives Centre, Ezra Pound W/W file 1953–1962).

143 EP to Agnes Bedford, August 6, 1932 (Lilly).

144 E. A. F. Harding to EP, September 13, 1932 (Beinecke).

145 E. A. F. Harding to EP, May 25, 1933 (Beinecke). The letter is dated June 25, 1933, but this is a mistake, as is confirmed by Pound's letter to Dorothy marking the date of the meeting, May 30, a Tuesday (EP to Dorothy Pound, May 30, 1933; Lilly).

146 EP to Agnes Bedford, May 16, 1933 (Lilly).

147 Ferrari's program did not proceed. EP to Agnes Bedford, May 31, 1933 (Lilly).

148 EP to Agnes Bedford, June 7, 1933 (Lilly).

149 Harding's removal from London for this dismal outpost was viewed by his colleagues as a demotion. However, Harding came into his own in the north of England. For all his interests in literature and foreign affairs while in London, he put the transfer to good purpose by inaugurating regional-based programming. Kenneth Adam, controller of the Light Programme of the BBC North Region, described the impact of Harding's arrival: "Within a few months the offices in Piccadilly [Manchester] had become the spearhead of new advances in technique, in programme ideas, in microphone performance. No one was safe from his all-conquering, all-embracing enthusiasm. Journalists, lawyers, insurance agents, income-tax inspectors, industrialists, and a whole heap of other workers and craftsmen found themselves somewhat to their surprise writing and reading, acting, and even singing for the BBC" (obit., *Manchester Guardian,* January 27, 1953).

150 Agnes Bedford to EP, October 17, 1933 (Lilly).

5

Minister of Kulchur in Utopia

1 Lambert, 186.

2 EP to D. F. Aitken, August 11, 1936 (BBC Written Archives Centre, R cont. 1, Pound Ezra RT & Listener Articles 1936).

3 D. F. Aitken to EP, August 27, 1936 (BBC Written Archives Centre, R cont. 1, Pound Ezra RT & Listener Articles 1936).

4 D. F. Aitken to EP, October 21, 1936 (BBC Written Archives Centre, R cont. 1, Pound Ezra RT & Listener Articles 1936).

5 D. F. Aitken to EP, June 30, 1936 (BBC Written Archives Centre, R cont. 1, Pound Ezra RT & Listener Articles 1936); letter from Pound to James Laughlin, September 2, 1936 (*Pound and Laughlin, Selected Letters,* 64). Pound's audience of three "millym" mistakenly referred to the subscriber base of *Radio Times* rather than *The Listener.* In 1936 there were 7.5 million radio licenses issued in the United Kingdom (Paulu, 413). According to Briggs, there were three million *Radio Times* subscribers in 1939, and 52,000 *Listener* subscribers in 1935 (Briggs, *BBC,* 114–115). A subscription to *The Listener* to be mailed to Rapallo was arranged by Aitken to begin November 1936. Pound's personal contact with the BBC came to an end in December 1936.

6 The broadcast from Italy to the United States took place on January 11, 1935 (de Rachewiltz, "Fragments of an Atmosphere," 160–161).

7 Ibid., 161.

8 One hundred twenty transcripts of the broadcasts are collected in *"Ezra Pound Speaking": Radio Speeches of World War II.*

9 "God damn destructive and dispersive devil of an invention. But got to be faced" (March 31, 1940, *The Letters of Ezra Pound,* 342–343). Regarding compromise in the music, the music of living composers was not generally subject to substitution, rewriting, omission, and reassignment to different instruments. Pound's music had been subjected to all of these. Had he mastered a foolproof music notation, he still could not have prevented his producer, conductor, and rehearsal coach from evaluating the music as the work of an amateur and in need of improvement.

Pound improved his technical language to communicate differences, for example, between diminuendi and ritards. He wrote that the ritards were written into the rhythm of the music, and the performer should use a metronome to insure correct tempi.

10 *"Ezra Pound Speaking,"* xi.

11 Beinecke, Ezra Pound Papers.

12 De Rachewiltz, 164.

13 The comment continued, "Art long. man prone to error, no need to stay ever supine. Labor, peine, of this appalling treatice, in part a due

penance for sin" ("Song," pp. 3–4, third draft; Beinecke, Ezra Pound Papers).

14 Ezra Pound, "Guido Cavalcanti," unpublished essay or radio speech in Italian, undated, but written in the 1940s. (Beinecke, Ezra Pound Papers.)

Postscript

1 Briggs, *History of Broadcasting,* vol. 2, 169.

2 Obit., *Manchester Guardian,* January 27, 1953.

3 Agnes Bedford to EP, November 26, 1948 (Beinecke).

4 Dorothy Pound to EP, July 13, 1933 (Lilly).

5 Martin Esslin, letter to author, January 18, 1996. A Brecht scholar and an expert on the theater of the absurd, Esslin became assistant head of Drama in 1961. The closing of the Features Department fell to him soon after he replaced Val Gielgud as head of Drama. His letter describes the mature Archie Harding: "He was a splendid man, a burly giant, very bohemian, friendly, with curly white hair."

6 Agnes Bedford to EP, February 23, 1953 (Lilly).

7 Pound was imprisoned in the U.S. Army's Disciplinary Training Centre, Pisa, on May 24, 1945.

Appendix: BBC Script for *The Testament of François Villon*

1 The announcer's text was marked out and another substituted. The latter has not been found. Because of the cancellation of preconcert talks due to elections news, the likelihood is that Harding elaborated on the introduction.

2 Lines 501–508 (?) and 520–524 of Villon's *Le grand testament* were cut by the BBC to avoid sexually explicit words.

3 Pound marked the score to indicate that the drums and nose flute should start before the Priest and be audible throughout his short scene.

4 It is not ascertainable whether crowd sounds were made live or were a prerecorded effect.

5 This line was added by Harding. It appears to be the only dialogue written by him.

6 The script is typed as performed by the BBC. Please see the body of this text for notes on Pound's conception of the "Voices."

7 The singers are identified as "Tenor, high tenor at octave above when suitable, Baritone, 2 Basses & Basso Profundissimo. 'Cello?" (margin notes by unidentified hand, *The Testament of François Villon;* Lilly).

8 "This trick gives effect of them going on singing though one can't hear them. It enables one to make a cut sound natural" (Harding's margin notes, *The Testament of François Villon,* Lilly).

9 A second cut was made in the same manner.

References

Published Works of Ezra Pound

ABC of Reading. New York: New Directions, 1960.

Antheil and the Treatise on Harmony. Chicago: Pascal Covici, 1927.

The Cantos of Ezra Pound. New York: New Directions, 13th printing 1995.

(and Ernest Fenollosa) *The Classic Noh Theatre of Japan.* New York: New Directions, 1959.

Ezra Pound and James Laughlin, Selected Letters. Ed. David M. Gordon. New York: W. W. Norton, 1994.

Ezra Pound and Music. Ed. R. Murray Schafer. New York: New Directions, 1977.

Ezra Pound and the Visual Arts. Ed. Harriet Zinnes. New York: New Directions, 1980.

"Ezra Pound Speaking": Radio Speeches of World War II. Ed. Leonard W. Doob. Westport, CT: Greenwood Press, 1978.

Ezra Pound's Poetry and Prose: Contributions to Periodicals. 10 vols. Ed. L. Baechler, A. W. Litz, and J. Longenbach. New York: Garland, 1991.

Ezra Pound: Translations. Intro. Hugh Kenner. New York: New Directions, 1963.

Four Plays Modelled on the Noh (1916). Ed. Donald Gallup. Toledo: Friends of the University of Toledo Libraries, 1987.

Guide to Kulchur. New York: New Directions, 1968.

Guido Cavalcanti Rime. Genoa: Edizioni Marsano, 1932.

The Letters of Ezra Pound, 1907–1941. Ed. D. D. Paige. New York: Harcourt, Brace and World, 1950.

Literary Essays of Ezra Pound. Ed. T. S. Eliot. New York: New Directions, 1968. Includes *Make it New,* collected essays by Pound (London: Faber and Faber, 1934).

Pound's Cavalcanti. Ed. David Anderson. Princeton: Princeton University Press, 1983.

Selected Prose, 1909–1965. Ed. William Cookson. London: Faber and Faber, 1978.

The Spirit of Romance. New York: New Directions, 1968.

Three Cantos. *Poetry* 10, no. 3 (June 1917): 113–121; 10, no. 4 (July 1917): 180–188; 10, no. 5 (August 1917): 248–254.

Unpublished Papers of Ezra Pound

"Coition the sacrament," n.d. Ezra Pound Papers—Addition, Yale Collection of American Literature, Beinecke Library.

"Guido Cavalcanti" (in Italian), 1940s. Ezra Pound Papers, Yale Collection of American Literature, Beinecke Library.

"Song," three drafts, n.d. Ezra Pound Papers, Yale Collection of American Literature, Beinecke Library.

Unpublished Music of Ezra Pound

Cavalcanti. Three-act opera, 1931–1933. Composed by Ezra Pound, words by Cavalcanti and Sordello. Edited by Robert Hughes.

Le Testament. One-act opera, 1923. Composed by Ezra Pound, arranged by George Antheil, words by François Villon. Beinecke Library, Yale University.

The Testament of François Villon. Radio script, BBC, 1931. Composed by Ezra Pound, words by François Villon, additional dialogue by Ezra Pound, produced by E. A. F. Harding. Beinecke Library, Yale University.

The Testament of François Villon. Radio script, BBC, 1931. Composed by Ezra Pound, words by François Villon, additional dialogue by Ezra Pound, produced by E. A. F. Harding. Lilly Library, Indiana University.

Recordings of Music by Ezra Pound

Ego Scriptor Cantilenae: The Music of Ezra Pound. Audio CD, 2002. Composed by Ezra Pound, words by François Villon, Guido Cavalcanti, Sordello; edited and conducted by Robert Hughes, produced by Charles Amirkhanian. Performing forces, S. F. Western Opera Theater, Arch Ensemble, Other Minds Ensemble. San Francisco: Other Minds. OM # 1005–2.

Le Testament. Audiotape, 1962. Composed by Ezra Pound, words by François Villon, edited by R. Murray Schafer, produced by D. G. Bridson. London: BBC Sound Archive Library.

Le Testament. 33 RPM record, 1972. Composed by Ezra Pound, words by François Villon, edited and conducted by Robert Hughes, produced by Nathan Rubin. Performing forces, S. F. Western Opera Theater. Berkeley: Fantasy Records #12001.

Le Testament de Villon. 33 RPM record, 1980. Composed by Ezra Pound, words by François Villon, conducted by Reinbert de Leeuw. Performing forces, ASKO Ensemble, ASKO-koor, Holland Festival. Holland: Philips #9500 927.

Archival Sources

BBC Written Archives Centre, Caversham Park, Reading, England.

Ezra Pound Manuscripts, Manuscript Collections, Lilly Library, Indiana University, Bloomington, Indiana.

Ezra Pound Papers, Yale Collection of American Literature, Beinecke Rare Book and Manuscript Library, Yale University, New Haven, Connecticut.

Ezra Pound Papers—Addition, Yale Collection of American Literature, Beinecke Library.

Olga Rudge Papers, Yale Collection of American Literature, Beinecke Library.

Selected Secondary Sources

Adams, Stephen. "Musical Neofism: Pound's Theory of Harmony in Context." *Mosaic* 13, no. 2 (Winter 1980): 49–69.

Adams, Stephen. "Pound in the Theatre: The Background of Pound's Operas." In Leon Surette and Demetres Tryphonopoulos, eds., *Literary Modernism and the Occult Tradition.* Orono, ME: National Poetry Foundation, 1996.

Antheil, George. *Bad Boy of Music.* Garden City, NY: Doubleday, Doran, 1945.

Arnheim, Rudolf. *Radio.* Trans. Margaret Ludwig and Herbert Read. London: Faber and Faber, 1936.

Ascoli, Albert Russell. "The Vowels of Authority (Dante's *Convivio* IV.vi.3–4)." In Kevin Brownlee and Walter Stephens, eds., *Discourses of Authority in Medieval and Renaissance Literature,* 23–46. Hanover, NH: University Press of New England, 1989.

Berghaus, Günter. *Italian Futurist Theatre, 1909–1944.* Oxford: Clarendon Press, 1998.

Bernstein, Michael André. *Tale of the Tribe.* Princeton: Princeton University Press, 1980.

Bird, Otto, ed. "The Canzone d'Amore of Cavalcanti according to the Commentary of Dino del Garbo." Text and commentary. *Medieval Studies* 2 and 3 (1940, 1941): 150–203, 117–160.

Boccaccio, Giovanni. *The Decameron.* Trans. Richard Aldington. New York: Covici, Friede, 1930.

Booth, Michael. *English Melodrama.* London: Herbert Jenkins, 1965.

Boyle, Andrew. *Only the Wind Will Listen: Reith of the BBC.* London: Hutchinson, 1972.

Bridson, D. G. "An Interview with Ezra Pound." *New Directions 17.* New York: New Directions, 1961.

Bridson, D. G. *Prospero and Ariel.* London: Victor Gollancz, 1971.

Briggs, Asa. *The BBC: The First Fifty Years.* Oxford: Oxford University Press, 1985.

Briggs, Asa. *The History of Broadcasting in the United Kingdom.* Vol. 2, *The Golden Age of Wireless.* Oxford: Oxford University Press, 1965.

Bush, Ronald. *The Genesis of Ezra Pound's Cantos.* Princeton: Princeton University Press, 1976.

Cantril, Hadley, and Gordon Allport. *Psychology of Radio.* New York: Harper and Brothers, 1935.

Carpenter, Humphrey. *A Serious Character.* Boston: Houghton Mifflin, 1988.

Catullus, Gaius Valerius. "The Poems of Catullus." In *Catullus, Tibullus, Pervigilium Veneris.* Trans. F. W. Cornish. Cambridge: Harvard University Press, 1995.

Catullus, Gaius Valerius. *The Poems of Catullus.* Trans. and notes Charles Martin. Baltimore: Johns Hopkins University Press, 1990.

Chase, Francis. *Sound and Fury.* New York: Harper and Brothers, 1942.

Compagni, Dino. *Cronaca.* Ed. Gino Luzzatti. Turin: Einaudi, 1968.

Cornell, Julien. *The Trial of Ezra Pound.* New York: John Day, 1966.

Cornish, Alison. "A Lady Asks: The Gender of Vulgarization in Late Medieval Italy." *PMLA* 115, no. 2 (March 2000): 166–180.

Corti, Maria. *La felicità mentale.* Torino: Einaudi, 1983.

Cowan, Lester, ed. *Recording Sound for Motion Pictures.* New York: McGraw-Hill Book, 1931.

Crook, Tim. *Radio Drama.* New York: Routledge, 1999.

Dante Alighieri. *De vulgari eloquentia.* Ed. and trans. Steven Botterill. Cambridge: Cambridge University Press, 1996.

Dante Alighieri. *De vulgari eloquentia.* Ed. and trans. Robert Haller. In *Literary Criticism of Dante Alighieri.* Lincoln: University of Nebraska Press, 1973.

Dekker, George. *Sailing after Knowledge.* London: Routledge and Kegan Paul, 1963.

De Rachewiltz, Mary. "Fragments of an Atmosphere." *Agenda* 17, nos. 3–4; 18, no. 1 (Autumn-Winter-Spring 1979–1980).

Doctor, Jennifer. *The BBC and Ultra-Modern Music, 1922–1936.* Cambridge: Cambridge University Press, 1999.

Drakakis, John, ed. *British Radio Drama.* Cambridge: Cambridge University Press, 1981.

Dudek, Louis, ed. *DK/Some Letters of Ezra Pound.* Montreal: DC Books, 1974.

Eckersley, Peter. *The Power behind the Microphone.* London: Jonathan Cape, 1941.

Eliot, T. S. "Matthew Arnold." In *The Use of Poetry and the Use of Criticism*. Cambridge: Harvard University Press, 1933.

Eliot, T. S. *On Poetry and Poets.* New York: Farrar, Straus and Cudahy, 1957.

Frost, Everett, and Margaret Herzfeld-Sander, eds. *German Radio Plays.* New York: Continuum, 1991.

Gallo, F. Alberto. *Music in the Castle.* Trans. Anna Herklotz. Chicago: University of Chicago Press, 1995.

Gallup, Donald. *Ezra Pound: A Bibliography.* Charlottesville: University Press of Virginia, 1983.

Gielgud, Val. *British Radio Drama, 1922–1956.* London: George G. Harrap, 1959.

Gilson, Étienne. *Dante the Philosopher.* Trans. David Moore. New York: Sheed and Ward, 1949.

Goldberg, RoseLee. *Performance Art, from Futurism to the Present.* New York: Thames and Hudson, 2001.

Gordon, Mel. *Dada Performance.* New York: PAJ Publications, 1987.

Gorham, Maurice. *Sound and Fury: Twenty-One Years in the BBC.* London: P. Marshall, 1948.

A Guide to Pound and Fenollosa's Classic Noh Theatre of Japan. Ed. Akiko Miyake, Sanehide Kodama, and Nicholas Teele. Orono: National Poetry Foundation, University of Maine, and Otsu, Japan: Ezra Pound Society of Japan, Shiga University, 1994.

Guralnick, Elissa. *Sight Unseen.* Athens: Ohio University Press, 1996.

Harrison, Robert P. *The Body of Beatrice.* Baltimore: Johns Hopkins University Press, 1988.

Hettinger, Herman, ed. *Radio: The Fifth Estate.* The Annals of the American Academy of Political and Social Science, 1935.

Huelsenbeck, Richard. *Memoirs of a Dada Drummer.* Trans. Joachim Neugroschel. New York: Viking Press, 1969.

Hughes, Robert. "Ezra Pound's Opera: Le Testament de Villon." *Paideuma* 2, no. 1 (Spring 1973): 13–16.

Kaes, Anton, Martin Jay, and Edward Dimendberg, eds. *The Weimar Republic Sourcebook.* Berkeley: University of California Press, 1994.

Kahn, Douglas. *Noise Water Meat.* Cambridge: MIT Press, 1999.

Kahn, Douglas, and Gregory Whitehead, eds. *Wireless Imagination, Sound, Radio, and the Avant-Garde.* Cambridge: MIT Press, 1992.

Kaye, Jacqueline. "Pound and Heresy." *Paideuma* 28, no. 1 (Spring 1999): 89–111.

Kenner, Hugh. "Ezra Pound and Homer." In *Historical Fictions.* San Francisco: North Point Press, 1990.

Kenner, Hugh. *The Pound Era.* Berkeley: University of California Press, 1971.

Kirby, Michael, and Victoria Kirby. *Futurist Performance.* New York: E. P. Dutton, 1971.

Lambert, Richard S. *Ariel and All His Quality: An Impression of the BBC from Within.* London: Victor Gollancz, 1940.

Lewis, D. B. Wyndham. *François Villon: A Documented Survey.* New York: Literary Guild of America, 1928.

Longenbach, James. *Stone Cottage.* Oxford: Oxford University Press, 1988.

Mack Smith, Denis. *Mussolini.* New York: Alfred A. Knopf, 1982.

Makin, Peter. *Pound's Cantos.* London: George Allen and Unwin, 1985.

Makin, Peter. *Provence and Pound.* Berkeley: University of California Press, 1978.

Marinetti, Filippo Tommaso. "Destruction of Syntax—Wireless Imagination—Words in Freedom." Trans. Richard Pioli. In *Stung by Salt and War: Creative Texts of the Italian Avant-Gardist F. T. Marinetti.* New York: Peter Lang, 1987.

Marinetti, F. T. *Selected Writings.* Ed. and trans. R. W. Flint. New York: Farrar, Straus and Giroux, 1972.

Marinetti, F. T. *Taccuini 1915–1921.* Ed. Alberto Bertoni. Bologna: Società editrice il Mulino, 1987.

Marinetti, F. T. *Teatro F. T. Marinetti.* Vols. 1 and 2. Ed. Giovanni Calendoli. Rome: Vito Bianco Editore, 1960.

Matheson, Hilda. *Broadcasting.* London: Thornton Butterworth, 1933.

McWhinnie, Donald. *The Art of Radio.* London: Faber and Faber, 1959.

Melzer, Annabelle Henkin. *Dada and Surrealist Performance.* Baltimore: Johns Hopkins University Press, 1994.

Miyake, Akiko. *Ezra Pound and the Mysteries of Love.* Durham: Duke University Press, 1991.

Moritz, William. "Americans in Paris: Man Ray and Dudley Murphy." In Jan-Christopher Horak, ed., *Lovers of Cinema: The First American Avant-Garde Film.* Madison: University of Wisconsin Press, 1996.

Nadel, Ira, ed. *The Cambridge Companion to Ezra Pound.* Cambridge: Cambridge University Press, 1999.

Nelson, Lowry Jr., ed. and trans. *The Poetry of Guido Cavalcanti.* New York: Garland, 1986.

Norman, Charles. *Ezra Pound.* New York: Macmillan, 1960.

Parker, Derek. *Radio: The Great Years.* London: David and Charles, 1977.

Paulu, Burton. *British Broadcasting: Radio and Television in the United Kingdom.* Minneapolis: University of Minnesota Press, 1956.

Pawley, Edward. *BBC Engineering, 1922–1972.* London: BBC Publication, 1972.

Perloff, Marjorie. *The Futurist Moment.* Chicago: University of Chicago Press, 1986.

Poe, Elizabeth. *From Poetry to Prose in Old Provençal.* Birmingham, AL: Summa Publications, 1984.

Quaresima, Leonardo, ed. *Walter Ruttmann: cinema, pittura, ars acustica.* Rovereto: Manfrini Editori, 1994.

Rainey, Lawrence. "The Creation of the Avante-Garde: F. T. Marinetti and Ezra Pound." *Modernism/Modernity* 1, no. 3 (September 1994): 195–219.

Rossetti, D. G. *The Early Italian Poets from Ciullo d'Alcamo to Dante Alighieri.* London: Smith, Elder, 1861.

Rotha, Paul. *The Film till Now: A Survey of World Cinema.* London: Vision Press, 1949.

Sacchetti, Franco. *Tales from Sacchetti.* Trans. Mary Steegmann. London: J. M. Dent, 1908.

Salaris, Claudia. *F. T. Marinetti.* Firenze: La Nuova Italia, 1988.

Salaris, Claudia. "Marketing Modernism: Marinetti as Publisher." Trans. Lawrence Rainey. *Modernism/Modernity* 1, no. 3 (September 1994): 109–127.

Scannell, Paddy, and David Cardiff. *A Social History of British Broadcasting.* Vol. 1, *1922–1939.* Oxford: Blackwell Publishers, 1991.

Schebera, Jürgen. *Kurt Weill, an Illustrated Life.* Trans. Caroline Murphy. New Haven: Yale University Press, 1995.

Schöning, Klaus. "The Contours of Acoustic Art." Trans. Mark Cory. *Theatre Journal* 43 (1991).

Shaw, J. E. *Guido Cavalcanti's Theory of Love.* Toronto: University of Toronto Press, 1949.

Sieveking, Lance. *The Stuff of Radio.* London: Cassell Publishing, 1934.

Stock, Noel. *The Life of Ezra Pound.* New York: Random House, 1970.

Surette, Leon. *Light from Eleusis.* Oxford: Clarendon Press, 1979.

Surette, Leon, and Demetres Tryphonopoulos, eds. *Literary Modernism and the Occult Tradition.* Orono, ME: National Poetry Foundation, 1996.

Terrell, Carroll. *A Companion to the Cantos of Ezra Pound.* 2 vols. Berkeley: University of California Press, 1980.

Thomson, Peter, and Glendyr Sacks, eds. *The Cambridge Companion to Brecht.* Cambridge: Cambridge University Press, 1994.

Thomson, Virgil. *Virgil Thomson.* New York: Alfred A. Knopf, 1966.

Valli, Luigi. *Il linguaggio segreto di Dante e dei "fedeli d'amore."* Rome: Biblioteca di Filosofia e Scienza, 1928.

Villani, Filippo. *Le vite d'uomini illustri fiorentini.* Firenze: Sansone Coen, 1847.

Villani, Giovanni. *Cronica.* Franc. Gherardi Dragomanni. Frankfurt: Unveränderter Nachdruck, 1969.

Villon, François. *The Complete Works of François Villon.* Trans., biography, and notes by Anthony Bonner. New York: Bantam, 1960.

Webster, Gwendolen. *Kurt Merz Schwitters: A Biography.* Cardiff: University of Wales Press, 1997.

Wells, Alan, ed. *World Broadcasting: A Comparative View.* Norwood, NJ: Ablex Publishing, 1996.

West, Robert. *The Rape of Radio.* New York: Rodin Publishing, 1941.

West, W. J. *Truth Betrayed.* London: Duckworth, 1987.

Whigham, Peter, ed. *The Music of the Troubadours.* Vol. 1. Santa Barbara, CA: Ross-Erikson, 1979.

White, Eric Walter. *Stravinsky: The Composer and His Works.* Berkeley: University of California Press, 1969.

Whitehead, Kate. *The Third Programme.* Oxford: Clarendon Press, 1989.

Wilhelm, James. *Dante and Pound: The Epic of Judgement.* Orono: University of Maine Press, 1974.

Wilhelm, James. *Il Miglior Fabbro: The Cult of the Difficult in Daniel, Dante, and Pound.* Orono, ME: National Poetry Foundation, 1982.

Willett, John, ed. and trans. *Brecht on Theatre.* New York: Hill and Wang, 1992.

Willett, John. *The Theatre of Bertolt Brecht.* New York: New Directions, 1968.

Media Sources

Weill, Kurt. *Der Lindberghflug* (1929) and *The Ballad of Magna Carta* (1940). Audio CD, 1990. Music by Kurt Weill, words by Bertolt Brecht, translation by Lys Simonette. Königsdorf: Capriccio 60012–1.

Berlin, Die Sinfonie der Großstadt (1927). DVD video, 1993. Directed and edited by Walter Ruttmann, concept by Carl Mayer, screenplay and photography by Karl Freund. Chatsworth, CA: Film Preservation Associates.

Rien que les heures (1926). VHS video, n.d. Directed, written, and edited by Alberto Cavalcanti. Distribution by Facets Video, Chicago.

Index